Education in Sierra Leone

**PRESENT CHALLENGES,
FUTURE OPPORTUNITIES**

AFRICA HUMAN
DEVELOPMENT SERIES

Education in Sierra Leone

PRESENT CHALLENGES,
FUTURE OPPORTUNITIES

AFRICA HUMAN
DEVELOPMENT SERIES

THE WORLD BANK
Washington, D.C.

ISBN-10: 0-8213-6868-0
ISBN-13: 978-0-8213-6868-8
eISBN-10: 0-8213-6869-9
eISBN-13: 978-0-8213-6869-5
DOI: 10.1596/978-0-8213-6868-8

Cover photo: World Bank/Lianqin Wang.

Library of Congress Cataloging-in-Publication Data has been requested

Contents

BOXES

FIGURES

TABLES

Foreword

This report for Sierra Leone is part of an ongoing series of country-specific reports being prepared by the World Bank in collaboration with the relevant governments and partner organizations. The general objective of these reports is to enhance the knowledge base for policy development. This report is intended to provide a basis for engaging a diverse audience in dialogue on issues and policies in the education sector and for developing a shared vision for the future.

In recent years, the development context for education has evolved in ways that increase the relevance and demand for this type of analytic work. Governments are striving toward poverty reduction and the Millennium Development Goals (MDGs), and the international donor community has pledged to provide the necessary financial assistance. Many countries have given education a central role in their economic and social development and have made great progress in the education sector. Throughout Africa, many new schools have been constructed, new teachers have been hired, free primary education is being implemented, and student enrollments have surged to record levels in the past few years. However, more still needs to be done to achieve the education MDGs: ensuring that all children complete a full course of primary schooling by 2015 and that gender disparity is eliminated at all levels of education. Challenges remain on all fronts: many children, particularly girls and those from poor families and living in rural areas, still do not have access to primary education; the quality of learning is poor and often declines in a period of rapid system expansion; secondary education is not equipped to accommodate the recent influx of primary graduates; and tertiary education as well as technical and vocational education have little relevance to the labor market.

To address these issues, a first step is to develop a country-specific knowledge base that sheds light on the key weaknesses and challenges in the education system. This report does so by consolidating the available information in a policy-relevant manner, documenting not only the traditional and basic indicators, such as gross enrollment rates and retention, but also including analyses to examine the performance of the education system in terms of access, quality, equity, management, and resource allocation and utilization. The report also includes a chapter on education governance and management, and puts an emphasis on policy implications at the end of each chapter.

It is also noteworthy that country-specific reports such as this one are prepared with the active collaboration of partners, particularly the national team. Such collaboration allows for considerable capacity building and lays the groundwork for stronger country ownership in subsequent follow-up with policy development and implementation. This particular report has benefited from the engagement of the national team in all phases of the work from the very beginning to the very end, including data collection, data analysis, chapter preparation, and presentation of the draft report to the stakeholders in the country. The national team has full mastery of the financial simulation model prepared as part of the report and which has now started serving as an instrument for planning and costing education-sector programs.

The completion of this report for Sierra Leone comes at an opportune time. The country is moving out of a postconflict period and is likely to face a decline in external financing. Yet the education sector is at a stage when it needs more resources than ever in its rapid system expansion and quality improvement and in its striving to achieve its many goals, including universal primary completion by 2015. To better plan the development of the education sector and mobilize more financial resources, the Ministry of Education, Science and Technology (MEST) has decided to develop a sectorwide plan. This report helps to lay down a strong analytic foundation to inform the development of the plan while also building technical capacity in MEST to take ownership for the plan's preparation. It highlights the country's educational progress to date and the challenges that need to be addressed. It does not provide solutions. Policy responses to the issues outlined in the report will be formulated in the education sector plan, which is the next step.

The publication of this report is intended to institutionalize our collective knowledge on education in Sierra Leone and share this knowledge as widely as possible. The report offers comprehensive information on education in Sierra Leone; it is, however, constrained by the limitations of the available data at the time the report was prepared. It is my hope that as new information becomes available during the course of development of the education sector, this report will be updated to track progress and draw lessons learned that may have broad applications in other African countries.

Yaw Ansu
Sector Director
Human Development Department
Africa Region
The World Bank

Acknowledgments

This report was prepared in a close collaboration of the World Bank and the Ministry of Education, Science and Technology (MEST) of Sierra Leone. The Bank team consisted of Lianqin Wang (task team leader), Ramahatra Rakotomalala, Laura Gregory, and Paul Cichello. The Sierra Leone team was led by Albert C. T. Dupigny, under the overall direction of Honorable Dr. Alpha T. Wurie, Minister of Education, Science and Technology, and consisted of Bidemi Carrol, Reginald King, Mohammed A. Jalloh, Musu Gorvie, and Abubakarr Tarrawallie.

Jee-Peng Tan (advisor to the Africa Human Development Network) provided overall technical guidance. Technical advice and significant input were received from Benoît Millot and Alain Mingat. Peer reviewers were Douglas Addison, Robert Prouty, and Christopher Thomas. Zeljko Bogetic, Elizabeth King, and Juan Prawda provided very thoughtful comments at the concept paper stage.

The report has benefited substantially from the support given by various individuals, directorates, divisions, and units of MEST, Ministry of Finance, Ministry of Youth and Sport, the University of Sierra Leone, Decentralization Secretariat, and various agencies and development partners in Sierra Leone. They include W. A. Taylor, Y. N. Gibril, S. A. T. Rogers, Ibrahim G. Kargbo, Ibrahim Dabor, Blanche Macauley, J. A. Swarray, J. Sumaila, Edward Pessima, Emmanuel Gaiima, Adam Jackson, and Alimamy Bangura. Contributing entities include the Sababu Education Project Co-ordination Unit; Basic Education Secretariat; Programs, Planning, Inspectorate, and Higher Education Directorates; Pre/Primary, Secondary, Technical/Vocational and Non-Formal Divisions; West African Examinations Council (WAEC); Economic Policy and Research Unit; the Budget Unit and Education Departments of Fourah Bay College; and Njala University College. Statistics Sierra Leone provided the population census data and Sierra Leone Integrated Household Survey (SLIHS) data. The Decentralization Secretariat provided data concerning a school survey. German Technical Cooperation (GTZ) funded the technical/vocational survey referred to in the report. Their support made the data analysis possible. The UNICEF Sierra Leone office facilitated the policy dialogue and supported the report throughout the process.

Many staff members at the Bank contributed to this report. James Sackey (country manager for Sierra Leone), Peter Darvas, Eunice Dapaah, William Experton, and Michael Drabble provided strong support to the process as well as insightful feedback on the report. William Lorie contributed to the analysis of the WAEC data. Pia Peters provided valuable input to the youth and employment issues. Yongmei Zhu and Katherine Whiteside provided helpful input on the decentralization process and related information. Excellent administrative support was received from Gertrude Mulenga Banda, Aissatou Chipkaou, Adriana Cunha Costa, Nancy Etuhu-Badmus, Fatu Karim-Turay, and Marietou Toure.

The team acknowledges the financial support received from the Norwegian Education Trust Fund and the Africa Region Education Program Development Fund.

Abbreviations

AER	Age-specific enrollment rate
AfDF	African Development Fund
AFRC	Armed Forces Revolutionary Council
AGD	Accountant General's Department
BECE	Basic Education Certificate Examination
CAR	Cohort access rate
CASS	Continuous assessment
CCM	Composite cohort method
CEC	Community education center
COMAHS	College of Medicine and Allied Health Sciences
CREPS	Complementary Rapid Education for Primary Schools
CTA	Community Teachers Association
DAC	Development Assistance Committee
DACO	Development Assistance Coordination Office
DEC	District Education Council
EC	European Community
EFA	Education for All
EMIS	Education management information system
EU	European Union
FTI	Education for All Fast Track Initiative
GCR	Gross completion ratio
GDP	Gross domestic product
GER	Gross enrollment ratio
GIR	Gross intake ratio
GTZ	German Technical Cooperation
HDI	Human Development Index
HIPC	Heavily indebted poor countries
HIV	Human immunodeficiency virus

HTC	Higher teachers certificate
IDA	International development assistance
IMF	The International Monetary Fund
IPAM	Institute of Public Administration and Management
IRCBP	Institutional Reform and Capacity Building Project
JSS	Junior secondary school
LGA	Local Government Act
MDG	Millennium Development Goal
MEST	Ministry of Education, Science and Technology
MOF	Ministry of Finance
MTEF	Medium Term Expenditure Framework
NCRDC	National Curriculum Research and Development Centre
NCTVA	National Council for Technical, Vocational and Other Academic Awards
NER	Net enrollment rate
NGO	Nongovernmental organization
NIR	Net intake rate
NPSE	National Primary School Examination
NVC	National vocational certificate
NVQ	National vocational qualification
ODA	Official development assistance
OECD	Organisation for Economic Co-operation and Development
OND	Ordinary national diploma
OTD	Ordinary teaching diploma
PCR	Primary completion rate
PETS	Public Expenditure Tracking Survey
PRGF	Poverty Reduction and Growth Facility
PRSP	Poverty Reduction Strategy Paper
PTR	Pupil-to-teacher ratio
RCM	Reconstructed cohort method
RREP	Rapid Response Education Program
RUF	Revolutionary United Front
SLIHS	Sierra Leone Integrated Household Survey
SMC	School Management Committee
SSS	Senior secondary school
TC	Teachers certificate
TEC	Tertiary Education Commission
TVC	Technical vocational center
TVET	Technical and vocational education and training
TVI	Technical and vocational institute

UBE	Universal basic education
UIS	UNESCO Institute for Statistics
UNDP	United Nations Development Program
UNESCO	United Nations Educational, Scientific and Cultural Organization
UNICEF	United Nations Children's Fund
UPE	Universal primary education
VTC	Vocational trade centers
WAEC	West African Examinations Council
WASSCE	West Africa Senior School Certificate Examination
WB	The World Bank

CURRENCY EQUIVALENTS

(Exchange rate 2004 average)
Currency unit: Leone (Le)
US$1.00 = Le 2,701

Executive Summary

S ierra Leone is a small country located on the west coast of Africa; it has 5 million people and possesses fertile land with an abundance of natural resources. The recent history of the nation is, unfortunately, characterized by a civil war between 1991 and 2002 in which 50 thousand citizens lost their lives and in which the country lost most of its social, economic, and physical infrastructure. Since the end of the war, Sierra Leone has made remarkable progress in rebuilding the country. It has made advances in all areas, from the restoration of security to the delivery of basic public services. The country has witnessed an unprecedented surge in student enrollments, as well as great efforts to rehabilitate and reconstruct schools that were destroyed, damaged, or abandoned. Notwithstanding the significant progress, the education sector is facing huge challenges. Many of them are long-term consequences of the war; others are new challenges evolving from recent developments.

Financial resources play a key role in delivering quality education services. Although it already claims a large proportion of public resources, the education sector requires much more if the system is to be expanded, quality improvements made, and national and international goals met. To mobilize more domestic funds and attract more international resources for education from the primary level upward, Sierra Leone needs to show clear evidence of the effective use of funds already available, together with a credible plan for utilizing future, additional resources.

The purpose of this report is to provide an analysis of the education sector that enables a shared understanding among stakeholders, and thus lays a foundation for the preparation of an Education Sector Plan. With this objective in mind, the study outlines the current status of the education sector and highlights issues that policy makers need to address to move the sector forward. It also simulates a few policy scenarios and their financial implications to facilitate discussions about future feasible, affordable, and sustainable policy options.

The coverage of this report—a stock-taking exercise based on data, studies, reports, and documents available up to the 2004/05 school year—is limited to key factors, including access, quality, equity, management, and finance, and has an emphasis on basic education. Because of inadequate data at the time this report was produced, it was not possible to perform in-depth analysis in several areas (including, for example, student learning outcomes, nonformal and adult education, and educational opportunities for disabled children). For the same reason, analysis of early childhood education, technical and vocational education and training (TVET), and tertiary education is brief. In addition, as in many developing countries, the data currently available, which come from a variety of sources, contain discrepancies. In sum, the reliability of the data needs to be improved. This report, therefore, serves as a starting point for policy-relevant analytical work. As better data become available in the future, it will become possible to perform a more accurate and comprehensive analysis.

PROGRESS IN THE EDUCATION SECTOR

Sierra Leone's education system has made a remarkable recovery in several key areas following the end of the civil war, as outlined below.

STRONG GOVERNMENT COMMITMENT

The ingredient that has most contributed to the revitalization and rapid recovery of the Sierra Leonean education system is the government's commitment to it. The Education Act 2004 requires all children to complete basic education: 6 years of primary school and 3 years of junior secondary school (JSS). This national priority is consistent with the internationally agreed-upon Millennium Development Goals (MDGs) on education (as set out in the United Nations Millennium Declaration of 2000): ensure that all children complete a full course of primary schooling by 2015, and eliminate gender disparity at all levels of education by 2015. The government has committed itself to achieving the MDGs and to improving the quality of education at all levels.

In keeping with the policy framework articulated in the Sierra Leone Poverty Reduction Strategy Paper (PRSP) and other documents that set education as one of the country's priorities, the government abolished school fees for all children in primary schools and for girls in JSS in the

Northern and Eastern Regions. Additionally, a substantial share of government expenditure has been allocated to the education sector. From 2000 to 2004 the share of current expenditure allocated to education stabilized at about 20 percent, a far larger share than for any other single sector. Because of improvement in macroeconomic conditions, government expenditure on education increased in real terms during that period. The Ministry of Education, Science and Technology (MEST) has maintained the focus on expanding access to basic education across the entire country, paying particular attention to disadvantaged groups, such as girls and the Northern and Eastern Regions at the primary and JSS levels. This emphasis has led to a remarkable increase in student enrollments in the years following the end of the civil conflict.

INCREASED ACCESS

With the government's commitment and the right policies in place, such as the introduction of the Free Primary Education Policy in 2001, student enrollments have increased rapidly at all levels. Enrollments doubled in primary school between 2001/02 and 2004/05. Enrollments in JSS and senior secondary school (SSS) also experienced significant increases. Many children and youths who previously had little or no opportunity to access formal education are now in school. An increase in enrollments has also been witnessed in tertiary education. The corresponding upward trends are reflected in the gross enrollment ratios (GER) across different levels of education. The current primary GER of about 160 percent[1] places Sierra Leone at the top of low-income countries in Africa, and the JSS GER of 44 percent is close to the average. Although GERs in the SSS (14 percent) and tertiary levels (less than 4 percent) are below the averages for low-income African countries, the gap would have been even larger if the system had not experienced recent growth. In addition to an expansion in general education, student enrollments in TVET also expanded rapidly. There were more than 30,000 students enrolled in the different programs of the TVET subsector and are now more than 16,000 students enrolled in tertiary education.

NO DECLINE IN PRIMARY EXAMINATION RESULTS

As a result of the rapid increase in primary school enrollments and the abolishment of fees for examinations at the end of primary school, the number of students taking the National Primary School Examination (NPSE) has tripled from about 26,000 in 2001 to 78,000 in 2005. The score required to pass the test was increased by MEST in 2005 to regulate access to JSS on the basis of available space and to try to ensure that a greater percentage of those progressing to JSS would be able to succeed in the program. If, for comparison purposes, the pass mark had not changed between 2001 and 2005, the proportion of students passing each year would have remained stable at about 80 percent. Unlike those for many comparable countries, the NPSE pass rates indicate that examination outcomes have not suffered from an influx of students in the education system. A review of the number of students passing the NPSE reveals an optimistic picture of the learning outcomes of primary school students. The number of qualified primary graduates, defined by MEST based on pass rates, has increased from 21,700 in 2001 to 55,800 in 2005, a 2.5-fold increase. Completing primary school is particularly important because it takes about six years of successful schooling to become literate in Sierra Leone, as indicated by the Sierra Leone Integrated Household Survey (SLIHS) (2003/04).

DECENTRALIZATION OF SERVICE DELIVERY

Like many other African countries, Sierra Leone is undergoing a major decentralization process that will transfer power and responsibility for the delivery of basic services to local governments. According to the decentralization schedule, school management was to be devolved from MEST to local district, city, or town councils, a process that has begun with the 2005/06 school year. These councils will have full control and supervision of all preprimary, primary, and JSS schools by 2008, including such functions as the recruitment and payment of teachers, the provision of textbooks and teaching materials, and the rehabilitation and construction of schools. If decentralization succeeds, the education sector should benefit from more efficient and effective public spending, better service delivery, and improved school performance.

MAJOR CHALLENGES AND POLICY DEVELOPMENT

Sierra Leone's education system is recovering from the debilitating destruction of war. In the years to come, the country will continue to deal with problems caused by the war and face new issues and challenges. Priorities will shift from implementing emergency programs for reestablishing basic service delivery to designing and achieving fiscally sustainable long-term development for the education sector. Key issues that policy makers will likely encounter and suggested areas for further policy development to address them are outlined below.

ACHIEVING EDUCATION FOR ALL

Despite great progress made recently in increasing access to education, the goal of all children completing primary education is still not a reality. About 25–30 percent of primary-school-aged children (more than 240,000) are currently not in school. To achieve the international MDG goal for all children to complete a full course of primary schooling by 2015, Sierra Leone will need to enroll these out-of-school children and then encourage them to stay in school until the completion of the cycle. The gross completion ratio (GCR) in primary education was 65 percent in 2004/05, considerably short of the goal of 100 percent. Children (particularly girls) from the poorest households and those from rural areas and the Northern Region are lagging behind.

The Education for All (EFA) goal for Sierra Leone stipulates universal basic education (UBE; 6 years of primary school and 3 years of JSS). This goal poses an even greater challenge than universal primary education (UPE) because the JSS GCR was only 31 percent in 2004/05. Disparities between male and female students, poor and rich households, urban and rural localities, and across geographical regions are much more pronounced at the JSS than at the primary level. The road to reach UBE in Sierra Leone is a very long one.

EFA is now defined by the international community as *quality* universal education. Enrolling students in school is not enough; quality materials must be made available in a well-structured learning environment dedicated to achieving superior learning outcomes. Most schools in Sierra Leone have very poor classroom conditions and still lack sufficient learning materials and adequately qualified teachers; learning in many schools is minimal. Learning outcomes need to be improved, as evidenced by the Basic Education Certificate Examination (BECE), which shows only a 40 percent pass rate when a criterion of four passes, including English language or mathematics, is employed for graduation to SSS. These challenges have implications for policy development, as outlined in the following sections.

Free and compulsory primary schooling. Although the government abolished school fees, primary education is still not completely free because many schools impose a variety of charges on their students. In a country where there is widespread poverty, EFA cannot become a reality without removing barriers to schooling, especially for children from deprived regions or poor families. At the same time, detailed strategies are required to ensure that schools receive the financial and administrative support they need to provide the basic educational services.

Careful planning for basic EFA. The government is committed to implementing 9 years of UBE. Given the enormous financial outlay and immense capacity required to enroll all children in JSS and then ensure they can complete it, a realistic and sustainable plan must be developed. A two-step approach could be followed. The first step would be to achieve primary education for all, and the second to implement basic education for all. However, it is preferable to gradually expand JSS capacity (as permitted by available resources) without waiting for completion of the first step. This strategy would alleviate the pressure on JSS caused by the large cohorts of children graduating from the primary level.

Improving classroom conditions and enhancing student learning. The top priority immediately after the war was to rehabilitate all destroyed and damaged schools. This mission is far from complete and requires diligent oversight. Very large class sizes, overcrowded classrooms (more than 60 students per classroom), and poor classroom conditions are still common in many areas. School furniture should be provided so that children are not obliged to sit on the floor or on bricks or planks of wood. Despite notable efforts in the provision of free textbooks in the past few years, many students still do not have the necessary learning materials. A dedicated nationwide effort will be needed to supply all children with textbooks. The ultimate measure of educational quality is student learning outcomes, which require significant improvement. Furthermore, an effective system to monitor student learning would allow Sierra Leone to assess the quality of the system. The quality and relevance of the examination system (NPSE and BECE) should be reviewed, and analysis of the results of these two examinations should go beyond just pass rates, which are more suitable for deciding student advancement than for determining what students have learned or how well.

Motivating teachers. Teachers have a critical and unique role to play in the provision of quality schooling. Being both knowledgeable and motivated are indispensable prerequisites. A teacher motivation and incentives survey found that there is a serious teacher morale issue in the country. Only about 30 percent of primary teachers in the survey are satisfied with their jobs. Most of these satisfied teachers are, unfortunately, unqualified teachers in government and government-assisted schools or private schools. Reasons for teacher dissatisfaction included late payment of salaries, unfair recruitment policies, poor working and living conditions in the rural areas, and a grievous lack of in-service training opportunities. An improvement in policies for hiring, training, housing, and paying teachers should be a priority.

EXPANDING POSTBASIC EDUCATION

Supplying teachers, increasing the pool of human capital, and establishing a knowledge-based economy all depend on an adequate postbasic education sector that produces quality graduates in sufficient quantity. Sierra Leone's student flow pyramid narrows rapidly toward the top of the education ladder. The gross enrollment ratios at SSS and tertiary levels are only about 14 percent and 4 percent, respectively. Despite growth in these subsectors over the past few years, these rates still are below average for low-income countries. Postbasic education will need to be expanded congruent with the explosion of growth in primary schooling and JSS. General education must be balanced with TVET. The analysis of TVET and tertiary education points out disturbingly poor learning conditions and outcomes, an outdated curriculum, and low relevance to the labor market.

These issues need to be addressed in a comprehensive and consistent way. The development and implementation of a TVET and tertiary education strategy could be a good way forward, following a two-staged approach:

1. *Identify human resources development priorities and labor market needs.* As suggested by the PRSP Education Sector Review in 2004 (Bennell, Harding, and Rogers-Wright 2004), it is imperative to identify the country's human resource development priorities and labor market needs through comprehensive study and wide consultation. The results will provide a clear sense of direction for SSS, TVET, and tertiary education.
2. *Develop a TVET and tertiary education strategy.* Based on the priorities established in step 1, the education sector should develop a TVET and tertiary education framework that redefines the objectives of these two subsectors. The framework should facilitate development of a solid plan for restructuring TVET and tertiary programs to support key growing sectors, reform the curriculum, expand student enrollments, address gender gaps and other subgroup disparities, retrain and upgrade the teaching force, improve physical conditions and facilities, and establish quality standards. Financial resources should be reallocated accordingly.

ENHANCING THE QUALITY OF TEACHERS

The war has left a deep scar on the teaching force. Notwithstanding the training efforts of the past few years, many teachers remain unqualified in the pretertiary sector (for example, 40 percent of teachers are unqualified at the primary level) and have outdated knowledge and skills at the tertiary level. It is impossible to enhance student learning outcomes without addressing the inadequacies of their teachers. To address this pervasive problem, a systematic approach must replace the ad hoc process now in place.

- *Reforming the in-service training system.* As suggested in the PRSP Education Sector Review, the teacher training system must be comprehensively reformed. MEST needs to formally build capacity through the use of a core group of in-service training officers covering main subject areas. MEST should develop an in-service training strategy and implementation plan based on the current status of the teaching force and on the various demands from schools. The in-service training should also facilitate teacher qualification standards and promotion structure. Training programs aimed at the large number of unqualified teachers in primary schools and JSS are urgently needed and should be the top priority of the in-service training plan. A distance-learning program has been popular and has expanded rapidly over the past few years, offering good potential for enhancement of teacher knowledge and skills. This may be a good time to review the program, to examine what has worked and what needs to be changed so that the program can be made more effective and relevant.

MANAGING DECENTRALIZATION

Decentralization can lead to improved efficiency, effectiveness, and delivery of services as well as increased school performance. However, none of these effects follow automatically from decentralization. The key challenges lie in the following areas:

- *Agreeing on strategy.* The decentralization process is treated differently by the Education Act and the Local Government Act (LGA). Clear lines of authority and accountability have not been drawn. For decentralization and devolution to work, the local governments and MEST will have to come to a shared understanding of the decentralization strategy, with a clear delineation of roles, authority, and functions for the local governments and MEST.
- *Building local capacity.* Local capacity is among many factors that play a key role in determining whether decentralization will lead to better education service delivery. Currently, the capacity in managing human, financial, and physical resources for the education sector is weak in most local councils. Local councils and MEST need to work together to

develop a capacity building plan to ensure that the devolved functions can be effectively managed and that schools and children truly benefit from the decentralization.

- *Strengthening MEST's capacity.* As decentralization progresses, the role of MEST in planning, formulating policy, and regulating service standards and curriculum development will strengthen and become more integral. But the present capacity may not allow MEST to play its desired role; substantial capacity building efforts will first have to be made. The decentralization reform should be seen as an opportunity to do a needs assessment on the current and desired levels of capacity—both managerial and technical. A well-developed continuous professional development program would be a worthwhile investment. In short, the issue of capacity is one of the most critical challenges facing Sierra Leone today, and a transformation in public sector pay and incentive structures may be necessary, along with an aggressive capacity building agenda.

ELIMINATING DISPARITIES IN EDUCATION

Disparities are wide across different groups in terms of access to schooling and public spending on education. Female children, rural children, children outside the Western Area, and those in poorer households all have reduced access to schooling; and the disparities become larger when climbing the education ladder. Consequently these disadvantaged subgroups receive a declining share of public spending from primary to tertiary education as their quotient in the student population decreases rapidly. To promote equity, government intervention could focus on:

- *Targeting the poor, rural children, and girls.* The government should build on the efforts already made to reduce gender disparity in access to primary schooling by extending these efforts to secondary education. Gender disparities are still very large at the JSS and SSS levels. As more primary-school students progress to JSS, it is important to ensure the parity of transition rates between girls and boys, and to ensure that girls are successfully completing both primary and JSS levels in equal proportions. MEST has already abolished fees for girls to attend JSS in the Eastern and Northern Regions, but this effort should be extended to other regions if cost considerations allow it. In many rural areas, attending primary school is still associated with the impediments of distance, affordability, and opportunity cost; and attending JSS remains very difficult. Attending SSS is almost impossible, and going to a tertiary institution is mostly a dream. Narrowing the gap between urban and rural children at all levels for accessing school should be an urgent priority. The Education Sector Plan could include a concrete strategy to foster more equal access regardless of gender, location, and family socioeconomic status.

• *Making the distribution of resources more equitable.* Improvement in distribution of public resources requires the allocation of public funds to those levels with the highest proportion of poor children. The prime target could include primary education in general but also involve basic skill training in TVET for the poor. JSS should also be targeted for the purpose of gradually implementing the basic EFA policy. Efforts will be required to ensure cost recovery at the tertiary level, combined with scholarship schemes for students from poor families. This is a complex and difficult area that the government needs to explore further, drawing on the experiences of other countries.

IMPROVING DATA

The lack of good data on the education sector is highlighted throughout this report. Data are important for various reasons, and planning, monitoring, evaluation, effective management, and policy making all call for timely, accurate, and reliable data on the education sector. In a decentralized system, it is particularly important that all subnational regions provide timely and quality data. Without the latter, MEST will not be able to perform its primary role of monitoring and supervision. In addition to an education management information system (EMIS), financial and human resource management systems would improve fiscal management and accountability.

MEST is in the process of establishing an EMIS system. The major components of the EMIS could include:

• *Annual school census.* One key function of the EMIS is to conduct a high quality school census every year to capture the required data for planning and policy-relevant analysis. The data produced from the school census should cover all subsectors of education. It is important to design a set of core education indicators to track progress toward the intended goals.

• *Sample-based student learning assessment.* In addition to the annual school census, a student learning assessment program could be introduced to carry out an in-depth survey of a nationally representative sample of schools. This survey would collect information on student learning outcomes and associated factors, such as school organization and management practices, school infrastructure, teacher characteristics and teaching practices, learning materials and equipment, and home environment. The purpose of such a survey is to assess the education system as a whole, rather than focusing on individual students.

- *Household survey.* The value to the education sector of a quality household survey cannot be underestimated. To maximize the benefit of household surveys, the education sector should take an active role in designing the questionnaire, so that the most pertinent questions are incorporated into the surveys.

MOBILIZING AND USING RESOURCES

Sierra Leone's education system is in transition from postconflict recovery to sustainable development. Expansion and upgrading of the education sector will require additional funding and more effective use of resources, given the immense tasks that face the nation in almost all areas, with emphasis on access, quality, equity, and management capacity. The following measures should be considered for improving the mobilization and management of resources:

- *Increasing the overall resource envelope for education through further donor support.* The government is already allocating a sizable proportion of its expenditure to education. Given the postwar needs of all sectors, there may be little scope for the government to increase the share of its spending on education. Households are already contributing a substantial amount to primary and secondary education. Therefore, further funding must be mobilized from the donor community. Joining the EFA Fast Track Initiative (FTI) would accomplish this.
- *Aligning allocations of public spending to subsectors with stated policies.* The government will need to review subsector allocations to align them with its policy priorities. For instance, if the government wants to prioritize technical and vocational education in addition to primary education, as stated in the PRSP, then the share of education spending that goes to this subsector should be increased. In fact, the TVET sector has experienced a recent decrease in expenditure both in absolute terms and as a share of total education expenditure.
- *Promoting public-private partnership and cost recovery at the tertiary level.* Competing for public funds among subsectors of education will

require the government to make trade-offs and seek alternative ways of financing education, such as promoting private schools and universities and engaging in cost recovery in tertiary education. The number of private primary and secondary schools is relatively small in Sierra Leone compared to other low-income countries in Africa, and there were no private universities at the time this report was prepared. Therefore, there is legitimate hope for increasing the share of private schools and universities in the future. In addition to promoting private partnership, the tertiary subsector could implement a sustainable cost recovery system. There are many different mechanisms for cost recovery; Sierra Leone should carefully study the experiences of other countries to find those mechanisms most suitable to its own situation.

POLICY SCENARIOS FOR LONG-TERM DEVELOPMENT

Long-term sustainability is important if the education sector is to move forward. Policy choices for development targets need to consider both fiscal affordability and implementation capacity. To facilitate discussions about policy choices, a policy simulation model is used to examine the relationship between targets and financial implications, which in turn helps in the formulation of achievable and sustainable education goals. Four policy scenarios are presented to illustrate the use of such a model and to facilitate policy discussions. Each of them takes into account existing education policies and goals in Sierra Leone, and all stipulate achievement of 100 percent primary school completion by 2015. The main purpose of the illustrative scenarios is to evaluate trade-offs among the targets, estimate the size of financing gaps, and assess the sustainability of the financial framework. The model projects the costs, revenues, and financing gaps for the education sector to 2015.

SCENARIO 1: EFA ACTION PLAN

This scenario includes most of the targets given in the Sierra Leone National EFA Action Plan developed in 2004. The focus of this scenario is on the government continuing to be the provider of education at all levels. The involvement of private providers is minimal. All targets are very ambitious: high enrollment at postprimary levels, small class sizes, and low pupil-teacher ratios. Little account is taken of in-country financial, human, and technical capacity. As a result, the financing gap is very large and sustainability is unlikely.

SCENARIO 2: ACHIEVABLE

This scenario focuses on what is achievable given the current situation in Sierra Leone. The enrollment rates, transition rates, and the degree of private involvement are all adjusted from scenario 1, bearing in mind incountry capacity and sustainability of provisions. The pupil-teacher ratios and class sizes are slightly higher than desired but are still acceptable, given Sierra Leone's stage of development. As a result, the financing gap is much smaller compared to scenario 1 and sustainability is more likely.

SCENARIO 3: OPTIMISTIC

The third scenario is somewhat more optimistic than scenario 2 and can be seen as a compromise between scenarios 1 and 2. It includes more government and government-assisted preprimary schools, smaller class sizes, and lower pupil-teacher ratios, increasing the gross enrollment ratio at JSS to achieve UBE more rapidly. As a result, the financing gap is larger than that of scenario 2 and sustainability is questionable.

SCENARIO 4: EFFICIENT

The final scenario is developed from scenarios 2 and 3. It requires the system to be more efficient, including a reduction of repetition rates and unit cost of teachers, as well as an augmentation of class sizes and pupil-teacher ratios. It results in a smaller financing gap than in scenario 3 and allocates more financial resources for each of the postprimary levels. Therefore, sustainability is more likely.

The financing gaps in 2015 for the four scenarios are US$171 million (scenario 1), US$46 million (scenario 2), US$69 million (scenario 3), and US$57 million (scenario 4). Whatever the scenario selected, the financing gap is substantial (more than 100 percent of the resource envelope in two of the four cases). Yet, the model results also suggest that there is some margin of maneuver, because the largest gap (scenario 1) is more than three times bigger than the smallest one (scenario 2). When interpreting the results, however, it should be kept in mind that the model focuses mostly on current expenditure. Therefore, if the capital costs of expansion are factored in, the real financial gaps will be even larger.

As domestic resources are clearly going to be insufficient to match the needs of primary education for all (let alone UBE), donor support will be required. However, even in the "best" case (scenario 2), the gaps may exceed what external partners are willing to pledge. In addition, heavy reliance on external financing would not be without problems. Therefore the model should continue to be used as a planning tool to discover a scenario that better balances the legitimate ambitions of the country and its still limited resources and capacity. More consultation with stakeholders is needed to agree on a sustainable long-term development policy scenario that could become the backbone of the Education Sector Plan being developed by MEST.

CONCLUSION

Four years after the war, the education system has achieved an extraordinary recovery, reflected in the doubling of student enrollments in nearly all levels, from primary to tertiary. With the government's strong commitment to education and favorable resource allocation to the sector, the education system has great potential for sustainable development. But major challenges remain, formidable issues that the government has to address in a comprehensive, innovative, and systematic way. The development of the Education Sector Plan should prove an effective way forward, grounded in credible, affordable, and sustainable policies that should be followed by forceful implementation strategies.

CHAPTER 1

Postconflict Context

Sierra Leone has recently emerged from a brutal civil war that lasted a decade (1991–2002) and destroyed most of the country's social, economic, and physical infrastructure. It left a multitude of scars in the education sector: devastated school infrastructure, severe shortages of teaching materials, overcrowding in many classrooms in safer areas, displacement of teachers and delay in paying their salaries, frequent disruptions of schooling, disorientation and psychological trauma among children, poor learning outcomes, weakened institutional capacity to manage the system, and a serious lack of information and data to plan service provision.

The country has made a remarkable recovery since the end to the war was officially declared in January 2002: increased security; sustained economic growth; and aggressive and effective restoration of public services, including education. Primary school enrollment has expanded impressively in the past 4 years. Poverty levels, however, are still very high, and indicators measuring economic and human development are some of the lowest in the world. The future holds promise, but the country still faces great challenges. The government has resolved to move the country forward and as part of this effort has prepared the PRSP (Government of Sierra Leone 2005) to pursue economic, social, and public rebuilding.

The PRSP recognizes that human resource development is the bedrock of poverty reduction and sustainable development. It asserts that the overall objectives of the education sector are to provide basic education[1] for all Sierra Leoneans and support manpower development in key sectors. The government is committed to the global initiatives of EFA (UNESCO 1990) and for every child to complete a course of primary education by 2015, the educational target set forth in the MDGs (United Nations 2000). Consistent with its commitment to education, the government has allocated a large portion of public expenditure to education. The

challenges for the education sector are to use the public finances efficiently and effectively. The rapid growth of the child and youth population in the years to come will add more pressure to the education system.

This report contributes to the ongoing dialogue on how to move the
education sector from postconflict recovery to sustainable development.
It is also intended to provide MEST with an analytical platform on which
to build its sectorwide plan. This chapter presents an overview of the
demographic, political, social, and economic contexts in which the education system operates, beginning with a summary in box 1.1. The purpose is to set the stage for a discussion of the issues, challenges, and
opportunities that the education sector faces.

BOX 1.1 SIERRA LEONE AT A GLANCE

Geography. Sierra Leone is a small country situated on the west
coast of Africa, bounded on the west and southwest by the
Atlantic Ocean, on the north and east by the Republic of Guinea,
and on the south by Liberia. It has an area of 27,925 square miles
(73,326 square kilometers), with a maximum distance of 315
miles from north to south and 228 miles from west to east. The
country has important mineral resources, including diamonds,
gold, bauxite, iron ore, and rutile. Seventy-five percent of the land
is arable. Of the arable land, 10 percent is cultivated, mainly for
food crops such as rice, cassava, yams, and other root crops.

People. The population of Sierra Leone is approximately
5 million and consists of a considerable number of diverse ethno-
linguistic groups. Thirteen distinct languages are spoken; while
English serves as the official language. In addition to traditional
African religions and customs, Islam and Christianity are widely
practiced in the country, and educational institutions sponsored
by both religions abound.

Politics. Sierra Leone gained its independence on April 27, 1961.
Recent political history in Sierra Leone has been marked by extreme
instability and violence. Starting in 1967, the country suffered
through five military coups and the most recent brutal armed conflict which lasted more than 10 years (1991–2002). During the last
civil conflict, 50,000 people were killed, 2 million displaced,
100,000 were mutilated, and 250,000 women were raped. The first
postconflict democratic election was held in 2002, and President
Kabbah was re-elected for a second term.

Administration. Sierra Leone is divided into 4 regions (the Northern, Southern, and Eastern Regions, and the Western Area), 13 administrative districts and 149 chiefdoms. Freetown, the capital city, is in the Western Area. The decentralization of central government services and the reestablishment of local government are the key political and administrative reforms of recent years. There are 19 local councils, and the first local government elections following the end of civil conflict took place in 2004.

Economy. Even though Sierra Leone is blessed with an abundance of natural resources, years of political instability and mismanagement have meant that the economic development of the country is limited and the majority of people are very poor. Per capita gross national income (GNI) of US$200 in 2004 is much lower than the average of US$600 for Sub-Saharan African countries. About two-thirds of the working-age population engages in subsistence agriculture. Manufacturing consists mainly of the processing of raw materials and of light manufacturing for the domestic market. The bauxite and rutile mines shut down during the conflict are due to be re-opened soon. Commercial agriculture, largely cocoa, coffee, and palm oil, was devastated by the civil conflict. The major source of hard currency is diamond mining.

POLITICAL AND ADMINISTRATIVE STRUCTURE

Sierra Leone gained its independence in 1961 and became a republic in 1971. Control was centralized in 1972, after the dissolution of the local councils: the District, Town, and Freetown City Management Committees were appointed by the central government rather than by local people. The centralization and the associated rise in corruption are viewed by many observers as one of the causes of the civil war (Government of Sierra Leone 2005, 1). The most significant political and institutional reform in recent years has been to decentralize governance after 33 years of central rule. The Local Government Act of 2004 established local councils and provides the legal basis for the devolution of basic service delivery—including the delivery of education services—to these councils. The first local government elections were held in 2004, and the resultant 19 local councils are the political authority for their localities, answerable to their local electorates. The various reasons behind the decentralization reform are related to issues of economic development, administrative efficiency, and participatory politics. A list of important events in the history of Sierra Leone is given in appendix table D.1. The regions, administrative districts, local councils, and educational districts are shown in appendix table D.2.

POPULATION STRUCTURE AND GROWTH

Sierra Leone's population has been steadily rising over the past four decades, as shown in figure 1.1. The population at the time of the last census (2004) was just under 5 million, with about 66 percent of the population living in rural areas (Government of Sierra Leone 2005, 20). The average growth rate between 1985 and 2004 was 1.8 percent per year. A rapid increase in the population is expected over the next few decades, resulting in a projected increase of about 75 percent by 2025.

All of the administrative districts in Sierra Leone experienced growth in their populations between the 1963 and 1985 population censuses, as shown in figure 1.2. The growth continued through to the 2004 census in all districts except Kono, a town in the Eastern Region, which saw its population decline by 14 percent between 1985 and 2004 (Kono was one of the districts most devastated by the civil war). Between 1985 and 2004, the largest increase in population occurred in Freetown (an increase of more than 300,000), and the largest relative increases were seen in the Western Rural Area and Pujehun District (where the populations almost

Figure 1.1 Total Population, 1963–2004, and Projected Population, 2005–25

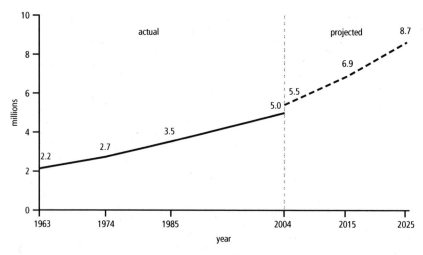

Sources: Actual statistics from Sierra Leone Population Census 2004; projected figures from the United Nations Population Division (medium variant).

Figure 1.2 Population by Administrative District, 1963–2004

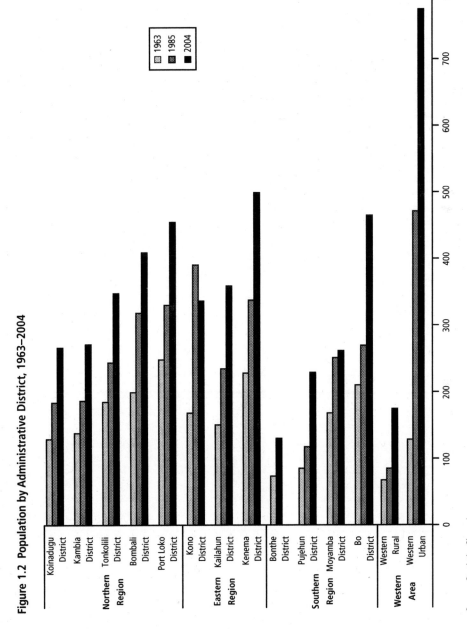

Source: Statistics Sierra Leone.

Figure 1.3 Population Pyramids, 2004 and 2015

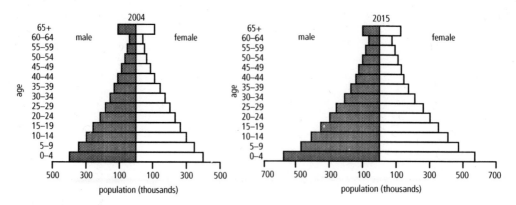

Source: Appendix figure D.1.

Table 1.1 Population Distribution by Age, 1963–2025

	Population aged less than 15		Population aged 15–34		Total population	
	(thousands)	(%)	(thousands)	(%)	(thousands)	(%)
1963	801	36.7	765	35.1	2,180	100.0
1974	1,110	40.6	861	31.5	2,735	100.0
1985	1,459	41.5	1,122	31.9	3,516	100.0
2004	2,088	42.0	1,682	33.8	4,977	100.0
2015	2,956	42.9	2,281	33.1	6,897	100.0

Sources: Statistics Sierra Leone 1963–2004; United Nations Population Division (medium variant 2015).

doubled) and in Bo District (where it increased by three quarters of its 1985 population). These changes were largely due to the movement of internally displaced persons during the war.

Children and youth make up a very large portion of the total population in Sierra Leone. Just over 40 percent of the total population is less than 15 years of age, and around 34 percent is between 15 and 34 years old (defined as youth in Sierra Leone). Between 1963 and 2004 both the numbers of children and youth and their share of the total population increased (table 1.1). A rapid expansion is projected for the younger age groups (due to high fertility rates) in the coming years, with little change in the size of the older population (due to stagnant and low life expectancy rates). These demographics can be seen in the population pyramids for 2004 and 2015 (figure 1.3).

POVERTY LEVELS AND WELL-BEING

The decade-long civil war intensified poverty in the population, placing the country at the bottom of the United Nations Development Program's (UNDP) Human Development Index (HDI). Poverty in Sierra Leone is defined at two levels: the food/extreme poverty line and the full poverty line.[2] Seventy percent of the population falls below the full poverty line, and 26 percent lives under the food/extreme poverty line (Statistics Sierra Leone 2003/04). The total expenditure of the average poor household is 29 percent below the amount required to meet their basic needs (Government of Sierra Leone 2005).

Poverty is heavily concentrated in rural areas, where nearly 80 percent of people are poor compared to 54 percent in urban areas. About one-third of the rural poor population lives below the food/extreme poverty limit. The expenditures of the rural poor are 37 percent less than the amount required to meet their basic needs, whereas the urban poor have a shortfall of 27 percent. Table 1.2 shows that the five rural areas with the highest incidence of poverty are in the districts of Kenema, Kailahun, Bombali, Port Loko, and Tonkolili.

Poverty in urban areas outside Freetown is also high, with the poverty incidence equal to the national average of 70 percent. Twenty percent of

Table 1.2 Incidence of Poverty by District and Locality, 2002/03

District	Urban			Rural		
	Food poor	Full poor	Poverty ranking	Food poor	Full poor	Poverty ranking
Bonthe	39.9	88.7	1	33.1	83.5	6
Tonkolili	36.4	87.7	2	31.0	84.2	5
Kailahun	25.7	86.2	3	54.9	94.6	2
Bombali	25.1	83.4	4	69.6	90.0	3
Koinadugu	28.6	81.1	5	29.2	76.3	8
Kenema	19.5	77.5	6	52.4	95.0	1
Kambia	. .	75.6	7	11.6	67.7	12
Port Loko	12.7	71.9	8	22.6	85.0	4
Bo	27.3	59.9	9	24.3	67.8	11
Pujehun	7.7	59.5	10	16.3	59.6	13
Moyamba	11.1	59.0	11	17.4	69.1	10
Kono	9.2	56.3	12	35.2	79.6	7
Western Area	3.2	17.1	13	26.3	70.1	9
Total	14.7	54.3	. .	32.8	78.9	. .

Source: SLIHS 2003/04.
Note: . . = nil or negligible.

people in these areas live in extreme poverty. Freetown, with a poverty incidence of 15 percent, recorded the lowest proportion of poor people. The five urban areas with the highest incidence of poverty are to be found in the districts of Bonthe, Tonkolili, Kailahun, Bombali and Koinadugu.

Agriculture is the largest employment sector in Sierra Leone, accounting for about 75 percent of the population (Government of Sierra Leone 2005, 32). Those working in this sector are among the poorest in the country. There are many factors contributing to the problems in this sector, including poor investment and weak capacity. The fishing industry is also a large employer with high rates of poverty, and it also suffered badly during the war. The poor performance of these major sectors contributes to the problem of families requiring their children to work, which in turn results in poor educational outcomes.

There is a strong relationship between poverty incidence and education attainment, as seen in table 1.3. More than 70 percent of households headed by an individual with no formal education are living below the full poverty line. The incidence of poverty decreases with the attainment of higher levels of education.

The country has one of the lowest levels of life expectancy in the world. Average life expectancy is only 39 years for men and 42 years for women, which is about 10 years shorter than the average for countries in Africa and 25 years shorter than that for the world. The decade-long civil conflict halted the previously increasing trend in life expectancy (figure 1.4).

The state of health in Sierra Leone is particularly concerning. Child mortality rates are among the highest in the world: 17 percent of children die before their first birthday, and 28 percent die before they reach the age of 5 (see table 1.4 for selected health indicators). The maternal mortality rate is the highest in the world at 2,000 maternal deaths per 100,000 live births. The number one killer in the country is malaria. A new national

Table 1.3 Poverty Incidence by Formal Educational Attainment, 2003/04

Educational level	Percentage below the poverty line[a]	
	Male-headed households	Female-headed households
None	74.5	72.2
Primary Education	63.2	57.9
Junior Secondary School	52.7	*
Senior Secondary School	45.2	28.2
All	70.2	67.6

Source: Government of Sierra Leone 2005, 24.
Note: * = sample size is too small to display a reliable estimate.
a. The poverty line is estimated at Le 770,648 per year (US$2 per day equivalent).

Figure 1.4 Life Expectancy, 1950–55 to 2000–05

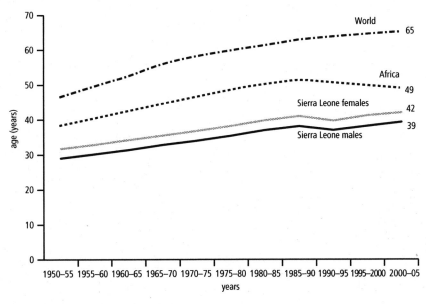

Source: United Nations Population Division.

Table 1.4 Selected Health Indicators

Indicator	Value
Life expectancy at birth (years), 2000–05	
Total	41
Male	39
Female	42
Total fertility rate, 2003 (births per woman)	5.6
Infant mortality per 1,000 live births, 2003	166
Under 5 mortality rate per 1,000 live births	284
Maternal mortality rate per 100,000 live births, 2000	2,000
Births attended by skilled health staff, 2000 (% of total)	42
Access to health service, 2002 (%)	40
Access to safe drinking water, 2002 (%)	57
Access to safe sanitation, 2002 (%)	39
Disability prevalence rate, 2002 (%)	7.0
HIV/AIDS prevalence rate, 2003 (%)	
National	1.4
Freetown	2.3
Outside Freetown	0.7

Sources: United Nations Population Division; World Bank 2005b; Government of Sierra Leone 2005, 37; UNAIDS 2002.

malaria protocol has been adopted, but effective treatment has not yet been implemented. In addition, tuberculosis (TB), acute respiratory diseases, diarrhea, Lassa fever (an acute viral illness), cholera, and other waterborne diseases all contribute to the high mortality rates. Compared to many African countries, Sierra Leone has a lower prevalence of HIV infection (1.4 percent). However, the prevalence in Freetown is much higher, at 2.3 percent (compared with 0.7 percent outside of Freetown). Overall, the extremely poor health outcomes reflect a failure to provide health services in the country. In 2004 there were only 33 nurses, 4.7 midwives, and 7.3 physicians for every 100,000 people in the country, or 0.45 medical personnel per 1,000 people, well below the World Health Organization standard of 2.5 per 1,000 (Medecins Sans Frontiers 2006).

ADULT LITERACY AND EDUCATIONAL ATTAINMENT

Literacy was defined in the population census of 2004 as being able to read and write in any language. Of those aged 10 years and older, only 39 percent are literate (Statistics Sierra Leone 2004). The rates varied greatly by age, gender, and region. Half the male population is literate, compared with only 29 percent of the female population (table 1.5). Literacy rates in the Western Area are twice as high as those in the other regions. In Sierra Leone, most children are literate after 6 years of education (figure 1.5), highlighting the importance of completing primary education.

Educational attainment across the population of Sierra Leone is low, with an average of less than 4 years of education completed for males (aged 15 years or older) and less than 2 years for females. Figure 1.6 shows that individuals in the younger age groups have more years of education than those in the older groups. The geographic divide is clear: men

Table 1.5 Literacy Rates, 2004

	Percent		
	Literate	Illiterate	Not stated
10 years and older	39	60	1
Male	49	50	1
Female	29	70	1
Eastern Region	31	68	1
Northern Region	31	68	1
Southern Region	34	65	1
Western Area	65	34	1
10–14-year-olds	58	41	1

Source: Statistics Sierra Leone Population Census 2004.

Figure 1.5 Literacy Rates by Grade, 2003/04

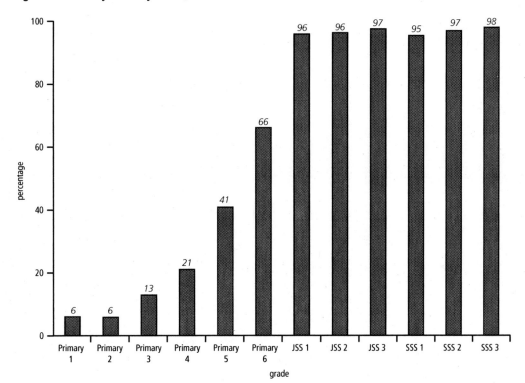

Source: SLIHS 2003/04.

in urban areas have about three times as many years of education as do men in rural areas, and the relative difference for women is even greater.

CHILDREN, YOUTH, AND YOUTH EMPLOYMENT

The years of war in Sierra Leone not only disrupted the education of children and youth, but left many of them disabled, separated from their families, or orphaned. Today many young people are illiterate and have no employment skills and little work experience.

Youth unemployment and underemployment is a key priority for both young people themselves and for the Government of Sierra Leone. A recent youth and employment study found that over three-quarters of youth worked in the agricultural sector, with about 60 percent of the 15- to 24-year-old workers and 40 percent of those between 25 and 34 years old being unpaid. The low productivity and incomes in the agricultural sector have exacerbated the migration of youth to cities and urban areas to seek employment opportunities. Most of the youth remain

Figure 1.6 Average Years of Education Completed by Age Group, Location, and Gender, 2003/04

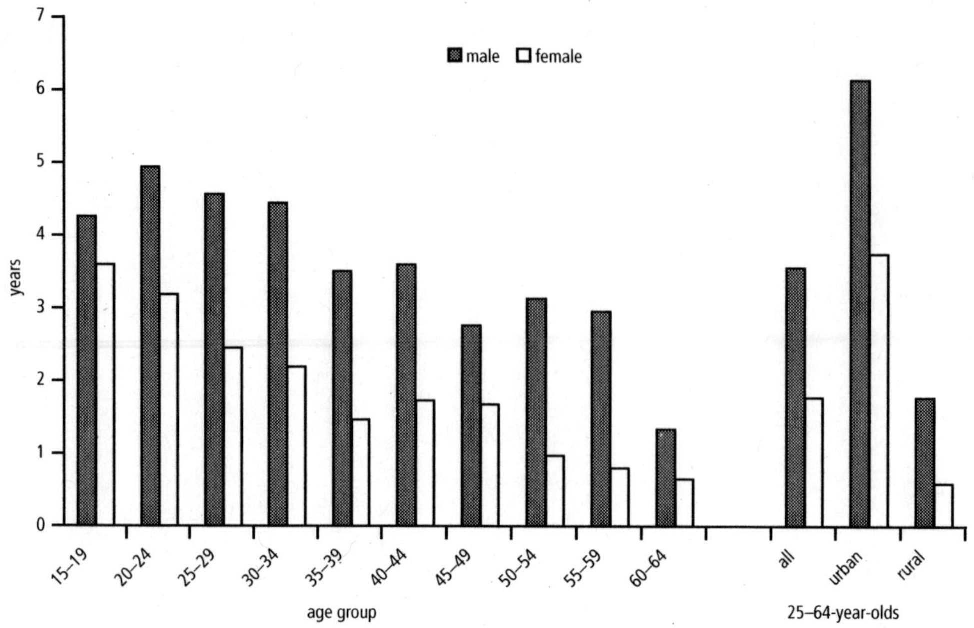

Source: SLIHS 2003/04.

unemployed and have joined the ranks of the urban poor. Focus groups from the Youth and Employment Study found that, although some youth would like increased skill development training (especially in such areas as business development), they tend to experience a gap between skills and available resources: they are trained but lack the tools to practice their trade, there is no demand for their skills in their communities, they lack resources to start their own businesses, or they lack resources to become certified to exercise their trades (for example, drivers).

Against this background, the government has prioritized the development of the youth population to sustain postconflict peace-building and poverty reduction (Government of Sierra Leone 2005, 2006). As emphasized in the PRSP, the medium-term objective is to promote the social and economic development of youth. The government's overall strategy is to ensure that all poverty reduction programs give priority to the employment and income needs of youths in urban and rural areas. Specific strategies for youth development include (1) setting up a framework for effective youth development and employment policy formulation and implementation, involving all stakeholders and the youth themselves at district and national levels; (2) training unskilled or semiskilled and unemployed youths, including former demobilized combatants, in the informal sector system and linking them to job opportunities in the private and public sectors; and (3) promoting the structures for effective social integration of young men and women into mainstream society.

The education of children cannot be separated from the broader context of poverty. For example, one of the main reasons for children not attending school is the economic difficulties of the family (see table 2.6). Although attendance of primary school is free, there are the hidden costs of travel and uniforms, plus the loss of work that the child may have been doing in support of the family during school hours (such as farm labor or domestic duties). In addition, early marriage is often encouraged due to economic difficulties, resulting in girls not attending school. The PRSP found that other challenges to child poverty include poor child protection services; a decline in family, cultural, and traditional values; and child powerlessness (Government of Sierra Leone 2005, 48).

OVERVIEW OF GOVERNMENT FINANCE

IMPACT OF WAR ON ECONOMIC DEVELOPMENT

Sierra Leone's economy collapsed after years of mismanagement and the civil war. During the 1960s and early 1970s, GDP grew steadily at 3–5 percent per year (table 1.6). The growth was mainly due to strong production in the mining and agricultural sectors. However, a decline in the output of the mining sector in the late 1970s led to a slow down in GDP growth to less than 2 percent per year. A further decline occurred in the late 1980s, primarily caused by poor macroeconomic and fiscal management policies of the government.

The onset of the rebel war in 1991 and the resultant general insecurity caused the economy to shrink substantially (figure 1.7). Apart from a period of structural adjustment in 1994 and a brief cease fire and elections

Table 1.6 Prewar Trends in Real GDP and GDP Growth Rates, 1963–88

Year	Real GDP (1963/64 = 100)	Average annual growth rate (%)
1963/64	100	
1968/69	117	3.2
1973/74	149	5.0
1978/79	161	1.6
1983/84	188	3.1
1988/89	182	−0.7

Source: Government of Sierra Leone 2005, 50.

Figure 1.7 War Impact on Real GDP Growth, 1991–2004

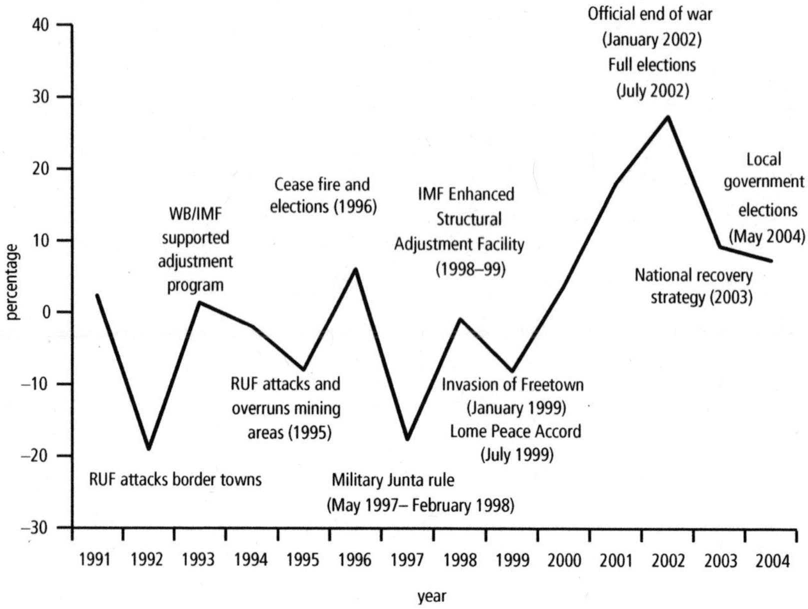

Source: Government of Sierra Leone 2005, and updated with IMF data April 2006.

in 1996, the 1990s were characterized by negative growth in the GDP. In addition to the destruction of social and economic infrastructure, major economic activities, including agriculture, mining, manufacturing, and service-related activities, were disrupted. Consequently, the annual GDP growth rate plummeted by 18 percent in 1997, stagnated in 1998, and fell a further 8 percent in 1999.

The contraction in economic activity resulted in a sharp decline in domestic revenues. At the same time, expenditure pressures persisted, driven mainly by security-related outlays. As a result, the budget deficit rose to more than 8 percent of GDP in 1999 (table 1.7). In the absence of external sources of financing, the deficit was financed mostly from the domestic banking system, thereby fueling inflation. Inflation rose to 35 percent at the end of the 1990s, and the exchange rate depreciated markedly. The decline in output during the period was attributed largely to a decline in investment and the disruptions to mining and agricultural activities due to rebel activities.

POSTCONFLICT RECOVERY PROGRAMS

Following the signing of the Lome Peace Accord[3] in July 1999, the government, in collaboration with multilateral and bilateral donors, elaborated

Table 1.7 Selected Economic Indicators during the War Years, 1990–99

	1990	1991	1992	1993	1994	1995	1996	1997	1998	1999
GDP (current, Le billions)	98.4	230.4	339.6	436.3	535.0	657.6	867.1	834.5	1,051.3	1,207.7
GDP (constant 2003, Le billions)	2,252.2	2,305.1	1,866.8	1,892.5	1,855.7	1,707.2	1,811.3	1,492.6	1,480.1	1,359.9
Real GDP growth rate (%)	—	2.4	−19.0	1.4	−1.9	−8.0	6.1	−17.6	−0.8	−8.1
Budget deficit (Le millions)	2,413	10,477	16,502	17,099	26,123	39,835	49,925	48,300	47,724	102,373
Budget deficit as a percent of GDP	2.5	4.5	4.9	3.9	4.9	6.1	5.8	5.8	4.5	8.5
Annual inflation rate (%)	111	103	66	22	24	26	23	15	35	34
Exchange rate (Le / $)	189	435	526	578	613	943	909	1,333	1,591	2,276
Exchange rate depreciation (%)		130.4	21.1	9.7	6.1	53.9	−3.6	46.7	19.3	43.1

Sources: IMF; MOF.
Note: Pre-2000 GDP figures are not directly comparable to post-2000 figures due to differences in accounting and statistical methods employed. — = not available.

an economic recovery program. The program was supported by the International Monetary Fund (IMF) under the Emergency Post Conflict Assistance Facility, by the World Bank through the first Economic Rehabilitation and Recovery Credit, and by the United Kingdom and European Union. The economic recovery program aimed at restoring macroeconomic stability, rehabilitating the economic and social infrastructure, and rebuilding the capacity for policy formulation and implementation (Government of Sierra Leone 2005).

With the improvement in security, the IMF approved a 3-year program in 2001 under the Poverty Reduction and Growth Facility (PRGF) in support of the economic recovery program. Sierra Leone began to receive Heavily Indebted Poor Country (HIPC) relief in 2002. The World Bank, the African Development Bank, the United Kingdom, the European Union, the Islamic Development Bank, and other development partners agreed to fund programs in support of strategic sectors, including governance, security, agriculture, education, health, capacity building, and public financial management (Government of Sierra Leone 2005).

The improved security and the reestablishment of government control and authority nationwide strengthened confidence in the economy and boosted economic recovery, as shown by the indicators in table 1.8. The postwar economic recovery benefited from large-scale reconstruction and rehabilitation activities, as well as improved economic management, including the implementation of key structural reforms. The annual growth rate in GDP was about 18 percent in 2001 and 27 percent in 2002, reflecting the postwar expansion in trade and commercial activities and

Table 1.8 Selected Economic Indicators during the Postwar Years, 2000–04

	2000	2001	2002	2003	2004
GDP (current, Le billions)	1,330	1,600	1,965	2,324	2,894
GDP (constant 2003, Le billions)	1,412	1,669	2,126	2,324	2,495
Real GDP growth rate (%)	—	18.2	27.4	9.3	7.4
CPI annual percentage change (%)	0.3	2.6	−3.7	7.5	14.2
Exchange rate (Le / $, period average)	2,092	1,986	2,099	2,347	2,701
Exchange rate depreciation (%)		−5.1	5.7	11.8	15.1

Source: IMF.
Note: Pre-2000 GDP figures are not directly comparable to post-2000 figures due to differences in accounting and statistical methods employed. — = not available.

Figure 1.8 Government Revenues and Expenditure, 1996–2006

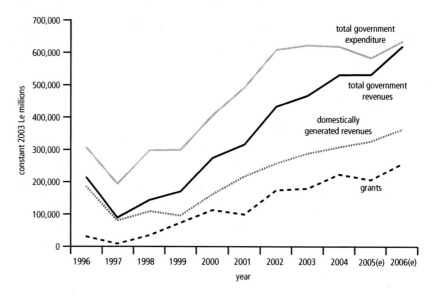

Source: Table D.3.
Note: Data for 2005 and 2006 are estimates.

the rehabilitation of industries. In 2003 and 2004, the growth rate slowed down a little, but was still high at 9 and 7 percent, respectively.

GOVERNMENT REVENUE AND EXPENDITURE

Government revenues, including both domestically generated revenues and donor grants, show an upward trend since the low of 1997. Between 2000 and 2004, total government revenues almost doubled in real terms (see figure 1.8), resulting in an increase in total government revenues from 19 to 21 percent of GDP. Estimates for 2005 and 2006 suggest that total revenues will continue to increase at this rate. Grants make up about 40 percent of the total government revenues, and these have also increased since the low in 1997. Domestically generated revenues were stable at about 12 percent of GDP between 2002 and 2004, which is relatively low compared with the average for low-income countries in Africa of 16 percent of GDP.

In line with the increase in revenues, total government expenditure also increased from the low in 1997, almost doubling between 2000

Table 1.9 Government Current Expenditure by Sector, 1996–2003

	1996	1997	1998	1999	2000	2001	2002	2003
% total current expenditure								
General public services	13.6	—	12.0	13.8	16.5	18.4	20.9	20.7
Defense	21.0	—	9.9	13.0	16.2	15.0	12.0	13.1
Education	14.2	—	16.5	18.5	21.7	18.6	18.3	19.9
Health	6.9	—	5.1	2.9	4.8	5.9	7.1	7.9
Social security and welfare	2.3	—	2.3	2.5	2.3	2.2	4.3	4.0
Housing and community amenities	0.4	—	0.4	0.2	0.3	0.4	0.4	0.3
Other community and social services	2.7	—	1.6	1.2	1.2	1.2	1.7	1.2
Economic services	10.1	—	6.6	5.7	5.4	7.2	6.9	7.7
Public debt interest and commissions	15.6	—	31.5	29.8	27.8	18.3	22.1	16.4
Other purposes	13.2	—	14.3	12.3	3.8	13.0	6.5	8.9
Total	100.0	—	100.0	100.0	100.0	100.0	100.0	100.0
% GDP								
General public services	—	—	—	—	3.7	4.6	5.0	4.5
Defense	—	—	—	—	3.7	3.7	2.9	2.9
Education	—	—	—	—	4.9	4.6	4.4	4.4
Health	—	—	—	—	1.1	1.5	1.7	1.7
Social security and welfare	—	—	—	—	0.5	0.5	1.0	0.9
Housing and community amenities	—	—	—	—	0.1	0.1	0.1	0.1
Other community and social services	—	—	—	—	0.3	0.3	0.4	0.3
Economic services	—	—	—	—	1.2	1.8	1.7	1.7
Public debt interest and commissions	—	—	—	—	6.3	4.5	5.3	3.6
Other purposes	—	—	—	—	1.5	1.4	1.8	0.9

Source: Ministry of Finance.
Note: The data used for this table did not exactly match the total current expenditures in table D.3. The small differences were adjusted in the "other purposes" category. — = not available.

and 2004. However, government expenditure decreased recently from 29 percent of GDP in 2001 to 25 percent of GDP in 2004 (see appendix table D.3). Ministry of Finance estimates for 2005 and 2006 suggest that government expenditure will remain steady at about the 2004 level.

Government expenditure has exceeded revenues in each year since 1996, with the deficit being more than 100 percent of total revenues in 1997 and 1998. The gap has narrowed substantially to just 16 percent of total revenues (including grants) in 2004. Ministry of Finance estimates for 2005 and 2006 indicate that the gap will narrow (mainly due to an increase in grants) but will persist at about 3–10 percent of total revenues.

PUBLIC EXPENDITURE BY SECTOR

Excluding debt payments, the largest share of government current expenditure goes to general public services and education (about 20 percent each in 2003), followed by defense (see table 1.9 on page 31). The share of total current expenditure for education increased markedly from 14 percent in 1996 to 20 percent in 2003. Education expenditure fluctuated around 4.4–4.9 percent of GDP between 2000 and 2003. The share of total public expenditure for defense went down from 21 percent in 1996 to 13 percent in 2003. However, this number is still high in relation to other countries: defense accounted for 2.9 percent of GDP in Sierra Leone compared with an average of 1.8 percent of GDP in Sub-Saharan Africa countries in 2003 (World Bank 2005b). Debt repayments have also decreased but still remain high at 16.4 percent of total current expenditure. Health expenditure is low at 1.7 percent of GDP compared to 2.5 percent of GDP in Sub-Saharan Africa countries in 2002. The share of total public current expenditure for health has increased from a low of 2.9 percent in 1999 to 7.9 percent in 2003. The government of Sierra Leone has made education a priority: there is clear alignment between government policy and expenditure on education.

CHAPTER 2

Student Enrollment, Completion, and Transition

Despite severe damage by the war, Sierra Leone's education system has made a remarkable recovery. Educational coverage at all levels, particularly primary education, has expanded impressively in the years since the war ended. The gross enrollment ratio in primary schools has surged to more than 100 percent as many older children come back to school to take advantage of the government's free primary education. With the current significant increases in primary enrollment, demand for further expansion in higher levels of education is inevitable. Compared to other low-income countries, Sierra Leone has slightly lower JSS, SSS, and tertiary gross enrollment ratios. Universal primary education is still a challenge, as around 25 percent of children aged 6–11 and 12–14 were out of school in 2004. Most of these children had never attended school. The GCR at the primary level was 65 percent—far from the EFA universal primary completion goal, although the rate is expected to increase rapidly given the recent surge in enrollments. Analysis of student flow reveals a low survival rate, with only slightly more than 50 percent of primary school entrants completing the sixth year without repeating a grade. More than 70 percent of primary completers go on to study at JSS schools, whereas only about half of the JSS graduates move on to SSS schools. Tertiary education is only available for a tiny portion of the relevant population. This chapter provides a detailed description of trends in enrollment and educational coverage at all levels and of student flow in primary and secondary education.

HISTORY OF THE EDUCATION SYSTEM

Sierra Leone has a rich educational tradition and occupies a prestigious place in history as having a series of firsts in Western style educational provision in Sub-Saharan Africa: the first school for boys (Sierra Leone Grammar School), founded in 1845; the first school for girls (Annie Walsh Memorial School), founded in 1849; and the first tertiary education institution (Fourah Bay College), founded in 1827. The country played an important role in the training of the first corps of administrators, doctors, and teachers in English-speaking West Africa in the first half of the last century.

At independence in 1961, Sierra Leone inherited a British-type education system, aimed largely at the urban middle class. The system was biased toward academically gifted students who entered tertiary education and found formal employment in government offices. In essence, the system was aimed at nurturing civil servants and government administrators. Most Sierra Leoneans were unable to access formal education or forced by circumstances to work before completing primary school. The Sierra Leone education system became an elitist system that excluded the majority of the population. Given this exclusive nature of the colonial education system, it is not surprising that literacy levels remained low and that, at independence, fewer than 15 percent of children aged 5–11 years attended school, and only 5 percent of children aged 12–16 years were in secondary school.

A change in direction for education in Sierra Leone had been recommended in a 1996 paper (Stuart et al. 1996), in which the need for increased access to quality primary education and greater emphasis on technical and vocational options was articulated. The Jomtien World Conference on Education in 1990 gave birth to the EFA movement and further buttressed the arguments for changes to education in Sierra Leone. Encouraged by trends in other English-speaking West African countries and around the world, the government adopted the 6-3-3-4 system of education (defined in the next section) in 1993. This step has been seen as a bold attempt to move the country away from a predominantly grammar school type of education, which takes neither the varied talents of the pupils nor the socioeconomic needs of the country into account. The establishment of the National Commission for Basic Education in 1993, the 1995 New Education Policy for Sierra Leone, and the Education Master Plan in 1997 can all be traced back to the Jomtien Conference.

At the heart of EFA is the right of all children to access the environments required to meet their basic learning needs. This reflects in the Constitution: "the government shall strive to eradicate illiteracy, and to this end, shall direct its educational policy towards achieving: free adult literacy programmes; free compulsory basic education at primary and junior secondary school levels, and free senior secondary education as and when practicable"

(Government of Sierra Leone 1991, 4). However the civil conflict adversely affected the achievement of these goals. Only after the war have tangible steps been taken, yielding promising results that have been reiterated in all EFA conferences. Notwithstanding the many and varied financial constraints, the government in 2001 took on the challenge of providing free basic education, starting initially with the primary grades for all students and for girls from the Eastern and Northern Regions at the JSS level.

STRUCTURE OF THE EDUCATION SYSTEM

The 6-3-3-4 education system is composed of 6 years of formal primary education, 3 years of JSS, 3 years of SSS, and 4 years of tertiary level education (see figure 2.1). Additionally, the Ministry of Education, Science and Technology (MEST) has focused on preprimary education in the past few years because of the overwhelming evidence that early childhood care, health, and education profoundly influence events later in life (Evans, Myers, and Ilfield 2002).

Figure 2.1 Structure of the Sierra Leone Education System

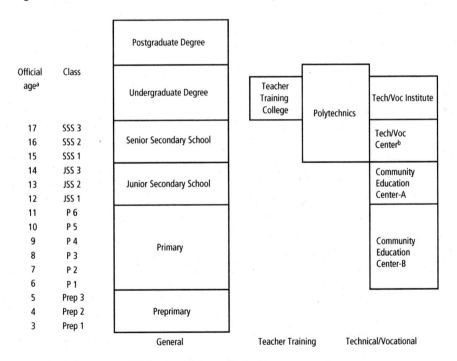

Source: Staff of the Ministry of Education, Science and Technology.
a. This is the official age for general education. However, there is a wide range of ages currently enrolled at the different levels of general education. These ages are not applicable to TVET programs.
b. The Vocational Trade Center is part of the Technical Vocational Center.

The current major policy objectives are to ensure 9 years (6 years of primary plus 3 years of JSS) of basic education for all and to fully implement the new 6-3-3-4 structure with its strong scientific and vocational orientation, focusing on quality, relevance, and gender equalities.

The official age for primary school students is between 6 and 11 years. All students at the end of the sixth grade are required to take and pass the NPSE designed by the West African Examinations Council (WAEC) to enable them to proceed to the secondary level, which is divided into two parts each of 3 years (JSS and SSS). Each part has a final examination: the BECE for JSS and the West Africa Senior School Certificate Examination (WASSCE) for SSS. Both are administered by WAEC. Successful candidates of WASSCE are admitted to a tertiary institution based on the number of course tests passed. In addition to the WASSCE, the National Vocational Qualification (NVQ) was introduced in 1999 to target students after BECE who demonstrate aptitude for and interest in TVET. Successful candidates of NVQ may be admitted to tertiary institutions.

TVET in Sierra Leone offers a mix of programs and certificates catering to a wide range of candidates, from those with no formal education to students having completed senior secondary education. Table 2.1 shows the current TVET programs.

The Complementary Rapid Education for Primary Schools (CREPS) system was instituted by MEST in the 2000/01 school year to enable the many individuals aged 16 years and older who had their education disrupted by the long civil conflict to resume schooling. The system covers primary education for 3 years, culminating in the NPSE to access JSS if

Table 2.1 Sierra Leone TVET Programs

Program	Entry requirement	Level	Duration
Community education center-B	No formal schooling	Nonformal / primary	2–6 months
Community education center-A	Completed primary education	Primary to JSS	2–6 months
Vocational trade center	Attempted the BECE	JSS to early SSS	6 months–2 years
Vocational trade center	Passed at least three subjects in BECE	JSS to SSS	6 months–2 years
Vocational trade institute	Attempted the WASSCE	SSS to post-SSS below tertiary	6 months–2 years
Polytechnics	Passed at least four subjects in WASSCE	Post-SSS to tertiary	2–3 years

Source: MEST.

successful. CREPS has started to be phased out as the backlog of war-affected children is absorbed into formal education.

STUDENT ENROLLMENTS

This section provides an overview of the numbers of students enrolled in each level of education from preprimary to tertiary, including recent trends. The next section provides further context by examining student enrollments in relation to the target population.

PREPRIMARY EDUCATION

The official age range for preprimary education in Sierra Leone is 3–5 years. According to the *Rapid Assessment of Early Childhood Care and Education* (MEST 2003b), preprimary education is mainly private and tends to be dominated by children from wealthier families in the urban and semiurban areas. Nearly two-thirds of the preprimary educational institutions are located in the Western Area, and more than 40 percent are not on permanent sites. Total enrollment in preprimary education remained steady at about 18,000–20,000 in the past few years (see figure 2.2); less

Figure 2.2 Preprimary Enrollment, 2003/04 to 2005/06

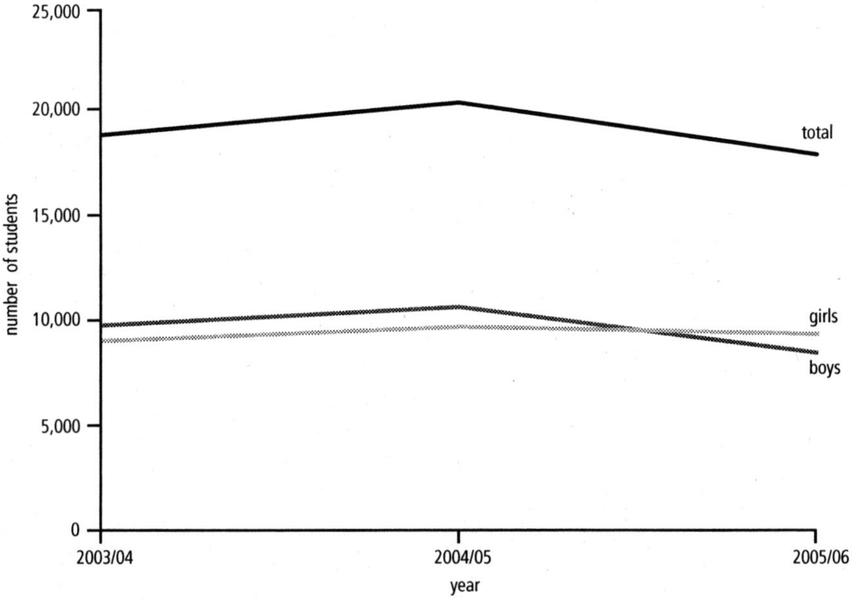

Source: Appendix table D.4.

than 5 percent of children have received preprimary education. Low enrollment rates at the preprimary level may be contributing to the problem of underaged enrollment in primary schools.

PRIMARY EDUCATION

Primary school enrollment was stable at close to 400,000 in the late 1980s, but declined to 315,000 in 1991/92 at the start of the war. There is limited information available on enrollment during the decade of conflict, but an estimate suggests that enrollment was about 370,000 in 1996/97, increasing to 660,000 at the end of the war in 2001/02. However, the effect of the war was different across regions, and increases in enrollment in one area may mask decreases in others. The end of the war and the government's decision to offer free primary education in 2001 led to a doubling in student enrollment between 2001/02 and 2004/05, reaching 1.3 million in 2004/05. However, figure 2.3 shows that a gender gap still exists, with girls

Figure 2.3 Primary School Enrollment Trends, 1987/88 to 2004/05

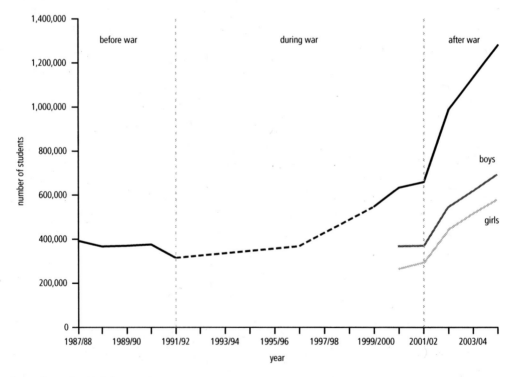

Source: Appendix table D.5.
Note: The dotted line means no data for the corresponding years.

comprising 45 percent of the total enrollment in primary schools in 2004/05.

The data used above are from the Inspectorate of the MEST. Because inspectors could not visit all schools to ascertain enrollment figures, there is a possibility that some institutions may have reported inaccurate numbers or overreported enrollment to take advantage of the government's capitation grant (fee subsidies) distributed directly to schools and based on enrollment numbers reported by schools. Possible overreporting of enrollment is indicated by the difference between grade 6 enrollments collected from some schools by the Inspectorate and the numbers registered for the NPSE in 2004. The former reported about 70,000 students (excluding repeaters) in grade 6 and the latter recorded 62,000 candidates taking the NPSE, a difference of about 13 percent. There may be other factors that contribute to this discrepancy, but it seems likely that some overreporting exists in the primary system.

According to the SLIHS (2003/04), about 25 percent of primary students are in government schools, about 70 percent are in government-assisted schools (which are primarily administered by religious bodies), and the remaining students (about 5 percent) are in private schools.

In addition to the surge of enrollment in regular primary schools, many older students were enrolled in the CREPS and Rapid Response Education Program (RREP) as part of the recovery program toward the end of the war.[1] The numbers of students who have participated in these programs are shown in table 2.2.

Table 2.2 Enrollments in the CREPS and RREP Programs, 2000/01 to 2004/05

Year	CREPS[a]			RREP[b]		
	Boys	Girls	Total	Boys	Girls	Total
2000/01	1,159	1,029	2,188	4,190	2,925	7,115
2001/02	3,865	2,895	6,760	3,852	2,562	6,414
2002/03	6,835	4,828	11,663	n.a.	n.a.	n.a.
2003/04	6,419	4,790	11,209	n.a.	n.a.	n.a.
2004/05	5,443	3,680	9,123	n.a.	n.a.	n.a.

Source: MEST.
Note: n.a. = not applicable.
a. CREPS was not introduced in some parts of the Southern Province (Bo, Bonthe, Moyamba, and Pujehun districts) and Northern Province (Tonkolili District). It has been phased out in the Kambia, Kono, and Kailahun districts and is in its final year in the Bombali, Kenema, Port Loko (Lungi), and Koinadugu districts.
b. RREP phased out at the end of 2002. Pupils were absorbed into the regular school system and the CREPS program.

SECONDARY EDUCATION

The expansion of the education system is reflected in both JSS and SSS. Because of lack of reliable enrollment data, an analysis can be based on data only from a few recent years. According to the Inspectorate of MEST, both JSS and SSS enrollments increased steadily between 2001/02 and 2004/05, with an annual growth rate of around 27 percent and 18 percent, respectively. JSS enrollment rose from 60,000 in 2000/01 to 155,000 in 2004/05, more than doubling in 4 years. SSS enrollment almost doubled in four years, from 23,000 in 2000/01 to 45,000 in 2004/05 (see figure 2.4). Although there was a rapid expansion in secondary schools, primary school enrollment was more than 6 times greater in 2004/05. The gender gap is wide in secondary school: in 2004/05, girls made up only 39 percent of JSS enrollment and 36 percent of SSS enrollment.

According to the SLIHS (2003/04), about 95 percent of JSS students are enrolled in government or government-assisted schools, and only 3 percent are enrolled in private schools (the remaining 2 percent are in

Figure 2.4 Secondary School Enrollment Trends, 2000/01 to 2004/05

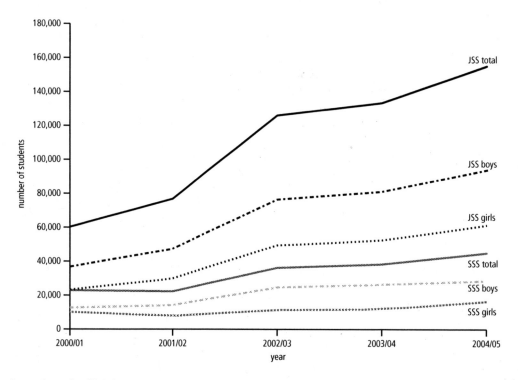

Source: Appendix table D.6.

schools administered by nongovernmental organizations [NGOs]). At the SSS level, about 92 percent of students are enrolled in government or government-assisted schools, 2 percent are enrolled in private schools, and 6 percent are in schools administered by NGOs.

TVET

A TVET survey in 2004 (GTZ/MEST 2004) and other sources from MEST and the National Council for Technical, Vocational and Other Academic Awards (NCTVA) show that more than 200 TVET institutions are currently in operation in the country. The total number of students in these institutions was approximately 30,000 in 2003/04. There are no historical data available to evaluate the trend of TVET enrollments. However, a large number of TVET institutions were recently established, which may indicate rapid growth in the TVET sector. Among the existing TVET institutions, about half were established in the 1990s and 30 percent have been established since 2000. The Western Urban and Bo Districts have the largest number of institutions and students (table 2.3). Female students made up more than 60 percent of enrollment in 2003/04; however,

Table 2.3   TVET Trainee Enrollments by District, 2004/05

Region	District	Formal			Nonformal			Total		
		Male	Female	Total	Male	Female	Total	Male	Female	Total
Eastern	Kailahun	274	496	770	..	381	381	274	877	1,151
Region	Kenema	1,098	1,973	3,071	293	439	732	1,391	2,412	3,803
	Kono	135	311	446	112	197	309	247	508	755
Northern	Bombali	590	523	1,113	183	304	487	773	827	1,600
Region	Kambia	108	202	310	10	45	55	118	247	365
	Koinadug	41	59	100	40	174	214	81	233	314
	Port Loko	629	776	1,405	13	136	149	642	912	1,554
	Tonkolili	430	576	1,006	43	193	236	473	769	1,242
Southern	Bo	2,339	3,297	5,636	768	946	1,714	3,107	4,243	7,350
Region	Bonthe	142	97	239	5	16	21	147	113	260
	Moyamba	232	412	644	10	40	50	242	452	694
	Pujehun	419	285	704	83	86	169	502	371	873
Western	Western Rural	198	611	809	126	173	299	324	784	1,108
Area	Western Urban	2,749	6,362	9,111	587	1,104	1,691	3,336	7,466	10,802
Total		9,384	15,980	25,364	2,273	4,234	6,507	11,657	20,214	31,871

Sources: TVET Survey 2004; MEST; NCTVA.
Note: . . = nil or negligible.

Figure 2.5 Distribution of Trainees by TVET Institution Type and Ownership, 2003/04

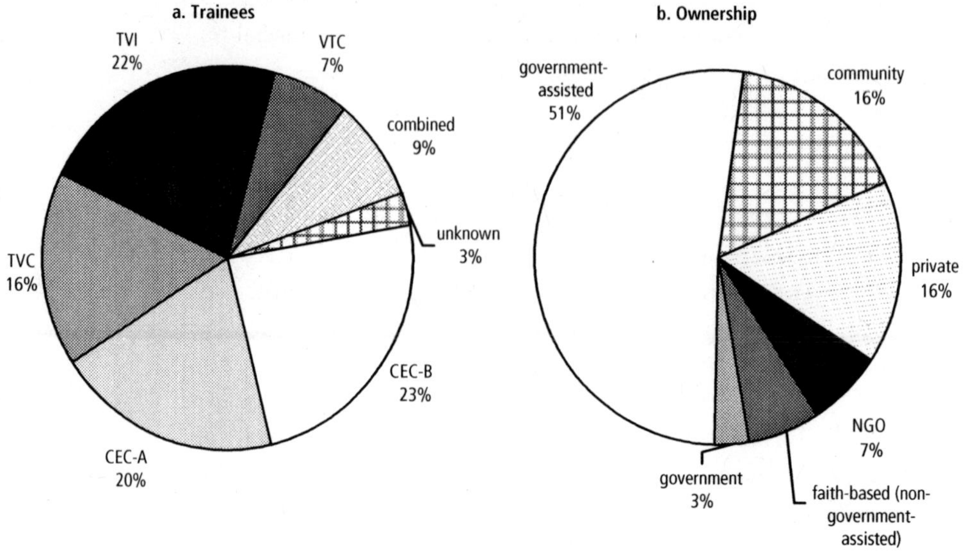

a. Trainees

TVI
22%

VTC
7%

combined
9%

unknown
3%

TVC
16%

CEC-B
23%

CEC-A
20%

b. Ownership

government-
assisted
51%

community
16%

private
16%

NGO
7%

government
3%

faith-based (non-
government-
assisted)

Source: TVET Survey 2004.

gender stereotyping by subject is still prevalent in TVET, with more than 95 percent of students in the technology options being male.

Enrollment by TVET program in 2003/04 is shown in figure 2.5. A large share of TVET trainees (44 percent) were enrolled in community education centers (CEC), including both CEC-B and CEC-A programs. Although the former has no entry requirements, the latter requires candidates to have completed at least primary education. About 16 percent and 22 percent were enrolled in technical vocational centers (TVC) and technical vocational institutes (TVI), respectively. Vocational Trade Centers (VTC) had a 7 percent enrollment share. The remaining trainees were enrolled in combined schools[2] (9 percent) or unknown (3 percent).

Figure 2.5 also shows the distribution of TVET institutions by ownership. Purely government institutions had the smallest enrollment share (3 percent), whereas government-assisted institutions had the largest (51 percent).[3] Community and private institutions both had about 16 percent of the total enrollment. The remaining 14 percent were evenly distributed between NGO and nongovernment-assisted faith-based institutions.

TERTIARY EDUCATION

The tertiary sector is composed of two universities with their constituents; three polytechnic institutions and constituent campuses; and two teacher training colleges. All are public institutions. Distance education is offered by one of the universities and the teacher training colleges. The Polytechnic Act of 2001 makes possible the establishment of two additional polytechnics, and the University Act of 2004 provides for the establishment of private universities, but none have been established so far.

Figure 2.6 shows that total enrollment in tertiary institutions more than doubled over the past 6 years, from about 6,000 in 1998/99 to more than 16,000 in 2004/05. Female students made up 36 percent of all enrollments in tertiary institutions in 2004/05. The large increase in tertiary students stems mainly from growth in university enrollment (58 percent in 2004/05; figure 2.7). Teacher training colleges and polytechnics experienced a steady but less rapid growth than the university sector. Distance education only commenced in 2001/02, but enrollment has increased more than tenfold since that date. In 2004/05, more than 2,000 students took part in distance education, about equal to the number of students in teacher training colleges and polytechnics combined, indicating a strong demand for distance education.

Figure 2.6 Tertiary Institutions Enrollment Trends, 1998/99 to 2004/05

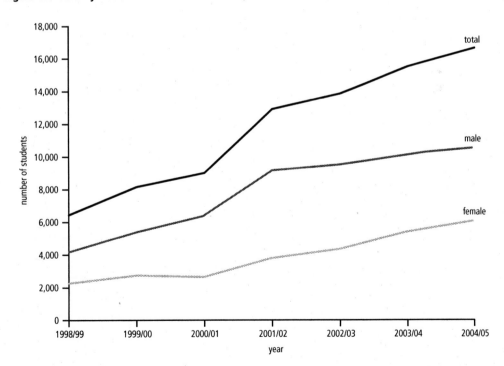

Source: Appendix table D.7.

Figure 2.7   Tertiary Institutions Enrollment Trends by Institution Type, 1998/99 to 2004/05

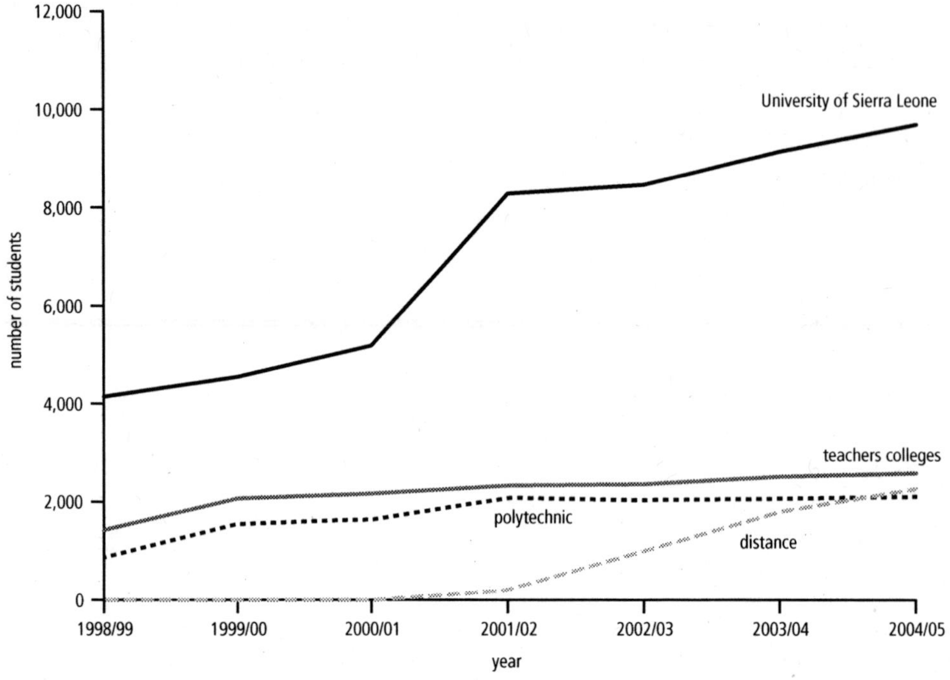

Source: Appendix table D.8.

Female enrollment in tertiary education was less than half that of their male counterparts. The gender gap is narrower in teacher training colleges and distance education; however, female student share in these institutions was still below 45 percent in 2004/05.

EDUCATIONAL COVERAGE

The previous section showed that many children and youth in Sierra Leone have been granted education opportunities since the war ended, with enrollments having increased rapidly across all subsectors of education. This section examines how the expansion in enrollment is related to the coverage of the school-aged population. The following indicators are used to examine coverage:

Gross enrollment ratio (GER): the number of students, regardless of age, enrolled in a given level of education as a percentage of the population in the official age range for that level.

Age-specific enrollment rate (AER): the number of students of a given age enrolled in school, regardless of grade and level, as a percentage of the population of that age group.

Net enrollment rate (NER): the number of students in the official age range for a given level enrolled in that level of education as a percentage of the population in the official age range for that level.

In Sierra Leone the official age ranges are 3–5 years for preprimary, 6–11 years for primary, 12–14 years for JSS, and 15–17 years for SSS. The age range used for computing tertiary rates is 18–21 years, although there is no official age in Sierra Leone for tertiary education.

GROSS ENROLLMENT RATIO (GER)

The rapid expansion in enrollments from primary to tertiary education between 2001/02 and 2004/05 is reflected in the increase in GERs (table 2.4). Based on MEST data, the GERs were 162 percent in primary school, 44 percent in JSS, 14 percent in SSS, and 4 percent in tertiary education in 2004/05, almost double the rates in 2001/02. The primary school GER is well over 100 percent, reflecting the occurrence of many older children coming back to school after the war, grade repeaters, and younger children attending the lower grades of primary. The high GER phenomenon will gradually diminish as the backlog of the war-affected children is accommodated.

The results of the SLIHS (2003/04)[4] and Population Census (2004) confirmed a high GER at the primary level; however, they differ considerably across the different sources. The MEST data yielded the highest GER, followed by SLIHS and then the Population Census. One explanation for the higher primary GERs from the MEST data is the possible data recording

Table 2.4 Percent GER, 2001/02 to 2004/05

Year	Based on MEST data				Based on surveys and population census			
	Primary	JSS	SSS	Tertiary	Primary[a]	JSS	SSS	Source
2001/02	89	23	7	2	—	—	—	
2002/03	131	38	12	3	—	—	—	
2003/04	146	39	12	4	123	50	32	SLIHS
2004/05	162	44	14	4	104	41	22	Population Census

Sources: MEST; SLIHS 2003/04; Statistics Sierra Leone Population Census 2004.
Note: — = not available.
a. The GER for primary from the SLIHS and Population Census are lower because students younger than 6 years of age are not included.

Figure 2.8 Primary and Secondary Gross Enrollment Ratios in Sub-Saharan Africa, 2004/05

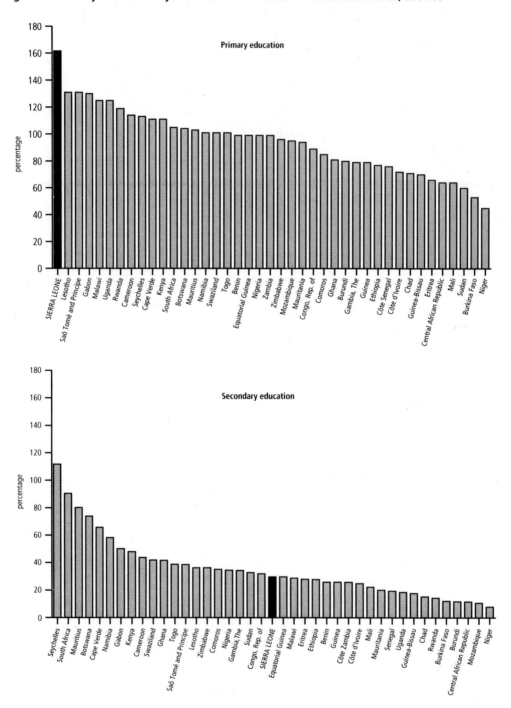

Sources: MEST staff for Sierra Leone and UNESCO Institute for Statistics for other countries.
Note: Data are for the 2004/05 or closest year (2003/04 for most countries).

and collecting errors discussed previously. In addition, there may be many other elements accounting for the divergences. The GERs for JSS are fairly similar across different sources (around 45 percent). For SSS, the GERs are substantially different, with the SLIHS and Population Census giving results up to twice as high as the MEST data. The SLIHS result may not be reliable because of the distribution of secondary schools in Sierra Leone and the survey design.[5] Based on the Population Census and the MEST data, the SSS GER can be assessed at about 20 percent.

International comparisons offer a useful perspective on where Sierra Leone stands in relation to educational coverage. Figure 2.8 shows the GERs for primary and secondary education in various Sub-Saharan countries. For the reasons given above, the primary GER in Sierra Leone is significantly higher than it is in other countries. At 30 percent, the secondary GER (which combines JSS and SSS) falls near the middle of its range for the selected Sub-Saharan countries.

Because the GER does not specify the fraction of the official age group that is in school, it can overestimate education coverage when there are multiple age cohorts in the system stemming from early or late entry to school and grade repetition. This distortion is particularly relevant for the primary GER, for which the value of more than 100 percent does not necessarily indicate that a high proportion of children aged 6–11 years are students (that is, it does not mean that Sierra Leone has achieved universal primary education).

AGE-SPECIFIC ENROLLMENT RATE (AER)

The AER reflects the share of children in a specific age group enrolled in school. Figure 2.9 shows AERs and the percentage of 6- to 17-year-old children and youth not attending school (SLIHS 2003/04; Population Census 2004).[6] The two data sources show fairly consistent patterns of educational coverage. Although most 6- to 11-year-olds were in school, more than 20 percent of the children in this group were not enrolled, with the lowest proportion of enrolled being among the 6-year-olds (about 60 percent). The AERs for children between 7 and 14 years old were similar, but the enrollment rates dropped between the ages of 14 and 17.

On average, about 25–30 percent of the primary-aged children (6–11 years old) were not enrolled in school (table 2.5). Similarly, around 25 percent of the JSS-aged children (12- to 14-year-olds) were not in school. For SSS-aged youth (15- to 17-year-olds), the proportion not enrolled in school is much greater at around 40 to 45 percent.

Figure 2.9 Age-Specific Enrollment Rate and Percentage of Out-of-School Children, 2003/04

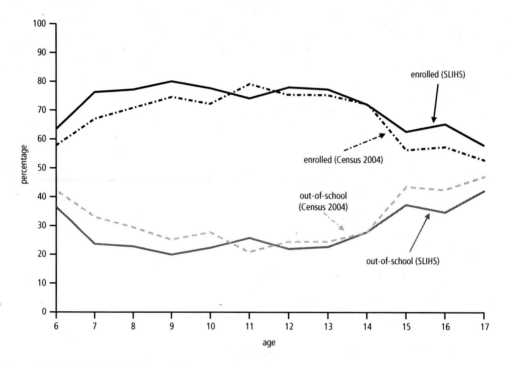

Sources: SLIHS 2003/04; Population Census 2004.

Table 2.5   Age-Specific Enrollment Rates and Out-of-School Children by Age Group, 2003–04
(percent)

Age (years)	SLIHS (2003/04)		Population Census (2004)	
	Enrolled	Out-of-school	Enrolled	Out-of-school
6–11	75	25	70	30
12–14	76	24	74	26
15–17	62	38	56	44

Sources: SLIHS 2003/04; Population Census 2004.

Based on the Population Census (2004) it is estimated that there were about 470,000 out-of-school children between ages 6 and 17, among whom 240,000 were 6- to 11-year-olds, 90,000 were 12- to 14-year-olds, and 140,000 were 15- to 17-year-olds. Most of the out-of-school children had never attended school. It is clear that achievement of the EFA and the Millennium Development Goal of universal primary education by 2015 will be very challenging.

Table 2.6 Community Perceptions on Why Children Do Not Attend School, 2003/04 (percent)

Primary reason	Primary			JSS		
	All	Urban	Rural	All	Urban	Rural
Economic difficulties	34	28	37	42	61	32
Parents do not care about children's education	31	40	27	8	11	7
School is too far away	13	7	17	37	11	51
School overcrowded/Not enough seats	6	4	7	1	0	1
Children are ill	4	5	4	0	0	0
Children are working	4	4	3	3	4	2
Children are incapable or do not like school	3	7	1	2	0	2
Other reason	4	5	3	8	13	5
Total	100	100	100	100	100	100

Source: SLIHS 2003/04.

One of the most common reasons cited for not attending primary school is economic difficulties (table 2.6). Although the government implemented free primary education in 2002/03, there are still hidden costs that some parents are unable to pay, such as uniforms, extracurricular activities, exercise books, and supplies. Additionally, the family loses the benefit of work the child may have provided during school hours. The government has made an effort to supply free textbooks; unfortunately, the quantity is not yet sufficient. The second reason cited for not attending primary school is that, in the opinion of other community members, parents do not care about their children's education, which may reflect supply- and demand-side factors that call for further study. The third reason is distance—schools are too far away from the prospective students; a serious problem in rural areas, particularly at the JSS level.

NET ENROLLMENT RATE (NER)

The NER differs from the AER in that it takes into consideration the level of schooling of the students. About 75 percent of 6- to 11-year-olds are enrolled in primary schools (table 2.7). This value equals that of the AER, indicating that virtually all students in this age group are at the primary level. As mentioned earlier, the high GER (123 percent) comes about because there are many primary-school students outside the official age for that level of schooling. As for the primary enrollment, the differences between NERs and GERs of JSS and SSS students show that most students

Table 2.7   Net Enrollment Rates, 2003–04
(percent)

Education level	Age range (years)	SLIHS (2003/04)	Population Census (2004)
Primary	6–11	75	64
Junior secondary school	12–14	13	12
Senior secondary school	15–17	7	6

Sources: SLIHS 2003/04; Population Census 2004.

are not within the official age groups for these levels of education (compare tables 2.4 and 2.7).

Given that many children entered school late and repeated grades, it is very likely that many older children in the 6- to 11-year-old group are still enrolled in the lower grades of primary education. By the time children graduate from primary and enter JSS and SSS, they are much older than the official ages for these levels. Table 2.8 shows the percentage distribution of ages within each grade of primary, JSS, and SSS education. The shaded cells show the proportion of students who are at the official age for each grade. In the early primary grades, there are high proportions of both younger and older children. For example, in primary grade 1, 19 percent of the children were under and 55 percent were over the official age (6 years). In the higher grades, the incidence of overaged students becomes very high due to late entry and repetition. For example, in SSS grade 3, 83 percent of students were older than the official age (17 years) and only 2 percent were younger than the official age. The incidence of over- and underaged students is also shown in figure 2.10. This figure highlights the extent of overaged students in the system: over 50 percent in all grades at all levels and over 80 percent in all grades at the JSS and SSS levels.

STUDENT FLOW IN PRIMARY AND SECONDARY EDUCATION

Schooling is a dynamic process and a challenging sequence in which children go through several critical phases, including entry into the education system, completion of each level, and transition between the levels. This section provides an assessment of this flow of students through primary and secondary education. It also includes information on repetition rates and a summary of the efficiency of the system.

ENTRY TO PRIMARY GRADE 1

Sierra Leone had a rapid growth in new entrants to primary grade 1 between 2001/02 and 2004/05, from nearly 200,000 to more than 300,000

Table 2.8 Age Distribution of Currently Enrolled Students by Grade, 2003/04 (percent)

Age (years)	Primary 1	Primary 2	Primary 3	Primary 4	Primary 5	Primary 6	JSS1	JSS2	JSS3	SSS1	SSS2	SSS3
5 or under	25	8	0	0	0	0	0	0	0	0	0	0
6	24	11	7	0	0	0	0	0	0	0	0	0
7	21	15	8	4	0	0	0	0	0	0	0	0
8	14	20	14	8	4	0	0	0	0	0	0	0
9	5	13	16	10	6	3	0	0	0	0	0	0
10	5	13	16	18	14	8	1	0	0	0	0	0
11	2	4	9	8	9	8	0	1	0	0	0	0
12	2	6	12	15	15	15	9	3	2	0	0	0
13	0	3	5	13	13	15	16	4	3	1	0	0
14	0	2	4	8	9	10	12	16	6	0	0	2
15	0	2	3	8	14	16	16	20	8	7	4	0
16	0	1	2	3	5	10	15	11	10	14	4	15
17	0	0	1	1	3	6	10	9	14	13	7	13
18	0	0	1	1	4	6	10	8	18	24	14	13
19	0	0	0	1	1	1	3	9	12	4	12	13
20	0	0	1	1	1	1	4	6	13	14	13	7
21	0	0	0	0	0	1	2	1	5	5	13	9
22	0	0	0	1	0	1	1	4	5	6	8	8
23	0	0	0	0	0	0	1	2	3	3	10	6
24	0	0	0	0	0	1	1	2	1	1	2	2
25+	0	0	0	0	1	0	2	2	0	8	14	24
All ages	100	100	100	100	100	100	100	100	100	100	100	100

Source: SLIHS 2003/04.

51

Figure 2.10 Percentage of Students At, Over, and Under the Official Age by Grade, 2003/04

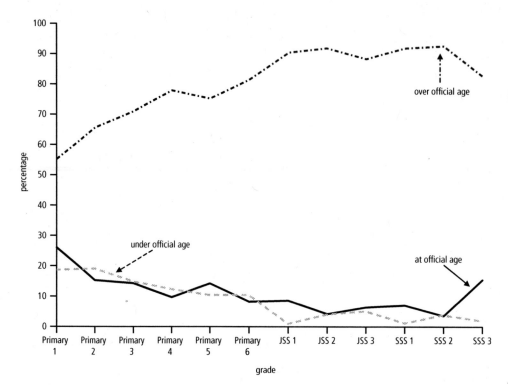

Source: SLIHS 2003/04.

students, according to the MEST data. The following three indicators are used to assess the effectiveness of the schooling system at this entry point: gross intake ratio (GIR), the net intake rate (NIR), and the cohort access rate (CAR).

The GIR is the ratio of new entrants to primary grade 1, regardless of age, to those who are at the official age of entry for primary grade 1 (6 years in Sierra Leone). According to the MEST Inspectorate data, the GIR was about 148 percent in 2001/02, increasing to 191 percent in 2003/04, and to over 200 percent in 2004/05 (table 2.9). The SLIHS (2003/04) produced a lower figure of 151 percent for the GIR. Both sources indicate a huge number of children entered primary grade 1 for the first time, although there is a discrepancy between the data sources for reasons discussed earlier.

The GIR tends to overestimate the share of children in one age cohort entering primary grade 1 because of the inclusion of multiple age cohorts in the numerator. In a system where there are multiple age cohorts entering

Table 2.9   Primary GIR, NIR, and CAR, 2001/02 to 2004/05
(percent)

Year	MEST data	SLIHS 2003/04		
	GIR	GIR	NIR	CAR
2001/02	148	—	—	—
2002/03	174	—	—	—
2003/04	191	151	35	82
2004/05	216	—	—	—

Source: MEST; SLIHS 2003/04.
Note: — = not available.

at the same time, the GIR can be misleadingly high. This is particularly true in Sierra Leone, given the high rates of late and early entry to school. The effects of the older age cohorts, who were responding to the newly available schooling opportunity, will gradually lessen, producing a lower GIR.

The NIR is similar to the GIR but only includes new entrants who are at the official age for primary grade 1 (6 years). Administrative data are not currently available for this indicator because it requires information on the age of the children enrolled. However, the SLIHS (2003/04) estimates that 35 percent of 6-year-olds are enrolled in primary grade 1. Compared to the GIR of 191 percent, this estimate shows that the vast majority of primary 1 new entrants are not at the official age of 6 years. From the NIR of 35 percent, it can be determined that the remaining 65 percent of 6-year-olds were not enrolled as new entrants in primary 1 for that year. These children (1) may have been in other primary grades in that year, (2) may have been repeating primary grade 1 in that year, (3) may enter primary school for the first time in subsequent years, or (4) may never enter primary school. The NIR tends to underestimate an age cohort share entering school, although it does provide information on the proportion of children entering primary grade 1 at the official age.

Both the GIR and NIR have pros and cons for measuring entry to primary grade 1, but another indicator, the CAR, is particularly suited to estimating the age cohort access rate for this grade, particularly in a system where children do not enter school at the official age. CAR is the share of children who have ever attended school by a certain age. In Sierra Leone the share of children who have ever been to school rises by age from 6 years to 9 years, flattens out between ages 9 and 13, and decreases after age 13 (figure 2.11). Thus children who have never been to school by age 13 are unlikely to ever enter school. Therefore, the share of children who have ever entered school by age 13 is an estimate of the cohort access rate to primary

Figure 2.11 Percentage of Children Who Have Ever Been to School, by Age, 2003/04

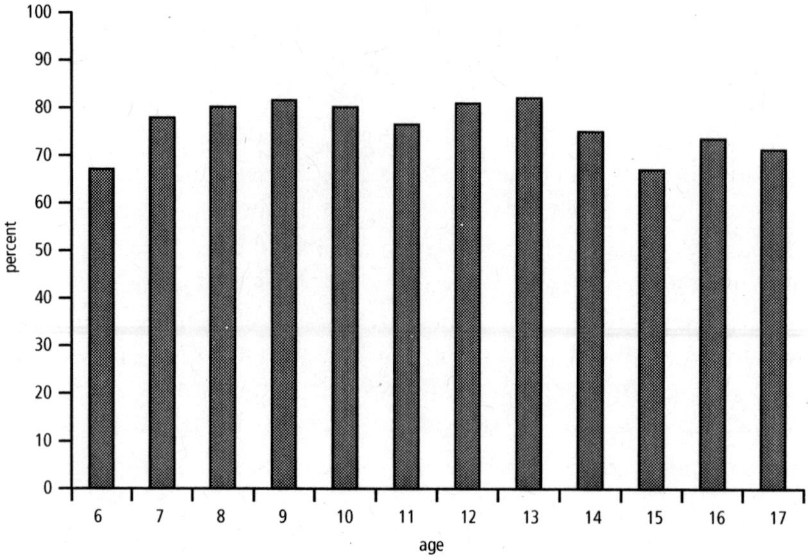

Source: SLIHS 2003/04.

grade 1. As shown in figure 2.11, the CAR was 82 percent in 2003/04, which is much higher than the NIR of 35 percent, implying that entry to primary grade 1 is still not universal in spite of the very high GIR (151 percent).

SURVIVAL, TRANSITION, AND COMPLETION

This section examines the efficiency of student flow after entry into primary grade 1, including rates of survival through the grades and transitions between the levels, as well as rates of completion of each level. However, the school system in Sierra Leone is itself in transition, which makes it difficult, if not impossible, to compute accurate survival and transition rates in the absence of a consistent and reliable data collection system. The massive influx of children coming into the school system at various grades significantly affects the flow of students from grade to grade. This section presents estimates of survival and transition rates based on data currently available. The results should be verified once the MEST establishes a reliable education management information system (EMIS).

Survival rates are the share of new entrants to the education system who eventually reach each successive grade. There are several ways to estimate survival rates, each based on several assumptions. The two examined here are the composite cohort method (CCM) and the reconstructed cohort method (RCM). Both methods use data from two consecutive years, so at present the MEST data are the only available source that can be used for these indicators. As a result, the computed values are not actual observed rates of survival but those that would be expected if the cohort were to experience the grade-to-grade progression that currently exists.

The CCM and RCM[7] yield similar estimates of grade-by-grade survival rates, although the RCM survival rate is slightly higher because of inclusion of repeated grades (figure 2.12). The survival rates show a steep downward slope throughout the primary grades and a much flatter trend in both JSS and SSS cycles. Slightly more than half of entrants to primary grade 1 are expected to reach primary grade 6, about 35 percent are likely to reach the final grade of JSS, and only 20 percent the final grade of SSS in the intended number of years. The dropout rate is high throughout primary grades 1–6. Although some of the dropouts may come back to school later, the data cannot identify such children. Such low survival rates may also be affected by the large number of older children coming back to the system and then leaving again. Students are much more likely to survive once they reach the first grade of JSS: nearly 90 percent of those who started JSS grade 1 reach JSS grade 3. The rates are even better at the SSS level: there is almost no dropout in SSS.[8]

The transition rate from primary grade 6 to JSS grade 1 in 2004/05 was about 73 percent, a quite large proportion of grade 6 students having the opportunity to enter the next level of education. However, such a transition

Figure 2.12 Estimated Survival Rates by Grade, 2004/05

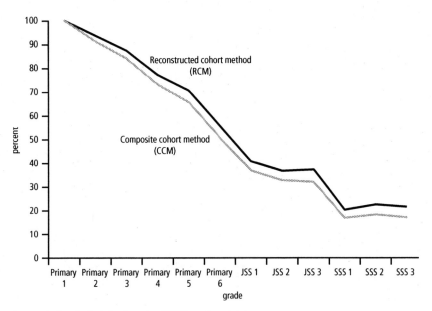

Source: Authors' calculation based on MEST enrollment data.

rate is probably not sustainable if the JSS level is not expanded to accommodate the much larger student body that will reach primary grade 6 in the next few years. The marked drop at the points of transition from JSS to SSS in figure 2.12 indicates that basic education is the end of schooling for many: only about 53 percent of students in the last grade of JSS enter SSS.

Completion rates measure the proportion of children who attain schooling of a given grade. In Sierra Leone, the important milestones are the completion of primary grade 6, JSS grade 3, and SSS grade 3 because they correspond to the completion of primary school, JSS, and SSS, respectively. The GCR is the number of students, regardless of age, completing the final year of each level of education divided by the population of the official completion age of the level. Due to the data limitations, the number of students enrolled in the final grade of each level (excluding the number of expected repeaters) is used as a proxy for the number of completers—an internationally accepted methodology. The proxy GCR may be an overestimate, because a small proportion of students enrolled in the last grade may drop out before completing it. The GCR depicts the current status of completion in the year the data were collected. For the primary level, it mainly reflects past intake rates into primary grade 1 as well as survival rates over the years that students were in school. Figure 2.13 shows the

Figure 2.13 Gross Completion Ratios by Level of Education, 2001/02 to 2004/05

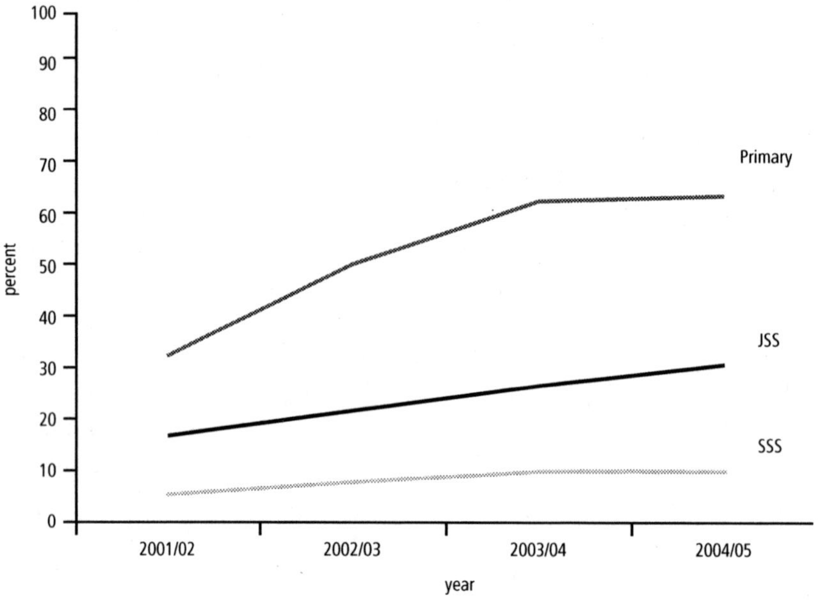

Source: MEST.
Note: Data are not available for JSS and SSS in 2002/03.

proxy GCRs for primary school, JSS, and SSS. The primary GCR almost doubled from 33 percent to 65 percent between 2001/02 and 2004/05. Given the primary enrollment surge in the recent years, GCR is expected to increase rapidly. During the same period, GCR for JSS increased from 17 percent to 31 percent, while that for SSS increased from 6 percent to 10 percent. Although the growth in GCRs is significant, the completion rates for JSS and SSS remain low. The rate of increase in primary completion was considerably faster than those in JSS and SSS completion.

The SLIHS (2003/04) data yielded similar GCRs for primary school (60 percent) and JSS (32 percent). However, the SSS GCR of 25 percent from the SLIHS appears to be too high, a result that may be distorted by the very high rates of completion in a few clusters in the Western Area.

Compared to the EFA target or the Millennium Development Goal of 100 percent completion of primary education, Sierra Leone faces a big challenge in enrolling all children in primary school and ensuring their completion. Compared to other countries in Sub-Saharan Africa, Sierra Leone is about average for primary school completion (figure 2.14).

Figure 2.14 Primary Gross Completion Ratios in Sub-Saharan Countries, 2004/05

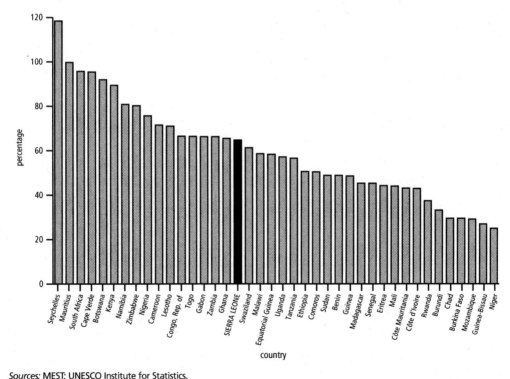

Sources: MEST; UNESCO Institute for Statistics.
Note: The completion ratios are the gross new entrant ratio to the last grade of the primary level. Data are for 2004/05 or the closest year (2003/04 for most countries).

Figure 2.15   Repetition Rates in Primary and Secondary Schools, 2003/04

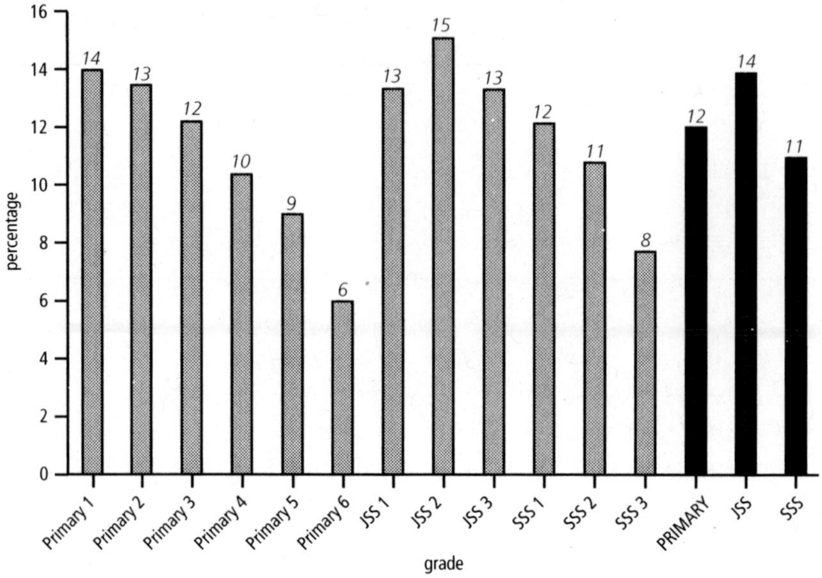

Source: MEST staff.

Grade repetition and dropout rates are two important indicators for measuring student flow efficiency. Based on the information from more than 1,000 schools that recorded student repetition, Sierra Leone has average grade repetition rates of 11–14 percent in primary and secondary schools (figure 2.15). Compared to other West African countries, Sierra Leone has relatively low repetition rates. However, it is much higher than that of many countries in the world. For instance, the average repetition rate for primary education in East Asia is only 1 percent. Thus reducing the repetition rate should be a policy of the government.

SUMMARIZING THE EFFICIENCY OF STUDENT FLOW

Sierra Leone is a country where resources are scarce and therefore not to be wasted. Inefficiency of student flow, characterized by high dropout and repetition rates, is a key source of such waste. The surge of student enrollments in primary school after the war granted many children an opportunity to obtain an education. However, the education service delivery has struggled to cope with the sudden and huge expansion of the system, which has resulted in a serious lack of trained teachers, classrooms, and teaching materials. These shortcomings might have contributed to the

Table 2.10 Efficiency of Student Flow in Primary Education, 2004/05

Grade	Number left from an initial cohort of 1,000 students	Repetition rate (%)	Pupil years invested with dropout and repetition
Primary 1	1,000	14	1,163
Primary 2	912	13	1,054
Primary 3	841	12	958
Primary 4	733	10	818
Primary 5	657	9	722
Primary 6	506	6	538
Cumulative pupil years			
without repetition and dropout	3,036		
with dropout only	4,648		
with dropout and repetition	5,252		
Index of efficiency			
Dropout-related	0.65		
Repetition-related	0.89		
Overall	0.58		

Source: Authors' calculations based on MEST data.

low survival and high repetition rates in primary schools. Table 2.10 uses the information on progression and repetition to assess the student flow efficiency in primary schools.

To illustrate the computation, a cohort of 1,000 students is used as an example. Of these students, only 506 remained at the end of primary education, based on the grade-by-grade survival rates in 2004/05. If there were no repeaters or dropouts, only 3,036 (506 × 6) pupil-years would be needed to produce these 506 completers of primary grade 6. Only taking into account dropouts, 4,648 pupil-years were invested to produce 506 primary completers. The ratio of 3,036 to 4,648 generates a dropout-related index of efficiency of 0.65. Thus 35 percent (100 − 65) of the resources were used on children who dropped out before completing primary schooling. Accounting for both repeaters and dropouts, 5,252 pupil-years were invested to produce 506 primary completers. The ratio of 4,648 to 5,252 yields a repetition-related index of efficiency of 0.89. In other words, 11 percent (100 − 89) of the resources were used on children who were repeating grades. Dropping out contributes more to resource wastage than does repetition, although the waste caused by the latter is also significant. The overall index of efficiency, considering both dropout and repetition rates, is 0.58. A system that operates at an efficiency rate of 0.58 misdirects much-needed resources.

Table 2.11 Index of Efficiency in Student Flow for JSS and SSS, 2004/05

	JSS	SSS
Dropout-related	0.95	0.98
Repetition-related	0.86	0.90
Overall	0.81	0.88

Source: Authors' calculations based on MEST data.

The system operates more efficiently in JSS and SSS schools (table 2.11). The efficiency indexes shown in the table indicate little wastage associated with dropouts, whereas there is still considerable waste caused by grade repetition. The overall indexes of efficiency for JSS and SSS are 0.81 and 0.88, respectively.

The method used here underestimates the efficiency of the system because, as previously discussed, the survival rate only captures those that complete primary school within the intended 6 years. In addition, the methodology assumes a stable system, which is not true for the postwar transitional period in Sierra Leone. The effect of this assumption is to overestimate the rate of dropouts in the system. These measures of completion also do not take account of the quality of the education received.

VISUAL REPRESENTATION

A visual representation of the student flow is shown in the student flow pyramid (figure 2.16), which is formed by four blocks that represent the four levels of education: primary, JSS, SSS, and tertiary; the arrows represent the transitions between the levels. The bottom of each block represents the gross entry ratio to that level and the top of the block represents the completion rate. The various trapezoidal shapes of the blocks indicate how well students survive from the first grade to the last grade within each level. The Sierra Leone student flow pyramid has a wide base, which indicates a high entry rate into primary grade 1. The pyramid narrows rapidly in the bottom block, reflecting a serious issue of student survival in primary school. The three small blocks above indicate a low access to secondary school and to tertiary education in particular.

POLICY IMPLICATIONS

The key issues having implications for further policy development on student enrollment, completion, and transition are discussed in this section.

Figure 2.16 Sierra Leone Student Flow Pyramid, 2004/05

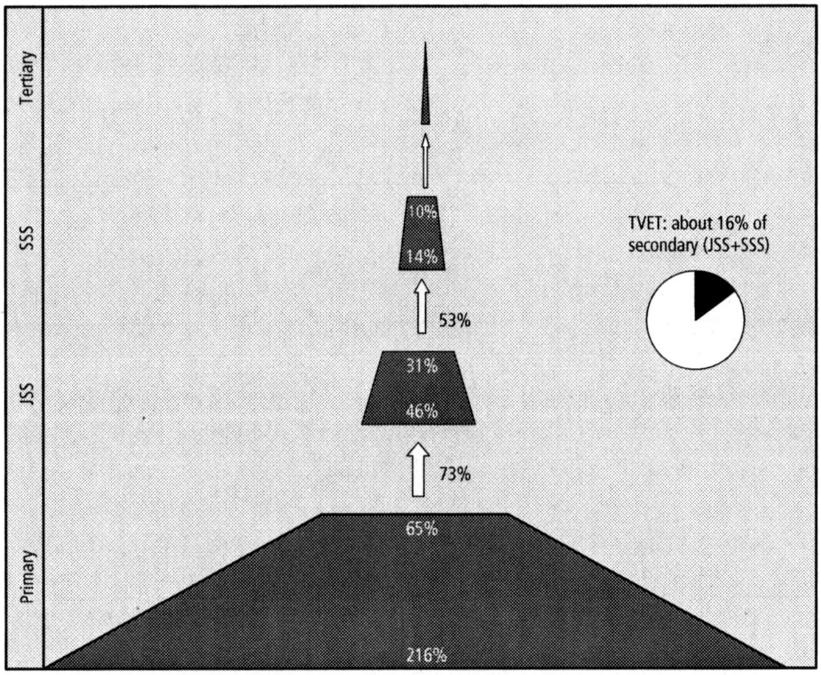

Source: Authors' calculations based on MEST data.

Significant Numbers of Children Out of School. Although many children enjoy their new-found educational opportunities, nearly 30 percent of those between the ages of 6 and 11 still remain out of school (240,000 children). This fraction poses a formidable challenge for Sierra Leone to reach the United Nations Millennium Development Goals on universal primary education (UPE) completion by 2015, a goal the country is committed to achieving. It takes 6 years for children to complete primary school (without taking into account repetition), which means that all suitably aged children must be enrolled in primary grade 1 by 2009 if they are to complete grade 6 in 2015. Enrolling children in primary grade 1 is only the first step; ensuring that children can complete primary education is another critical step, one that requires close monitoring by the government. Given the current low survival rate in primary school, the challenge of reaching UPE by 2015 becomes even greater. While celebrating the immense progress made after the war, the government of Sierra Leone needs to continue the implementation of free primary education by developing additional strategies to deal with the 20 percent of children who are still not entering the nation's education system. Most of the absent children belong to disadvantaged groups (see chapter 5) who will need special government efforts to include them; at the same time, supply and demand factors associated with schooling warrant further analysis whose results should benefit policy formulation.

Low Efficiency in Student Flow in Primary Education. Low efficiency in student flow is characterized by high repetition rates across all levels from primary to senior secondary education (about 12 percent on average). The low efficiency has profound effects throughout the system, which might have contributed to low survival rates in primary school. Many children started their schooling but soon dropped out. Overaged children, particularly girls, may also tend to drop out more readily because of such personal and family pressures as marriage, work, and looking after their siblings. The influx into the school system of those who lost educational opportunities during the war is encouraging, but the government should be mindful that these students, being older than the official age, are more likely to drop out. About 20 percent of younger children in the low grades of primary schools may also contribute to the high repetition and dropout rates. Thus intervention for improving efficiency of student flow becomes critical in achieving universal primary completion and other education objectives. Such intervention must focus on improvement of overall quality, such as improving teachers' qualifications, reducing class size, increasing accessibility to teaching materials, and better school management. Given the importance of preprimary education to children's educational success in later years, as evidenced by various research results, tangible and realistic steps need to be taken by the government to allow more children to access preprimary education in Sierra Leone.

Lack of Reliable and Sufficient Data in the Education Sector. During the preparation of this report, the team experienced a deficit of data for a comprehensive basic analysis. When data were available, its inaccuracy and inconsistency often caused serious problems. The conclusion from the UNESCO Institute for Statistics (2004) report on Sierra Leone still pertains:

> The data collection in Sierra Leone is very fragmented and each division collects its own data according different procedures. There is no specific strategy and there is no data capture. All data collected are processed manually. . . . The current system is unable to provide accurate, timely and relevant information for management decision-making, budget preparation, and monitoring the progress towards Education for All.

Hence there is an urgent need to establish an EMIS that will allow the MEST to have complete and reliable information to plan, monitor, and evaluate the performance of the education sector. The MEST is planning to establish such a system. One key element of the EMIS is to conduct a high-quality school census every year to capture relevant data for analysis. The data produced from the EMIS must cover all subsectors of education and facilitate planning, monitoring, and evaluation. Once such a system becomes available, the information in this report should be updated. In addition to an annual school census, a student learning assessment program could be introduced to conduct an in-depth survey of a small sample of schools, collecting information on student learning outcomes as well as school, home, and community factors associated with learning. This option is further discussed in chapter 3. To maximize the benefit of household surveys, the education sector should help design the questionnaire to incorporate the most relevant questions regarding education. So far, there are no direct questions in any surveys in Sierra Leone about children's schooling status in the previous year. If appropriate questions were included, two consecutive years of data (previous year plus current year) could be used to estimate many indicators, such as repetition, dropout, survival, and transition rates, which would greatly increase the value of household surveys.

CHAPTER 3

Learning Environment and Outcomes

In the previous chapter, the efficiency of the education system and its ability to move students successfully through the system was examined. Providing children with access to education is vital; providing them quality education is even more important. The decade-long war destroyed the infrastructure of the country's education system: the quality of teaching and the learning environment reached the lowest levels seen in the world. The government has doubled enrollment since the war ended. However, without ensuring effective learning, efforts to increase enrollment are pointless. The government has committed itself to creating an acceptable school environment in which children can learn. Progress has been made recently, but great challenges remain. The rapid expansion of enrollment in primary schools places pressure on the secondary school system, prompting questions about how to continue expanding enrollment while also improving the quality of education (box 3.1). There are many factors that contribute to quality in education. This chapter examines two of these factors: the learning environment and learning outcomes. The discussion on learning environment includes the availability and condition of educational facilities and materials, as well as the quality of the curriculum and teaching staff. Student examination results are used as a proxy for measuring learning outcomes in primary and secondary education.[1]

PREPRIMARY, PRIMARY, AND SECONDARY EDUCATION

The Ministry of Education, Science and Technology (MEST) has, in the past five years, recognized preprimary education not only as a means of improving the quality of education, but also of giving children from deprived backgrounds an early opportunity for structured learning.

BOX 3.1   INTERNATIONAL LESSONS ON ENROLLMENT EXPANSION WITHOUT QUALITY DECLINE

Following the expansion of primary education, one of the main challenges for Sierra Leone is expanding access to secondary education while also improving quality and relevance, so that young people have the necessary skills to participate in a changing labor market. Many other countries are, or have been, in a similar situation and their experiences offer lessons on what is commonly perceived as a trade-off between educational coverage and quality.

India saw a significant expansion of primary education in the 1990s, which extended to secondary education in the 2000s. Eight years of elementary education became a fundamental right of every child in 2002 through the National Program for Universal Elementary Education. Since then, the number of out-of-school children has fallen from 25 million in 2003 to fewer than 10 million in 2005. However, the country still faces many challenges in secondary and vocational and technical education with access, quality, and relevance. The government has therefore devised strategies including greater private sector provision, financial assistance for girls, revision of the curriculum, and improving teacher quality.

Many countries in Latin America have large differences in secondary school participation between the urban and rural populations. Mexico has reduced this gap through a special distance education program (Telesecundaria), which used microwave and then broadcast satellite technology to provide a package of learning materials to support teachers and students.

Once one of the poorest countries in the world (following war in the early 1950s), Korea now has an education system comparable to those in developed countries, with students who achieve some of the top results in mathematics and science in international studies. Success has been attributed to comprehensive government plans for primary education in the 1960s, secondary in the 1970s, and tertiary in the 1980s; concentration on equity issues through some innovative and often controversial policies; increased spending, with four-fifths of the education budget going to primary education in the 1960s; and significant private participation

(55 percent of secondary school enrollment and 78 percent of tertiary), with support from the government through tax incentives.

Also in the East Asia region, Vietnam has substantially increased enrollment at the secondary level while also improving quality through effective self-financing policies for schools. Policies to enhance quality, together with targets for promotion, have improved both enrollments and quality in Cambodia. In contrast, Indonesia experienced rapid increases in primary and lower secondary enrollments, but the quality remained low. Lessons learned from their experience include considering quality from the outset when expanding the system; receiving timely donor support; ensuring that pilots of ways to improve learning outcomes can be scaled up if successful; going beyond a central government push for quality to the involvement of local communities; and clearly delineating responsibilities and objectives prior to decentralization.

Sources: World Bank 2003b; 2005c, 41–55; 2006.

According to the Rapid Assessment of Early Childhood Care and Education (2003), preprimary education in Sierra Leone is mainly private and tends to be dominated by children from wealthier families in the urban and semiurban areas. Nearly two-thirds of preprimary education institutions are located in the Western Area. Development of preprimary education is therefore at an early stage, given the lack of coverage and the fact that more than 40 percent of existing preprimary schools are currently not on permanent sites.

In 2004/05, Sierra Leone had 4,600 primary and secondary schools recognized by MEST,[2] including government-owned, government-assisted, and private schools (figure 3.1). The count does not include institutions that offer only technical and vocational education, but it does include those schools established, managed, and funded at the initial stage by the village community and later categorized as government-assisted schools. Private schools make up a small portion of all recognized schools (less than 5 percent of primary and secondary schools; table 3.1). The number of schools has rapidly increased (figure 3.1), particularly since 2000. About 30 percent of the recognized schools were added between 2000/01 and 2004/05, largely as a result of the government's commitment to education, the recognition of "feeder" schools as

Figure 3.1 Number of Recognized Primary and Secondary Schools, Pre-1962 to 2004/05

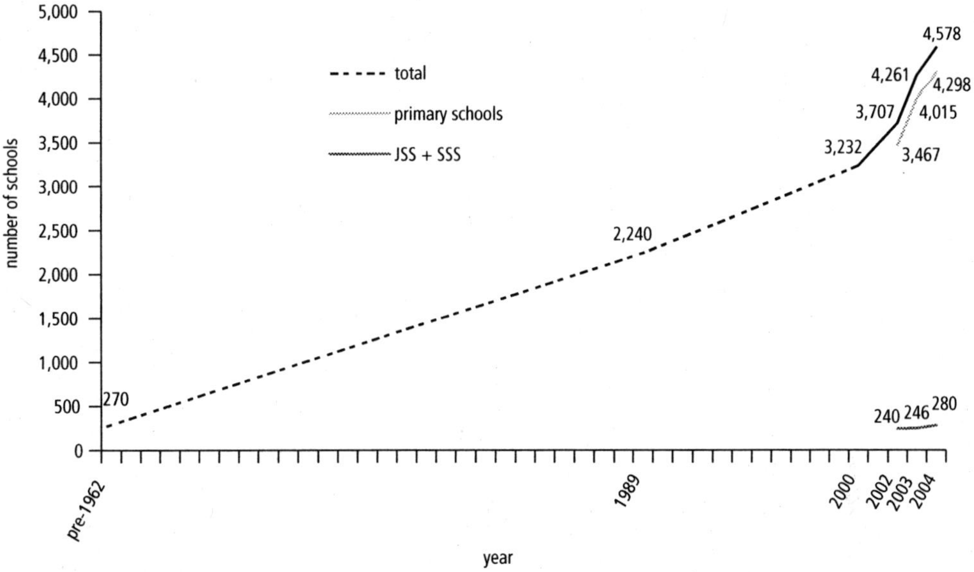

Source: Inspectorate, MEST.
Note: Includes government-owned, government-assisted, and private schools recognized by MEST. Until 2002, no separate data were available for primary and secondary schools. The dotted line means no data for the corresponding years.

Table 3.1 Percent of Recognized Primary and Secondary Schools by Ownership, 2004/05

Efficiency index	Government-owned	Government-assisted	Private	Total
Primary	11	85	4	100
Secondary	7	90	3	100

Source: Inspectorate, MEST.

schools in their own right, the recognition of many community schools that started in rural areas during the period of civil conflict, and the increased demand for schooling.

SCHOOL CHARACTERISTICS

This section identifies some of the main characteristics of schools in Sierra Leone. It examines the average school and class sizes and pupil-teacher ratios, the shift system and instructional hours, and the availability of learning materials and school equipment. Key regional differences are highlighted for all schools in general but in particular for the government-owned and government-assisted schools, which constitute the majority.

Average School and Class Size. The increase in enrollment has contributed to overcrowding in schools and classes. To address the problem, MEST has enacted policies limiting primary class sizes to 50 pupils and schools to a maximum enrollment of 1,500. This policy has been accompanied by school construction programs funded by the government and external development partners. However, overcrowding is still a serious issue for public schools in the Western Area because of increased migration to this area during the war. Most schools in the Western Area are large, often having classes large enough to adversely affect the quality of teaching and learning.

At the junior secondary school (JSS) level, MEST now stipulates a maximum of 1,500 pupils per school and 30 pupils per class. Most JSS outside the Western Area have yet to reach the upper limit for school size, but more than 60 percent of schools in the Western Area are above the limit, and many classes have more than 60 pupils. For senior secondary schools (SSS), the ceilings are 1,200 pupils per school and 25 pupils per class. In the Western Area, 70 percent of SSS already have student populations greater than 1,200 and many classes have more than 45 pupils.

School Facilities. The inadequacies of such physical infrastructures as school buildings, classroom furniture, and teacher accommodations continue to be major challenges in Sierra Leone. The war destroyed most of the infrastructure of the education system. Although the government and development partners are making great efforts to rehabilitate school buildings and to build new schools, by 2004, 60 percent of primary schools and 40 percent of secondary schools still had a damage index of 3 or 4 (that is, they needed major rehabilitation or reconstruction).[3] In some districts, the portion of schools with high damage indexes exceeded 80 percent (figure 3.2).

The provision of such sanitary facilities as latrines and sources of clean drinking water is a concern in Sierra Leone, with about 30 percent of schools recently surveyed having no toilet and 20 percent depending on a stream or river for their water supply (IRCBP 2004).

Classroom furniture for pupils and teachers is provided by the government and, to a lesser extent, school proprietors. Furniture is supplied to schools almost annually, but increasing enrollment and the poor quality of much of the furniture results in a very short lifespan (often less than 6 months). Thus classroom furniture is inadequate in many schools and pupils often resort to sitting on stones or standing. It is possible that, without additional effort, the ratio of students to chairs or benches will remain stagnant or even worsen in the immediate future, given the trend of increasing enrollment.

Figure 3.2   Distribution of Primary School Damage Index, 2004

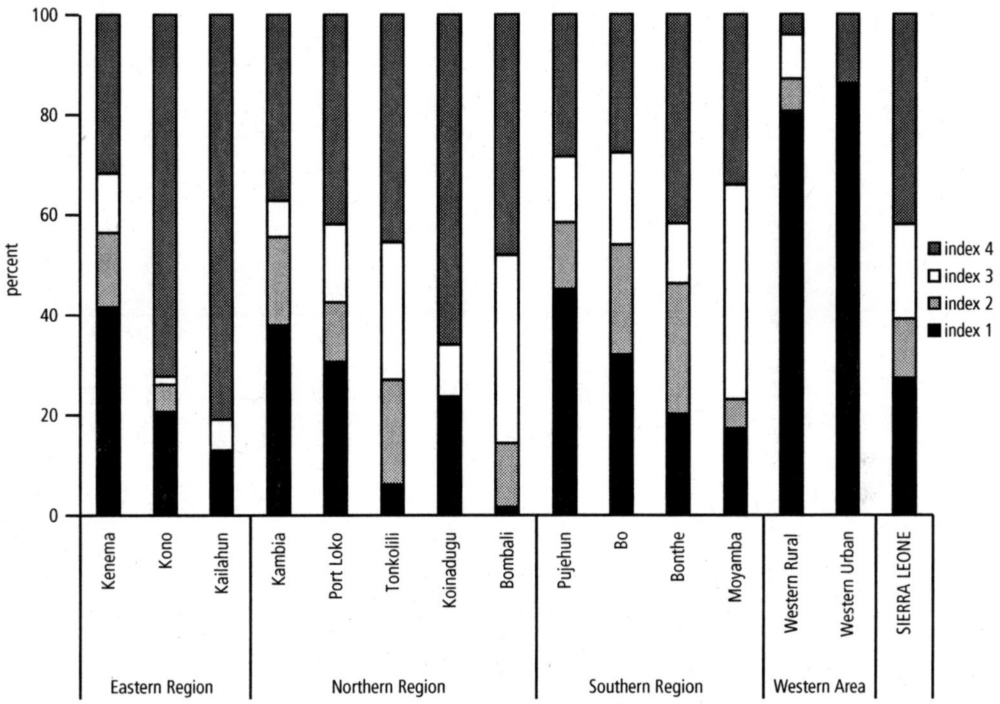

Source: Development Assistance Coordination Office (DACO) database.

Teaching and Learning Materials. An important factor in the realization of the objective of quality education for all, as stated in the 2004 Education for All National Action Plan, is textbook availability to students. The official policy of the Sierra Leone government is to provide without charge primary grade textbooks in the four core subjects (a set) and to reach a student-textbook ratio of 2:1. The government and development partners have made efforts to provide textbooks, but significant challenges remain. The Poverty Reduction Strategy Paper (PRSP; Government of Sierra Leone 2005) estimated that, in 2004, a ratio of 1 set of textbooks to 3 pupils in urban areas and 1 set to 6 pupils in rural areas had been reached. There are not enough textbooks to meet demand; textbooks are often stolen and sold at street corners. The situation is improving as the government and development partners continue to supply free textbooks. The Rehabilitation of Basic Education project (commonly referred to as Sababu), supported by the World Bank and African Development Bank, plans to provide more than 1 million books to primary schools and JSS nationwide. Table 3.2 shows the total sets of textbooks distributed since 1999/2000.

Table 3.2 Sets of Core Textbooks Distributed to Primary Schools, 1999/2000 to 2005/06

Efficiency index	MEST—Mainstream 1999/00 to 2004/05	MEST—Sababu 2005/06
Primary	2,240,278	916,865
JSS	. .	73,072

Sources: MEST Textbook Taskforce; Sababu Education Project.
Note: . . = nil or negligible.

Table 3.3 Intended Instruction Time, 2005
(hours per year)

School system	Primary		Secondary	
	Government-owned and assisted[a]	Private[b]	Government-owned and assisted[c]	Private[d]
Single shift	933	1050	933	1067
Double shift	700	n.a.	800	n.a.

Source: Authors' calculations.
Note: n.a. = not applicable.
a. Average of 8 daily periods of 35 minutes each in single shift schools; and 7 daily periods of 30 minutes in double shift schools, in a school year of 200 days.
b. Average of 9 daily periods of 35 minutes each in single shift schools, in a school year of 200 days. No double shift schools for private sector.
c. Average of 8 daily periods of 30 minutes each in double shift schools; and 8 daily periods of 35 minutes each in single shift government owned and assisted secondary schools in a school year of 200 days.
d. Average of 8 daily periods of 40 minutes each in single shift, in a school year of 200 days.

In private and public SSS, students must buy the textbooks required by the school. These books are relatively expensive and, because many students cannot afford them, alternative low-cost "pamphlets" are now widely available. These are written by teachers and draw heavily on material found in the standard texts. Most, unfortunately, are based on the examinations rather than the teaching syllabus and are of poor quality; others contain significant amounts of plagiarized material. In addition, the science and technical subjects suffer from a shortage of equipment and where equipment is available, teachers and technicians trained to use it. The cost of some of the equipment is a restraining factor.

Instructional Hours and the Shift System. The government introduced a double-shift system in urban areas as a temporary measure to address the rural-to-urban migration of school-aged individuals during and immediately after the civil conflict and to accommodate the rapid increase in enrollments over the past few years. The shift system is largely an urban phenomenon and has led to a reduction in the number of instruction hours in the school day. Instructional time is highest for private schools and lowest for public schools with a double-shift system (see table 3.3).

On average, private schools have 350 more instructional hours in the year than do public primary schools with a double shift, and 117 more hours than in public schools with a single shift.

In real terms the number of actual instructional hours is lower for all schools, as there are many public holidays and school event days throughout the year. Out of the possible 200 days available for schooling, approximately 23 days are public holidays or are taken up by other school activities (sports days, thanksgiving days, and so on). The Education for All Fast Track Initiative (FTI) set a benchmark for annual instructional time of more than 850 hours a year. Table 3.3 shows that double-shift schools fall below this recommendation.

Teachers in secondary schools may be underutilized, with most teaching less than 20 hours even though the expected minimum is 30 out of a possible 42 periods a week. Primary school teachers, however, are overstretched, as they both perform the administrative duties of a class teacher and teach every period of each school day.

The literature on time and learning shows a relationship between academic learning time (time-on-task) and achievement. Thus the goal is to maximize the time that students spend learning, which is partly dependent on the quality of the teacher.

TEACHING STAFF

Teachers are essential for delivering education services and improving student learning outcomes. This section examines the adequacy and quality of the teaching force.

Characteristics of Teaching Staff. In 2004/05 there were about 19,300 teachers in primary school and 5,600 teachers in secondary schools (table 3.4). Female teachers make up around 30 percent of the primary

Table 3.4 Distribution of Teachers by Gender and Qualification, 2004/05

Region	Primary schools			Secondary schools		
	Number of teachers	Percent female	Percent unqualified	Number of teachers	Percent female	Percent unqualified
SIERRA LEONE	19,316	32	41	5,580	19	10
Northern Region	5,706	26	51	1,184	9	14
Southern Region	5,650	25	44	1,236	14	5
Eastern Region	4,232	34	39	835	—	—
Western Area	3,728	49	23	2,325	28	8

Source: MEST.
Note: — = not available.

and 20 percent of the secondary school teaching force.[4] Compared to the average of 38 percent for 20 other countries in Africa, Sierra Leone has a lower share of female teachers in primary schools. However, there is a large regional variation in the share of female primary teachers, ranging from 49 percent in the Western Area to 25 percent in the Southern Region.

Unqualified teachers are defined in Sierra Leone as those teaching at a level higher than appropriate for their academic qualification (for example, those holding a Primary Higher Teacher Certificate [HTC-P] teaching at the secondary level). Teachers who do not possess a formal teaching qualification are referred to as untrained (for example, a B.S. graduate teaching at a secondary school but possessing no teaching certification). Presently about 40 percent of primary school teachers are unqualified, which translates to about 8,000 unqualified teachers. The share of unqualified teachers exceeded 50 percent in the Northern Region. Figure 3.3 shows the number of unqualified teachers by district. Although this problem is less severe at the secondary level, there are still many teachers who are unqualified. The government, assisted by development partners, is

Figure 3.3 Number of Unqualified Teachers in Primary Schools by Education District, 2004/05

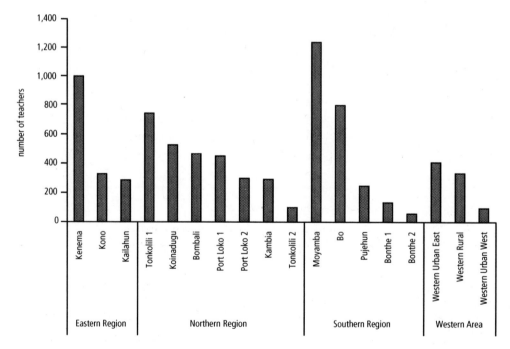

Source: MEST.

providing in-service training for unqualified teachers, but the progress has been slow and the capacity is limited.

The large number of unqualified teachers is to some extent the consequence of the civil conflict. During 1990s many qualified teachers fled Sierra Leone for safety and employment in other countries, particularly The Gambia. Many of those in rural areas and others unable to move out of the country during this time migrated to Freetown or to urban areas where they felt relatively safe.

Pupil-to-Teacher Ratios (PTRs). There was an average of 66 pupils for every teacher at the primary level in Sierra Leone in 2004/05 (table 3.5). This figure is significantly higher than that for Sub-Saharan countries (45), and higher than the target of 50 stipulated in the Sierra Leone government's policy documents New Education Policy (Government of Sierra Leone 1995) and Teacher Ceiling Gazette (MEST 2004). Although there are variations across the four regions, all have high PTRs, with the Northern Region having the highest (78). High pupil-teacher ratio affects the efficiency of the learning environment, as it can cause teacher work overload, which in turn may lead to stress, increased absenteeism, and high teacher attrition rates. The high PTRs are partly caused by the recent surge in student enrollment; they will gradually decline with the elimination of multiple cohorts of students (as long as the number of teachers does not fall). Reducing repetition would be one way to lower the PTRs. More appropriate teacher deployment would also help alleviate the high PTRs in the Northern Region and rural areas, where attracting and retaining qualified teachers is particularly challenging. To address the problem, "remote area" allowances are being instituted for those willing to teach in rural areas. Table 3.5 also shows the pupil to qualified teacher ratios, which are extremely high, indicating the urgency of addressing the issue of teaching force quality. The government has started a distance education program for teachers, and short in-service training programs continue.

Table 3.5   Pupil-Teacher Ratio in Primary Schools, 2004/05

Region	Number of students	Number of teachers	Pupil-teacher ratio	Pupil–qualified teacher ratio
SIERRA LEONE	1,280,853	19,316	66	112
Northern Region	446,567	5,706	78	160
Southern Region	316,243	5,650	56	100
Eastern Region	314,496	4,232	74	121
Western Area	203,547	3,728	55	71

Source: MEST.

The PTRs are much closer to the MEST standards of 30 and 25 students per teacher at the JSS and SSS levels, respectively (although many schools in the Western Area have overcrowding problems). Similar to the primary level, there is a relatively small percentage of qualified teachers in JSS and SSS.

Preservice Teacher Training. The two universities, three polytechnics, and two teacher colleges that train teachers in Sierra Leone are all government owned. The recent Universities Act 2004 provides for private universities, so that private institutions for training teachers will be possible. Programs range from the Teacher Certificate offered by teacher colleges to the Masters in Education offered by universities (table 3.6). Preservice certification of teachers was made the responsibility of the National Council for Technical, Vocational and Other Academic Awards (NCTVA) in 2002.

The training of teachers for primary schools has traditionally taken place in teacher colleges. Before the enactment of the Polytechnics Act in 2001, there were five teacher colleges. The Act specified that these colleges (with the exception of Bo Teachers College) eventually be transformed into polytechnics by merging with technical and vocational education and training (TVET) institutions. The Bo Teachers College has now been incorporated into the School of Education of Njala University under the

Table 3.6 Teacher Education Programs

Qualification	Entry requirement	Duration (years)	Institutions	Target levels
Teachers Certificate (TC)	SSS completion + college exam	1	Teacher colleges and polytechnics	Primary 1–6
Higher Teachers Certificate (HTC) (primary)	4 GCE O level or WASSCE or TC with credit + 3 years teaching	3	Teacher colleges and polytechnics	Head and specialist subject
Higher Teachers Certificate (secondary)	4 GCE O level or WASSCE or TC with credit + 3 years teaching experience	3	Teacher colleges and polytechnics	JSS
Bachelor of education	5 GCE O level or WASSCE with a credit grade in English language	4	Polytechnics and universities	JSS, SSS, TVET, colleges, and polytechnics
Postgraduate diploma in education	A university first degree	1	Universities	JSS, SSS, TVET, colleges, and polytechnics
Masters in education	A university first degree and teaching experience	1	Universities	Higher TVET, colleges, and polytechnics
Ph.D.	A 2.1 or 1st class honors degree or a masters degree at a prespecified grade	3	Universities	Polytechnics and universities

Source: MEST.

2004 Universities Act. The number of graduates from these institutions was relatively low until 2000, mainly because of the weak absorptive capacity of the institutions and low interest in the teaching profession resulting from poor conditions of service. The major incentive for entry into the profession has been the granting of scholarships.

Until very recently only one teacher college offered the Secondary Higher Teachers Certificate (HTC-S) program. This program is now offered by all teacher colleges and polytechnics. The Bachelor of Education program offered by polytechnics and the Njala University is also meant for secondary school teachers, but many pursuing this program do it only as a means of obtaining a degree and have no intention of working in the classroom.

Not enough mathematics and science teachers are being produced by the universities and colleges; therefore TVET graduates are increasingly being used to fill the gap. However, recent visits to schools by personnel from MEST revealed that most of the teachers do not have expertise in their subjects. One consequence is that students fail examinations, and fewer of them pursue science courses at the tertiary level, leading to an even greater shortage of mathematics and science teachers.[5]

The official student to teacher/lecturer ratio for teacher colleges and polytechnics is 20:1. This value is usually exceeded for arts and social science courses but can be lower than 7:1 for sciences and TVET courses. In fact on occasion some colleges do not graduate any students in physics and TVET because no students took the courses.

Many graduates of teacher training institutions do not enter the teaching profession, and a significant number of those who do stay for less than 4 years. Many who exit the profession join the police force to train as officers or work for NGOs, which they believe offer better conditions of service. Additionally, many teachers who graduate from institutions in the capital and district headquarter towns do not return to their home areas to take employment. As a consequence, rural areas are deprived of trained and qualified teachers.

The negative perception of the teaching profession could be improved by the government paying salaries on time, granting teachers loan facilities, and including more teachers in its annual national awards.

In-Service Teacher Training. There is a new emphasis on a distance education program for teachers in part to reduce the number of untrained and unqualified teachers (especially in rural areas). The 2005 NCTVA examinations for the teaching certificate (TC) indicate that more than 60 percent of candidates were pursing the TC by distance. Evidence suggests that the vast majority of candidates for the TC will come from the distance program. That these candidates do not have to leave their settings—apart from 2 weeks each in December and April and 6 weeks in July/August—as well as the guarantee of jobs and salaries are attractive incentives for the TC by distance.

Several initiatives are undertaken by MEST in collaboration with partners to design and implement in-service courses for primary and secondary school teachers. These courses focus on curriculum and emerging issues, such as HIV/AIDS, peace and conflict studies, and guidance and counseling. These courses have been very useful, but the participation of the teachers does not increase their salaries or enhance certification. Thus a need exists to properly coordinate the in-service courses and develop a credit system beneficial to the participants. MEST has appointed a Committee on In-Service Training as a first step to establishing a body to coordinate this activity.

Teacher Motivation. In addition to the knowledge and skills, teacher motivation is a critical prerequisite for quality teaching. A recent study on teacher motivation and incentives found a serious teacher motivation crisis in Sierra Leone, with only 30 percent of the primary school teachers surveyed being satisfied with their jobs (Harding, Beryl, and Mansaray 2005). Most of these satisfied teachers were either unqualified or worked in private schools. The reason for dissatisfaction is thought to stem from late payment of salaries, inadequate pay structure, and an unfair teacher recruitment policy.

CURRICULUM

This section examines the content of the curriculum in primary and secondary schools, the policy on language of instruction, and issues related to HIV education.

Curriculum Content. Curriculum development in Sierra Leone is the responsibility of the National Curriculum Research and Development Centre (NCRDC). This body is responsible for controlling and evaluating the provision and use of curricula, syllabuses, and textbooks within the system (Government of Sierra Leone 1995). The curriculum of primary schools emphasizes communication competence and the ability to understand and manipulate numbers. At the JSS level, the curriculum is general and comprehensive, encompassing the whole range of knowledge, attitudes, and skills in the cognitive, affective, and psychomotor domains. The core subjects of English, mathematics, science, and social studies are compulsory for all pupils. At the SSS level, the curriculum is determined by its nature (general or specialist) or its particular objectives.

On the whole, however, students are offered the set of core (compulsory) subjects with optional subjects based on the specialization of the student.

Teaching is guided by the teaching syllabuses and influenced by the external international examinations that students are required to take at the end of the 3-year course. Syllabuses clearly state the objectives of the lessons, support teaching/learning activities, materials, and means of evaluation. The examination syllabuses are produced by the West African Examinations Council (WAEC). In general both teaching and examination syllabuses are considered unrealistic in the breadth of their content.

Language of Instruction. English is the language of instruction at all levels of schooling. For primary grades 1 and 2, however, the medium of instruction can be both the community language and English. So that the national languages are not completely lost, the education policy encourages the teaching of national languages throughout the school system, teacher colleges, and university. In support of this policy, the National Institute of Sierra Leone Languages was established to promote the development and use of Sierra Leone languages both in the education system and in the community at large.

HIV and Education. The problem of HIV/AIDS does not appear to be as great in Sierra Leone as it is in some other African countries, but it is still an issue. Programs to increase awareness of, prevent, and treat HIV/AIDS are under way. Young and old are dying of the effects of AIDS, but it is rarely reported as the cause of death. Youth have been targeted in the ongoing sensitization campaign, and MEST has taken steps that include the establishment of an HIV/AIDS focal point at MEST, integrating the topic of HIV/AIDS into the school and teacher college curricula, and inclusion of sessions on HIV/AIDS in in-service training courses.

STUDENT LEARNING OUTCOMES

Sierra Leone does not have a student learning assessment system designed specifically to assess the entire education system, but there are plans to develop one. The country does have a public examination system that focuses on the assessment of individual students. This report uses student examination results as a proxy for measuring learning outcomes in primary and secondary education. For each of the primary, JSS, and SSS levels of education, this section briefly describes the examination system and then presents information on trends in the performance of students in these nationwide examinations.

Primary Education. At the end of primary grade 6, all students take the National Primary School Examination (NPSE) conducted by WAEC. The result of this examination, including continuous assessment (CASS) scores, is used for placement into JSS.

The NPSE tests students in mathematics, English, verbal aptitude, quantitative aptitude, and general studies. The last of these is a mixture of science and social studies. The tests are designed to be comparable from year to year. The individual NPSE subtest scores are standardized yearly and within country to have a mean of 50 and standard deviation of 10; the sum of these is an aggregate score. The total NPSE score is then a weighted composite of this aggregate score and the CASS scores, with the weights being 90 and 10 percent, respectively. CASS scores are based on school marks, which are also standardized and statistically adjusted, based on NPSE scores.

The number of candidates taking the NPSE has been rising steadily (figure 3.4), almost quadrupling between 2000 and 2005. No NPSE was conducted in 1997 as a consequence of a military coup. Two sets of candidates took the examinations in 1998; hence the increase in candidates that year. The low of 1999 was due to an onslaught on the Western Area and expansion in the occupation of the north by an alliance of rebel forces. The introduction of free primary education and the free NPSE partly explains the post 2001 increase in candidate numbers. The rates of increase have not been the same for male and female students. As a proportion of total test takers, in fact, the percentage of female students

Figure 3.4 Number of Candidates Taking the NPSE by Gender, 1995–2005

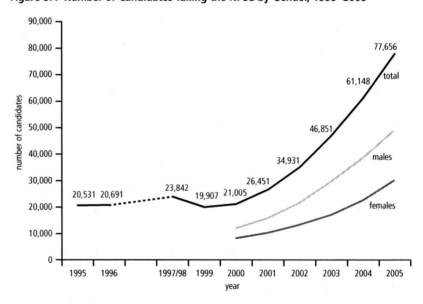

Source: West African Examinations Council.
Note: There was no exam in 1997 as a result of the civil war. The dotted line represents the lack of data for that year.

has been decreasing. The reasons for this decline are not entirely clear, but are worth investigating.

The NPSE pass mark is determined yearly by MEST. It has been gradually increased as the number of candidates taking the examination increases. According to MEST, the philosophy behind increasing the standard is to gradually raise expectations as educational capacity increases. The pass mark was set at a total score of 200 from 1995 to 2000. In 2001, it was increased to 220, and then again in 2005 to 230. Actual pass rates fell significantly when the pass marks were reset (figure 3.5). For comparison, the trend in pass rates is also displayed under a scenario in which the pass mark is fixed at a total score of 200. This hypothetical trend yields a more accurate picture of cohort-to-cohort change in achievement, separating out the effects of MEST policy changes. Clearly, the decrease in pass rates has been largely policy driven.

A review of the number of students passing the NPSE reveals a more optimistic picture of primary school student learning outcomes. Although the percentage of students passing the NPSE has decreased as standards have become more rigorous, the system has been producing drastically increased numbers of qualified candidates (as defined by MEST); between

Figure 3.5   NPSE Actual and Hypothetical Pass Rates if Pass Mark Retained at 2001 Level, 1995–2005

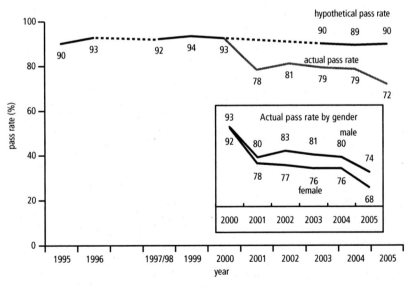

Source: West African Examinations Council.
Note: The pass mark increased from 200 (1995 to 2000) to 220 in 2001 and 230 in 2005. The percentage that would have passed if the pass mark had stayed at 200 is shown in this figure as well as the percentage that actually passed each year. The dotted line means no data for the corresponding years.

Figure 3.6 NPSE Pass Rates by Region, 2003–05

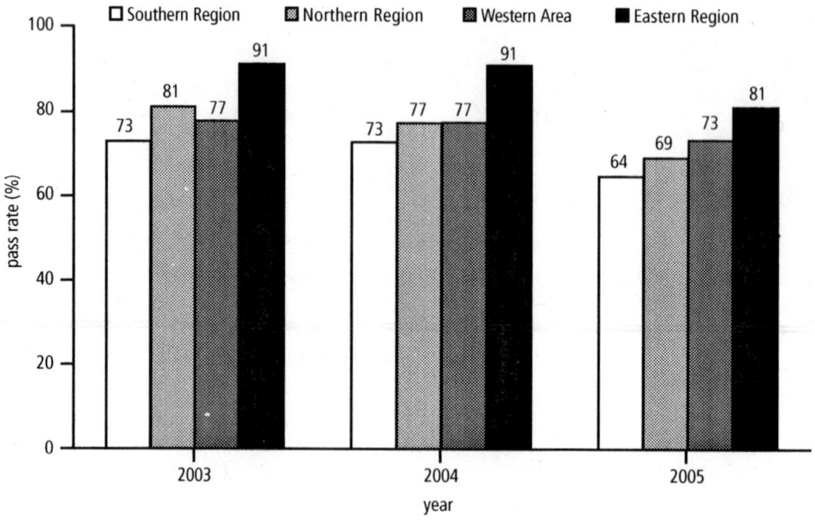

Legend: □ Southern Region ▨ Northern Region ▧ Western Area ■ Eastern Region

y-axis: pass rate (%)

2003: 73, 81, 77, 91
2004: 73, 77, 77, 91
2005: 64, 69, 73, 81

x-axis: year

Source: West African Examinations Council.

2001 and 2005, the total number of students passing the NPSE more than doubled (from about 21,000 to 56,000).

The gap between the numbers of boys and girls passing the NPSE (as well as the percentages) increased after 2000. In 2000, almost 93 percent of boys and 92 percent of girls passed the NPSE. By 2005, the gap in achievement had grown to 6 percentage points in favor of boys. It would be worthwhile for MEST to uncover the causes of these disparities and identify ways to address them.

There are significant regional differences in NPSE pass rates (figure 3.6), with the Eastern Region having the highest rates. For many years, candidates from the Northern Region performed worse than all others. The interventions by MEST in terms of teaching materials and a massive campaign on the benefits of education have turned around the Northern Region, which is now comparable with other regions.

Junior Secondary Education. JSS ends with the Basic Education Certificate Examination (BECE) conducted by WAEC. In this examination each candidate is tested in eight subjects, four of which are compulsory (language arts, mathematics, science, and social studies). BECE papers are marked and standardized on a seven-point scale. A score of 1–4 is a credit, 1–6 is a pass, and 7 is a fail. An aggregate score is determined by summing six subjects: four compulsory, one prevocational, and one other subject.

Figure 3.7 Number of Candidates Taking the BECE by Gender, 2000–05

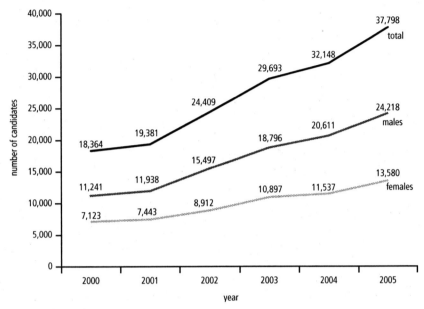

Source: MEST.

The CASS scores of the school constitute part of the final BECE scores with a weight of 20 percent.

The number of candidates taking the BECE more than doubled between 2000 and 2005 (figure 3.7). Significantly fewer girls than boys sit for the BECE, and the gender gap has widened over the past few years. In 2005, girls made up around 35 percent of BECE candidates. Almost half of all BECE candidates were from the Western Area in 2005, and it is known that many candidates from other areas go to the Western Area for JSS because the schools are believed to be of better quality. Thus the competition for places in SSS in Freetown is very severe and student population pressure affects the size of classes.

The number of students passing the BECE (defined as achieving four or more passes including language arts or mathematics) increased from about 9,000 to 15,000, almost doubling between 2000 and 2005. As a result there are significantly more qualified JSS graduates (as then defined by MEST). However, BECE pass rates actually declined between 2000 and 2005, from 50 to 40 percent, mainly because of a decrease in the performance of boys (figure 3.8). The girls' pass rates fluctuated during the same period. Although the gender gap is narrowing, boys still had an average pass rate about 6 percentage points higher than girls in 2005. Among

Figure 3.8 BECE Pass Rates, 2000–05

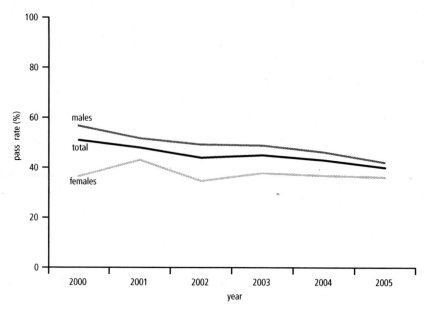

Source: MEST.
Note: The pass rate indicates passes in four or more subjects, including language arts or mathematics.

the four regions, the Western Area had the highest pass rate at 47 percent in 2005, followed by the Eastern Region at 41 percent (figure 3.9). The Southern and Northern Regions had the lowest pass rates at 33 and 31 percent, respectively.

In addition to the large proportion of fails (scores of 7), the BECE score distributions are highly skewed, and there are many students who received scores of 6 (barely satisfactory). Relatively many fewer students received scores of 1–5. This skewing holds for the four main content areas: language arts, mathematics, science, and social studies (figure 3.10). The majority of students either obtained score 6 or barely passed in each of these four subjects, suggesting that the quality of learning outcomes at the JSS level needs to be significantly improved.

Senior Secondary Education. SSS ends with the West Africa Senior School Certificate Examination (WASSCE). The number of candidates taking the WASSCE has been increasing, with more than 13,300 in 2005 (figure 3.11). Female candidates make up only 30 percent of the test takers. Pass rates (defined as credits in four or more subjects) are extremely low, with only 10 percent of male and 6 percent of female candidates passing the WASSCE in 2005 (figure 3.12). The Eastern Region performed particularly well on the WASSCE in 2003, but in

Figure 3.9   BECE Pass Rates by Region, 2003–05

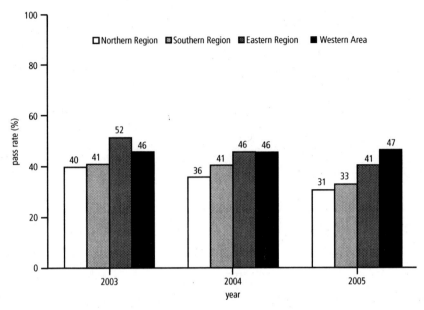

Source: MEST.
Note: The pass rate indicates passes in four or more subjects including language arts or mathematics.

Figure 3.10   BECE Score Distribution in Core Subjects, 2005

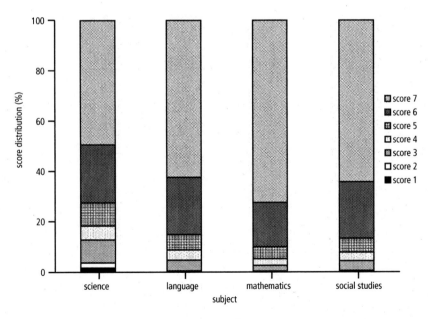

Source: MEST.

Figure 3.11   Number of Candidates Taking the WASSCE by Gender, 2000–05

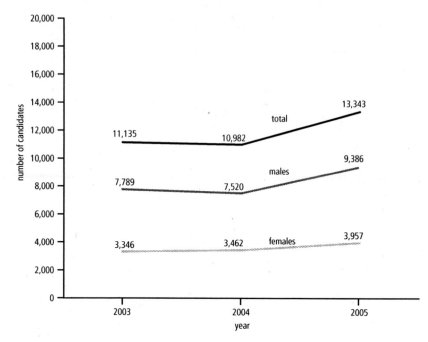

Source: MEST.

Figure 3.12   WASSCE Pass Rates by Gender, 2003–05

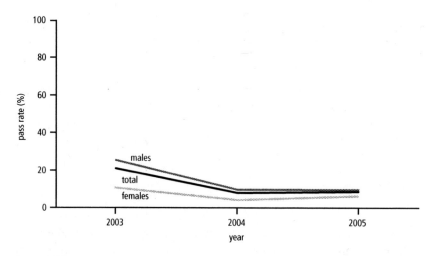

Source: MEST.
Note: A pass is defined as credits in four or more subjects.

Figure 3.13 WASSCE Pass Rates by Region, 2003–05

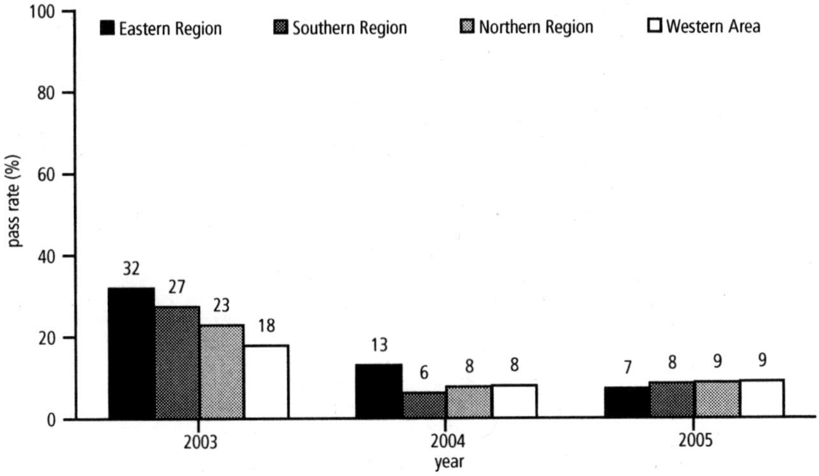

Source: MEST.
Note: A pass is defined as credits in four or more subjects.

2005, all regions had very low pass rates (between 7 and 9 percent; figure 3.13).

TECHNICAL AND VOCATIONAL EDUCATION AND TRAINING

POLICY ENVIRONMENT

The 6-3-3-4 system of education adopted in 1994 was mainly aimed at developing the human resources needed to meet the development challenges of the nation. Its implementation strategy emphasized the need to reduce wastage and enhance articulation between the different layers of the system. It placed TVET at the center of the education program for development in Sierra Leone. However, only in 2001 was the NCTVA Act established, which laid out the government's vision for the sector.

TVET DELIVERY SYSTEM

TVET programs are delivered by government, government-assisted institutions, NGOs, and private organizations or individuals. TVET programs are generally available at all levels of education, from the basic (National Vocational Certificate) offered by community education centers to the highest level (Higher National Diploma) in polytechnics. TVET is provided not only by specialized institutions but also by general schools that offer the JSS and SSS levels of classes. MEST policy requires that prevocational courses, such as introductory technology and business studies, are taught at the JSS level and that all candidates at BECE are offered at least one prevocational subject. The SSS curriculum includes a list of TVET subjects, but very few schools are able to offer the technology subjects because they lack the equipment and teachers. Most can and do offer business subjects. A few SSS institutions have been designated senior technical/vocational schools. These offer National Vocational Qualification (NVQ) courses as well as some WASSCE courses.

A survey carried out in 2004 (and other sources from MEST and NCTVA) indicates that more than 200 TVET institutions are currently in operation in Sierra Leone. Of these institutions, about 4 percent are government-owned and 37 percent government-assisted (figure 3.14).

Only institutions in the Western Area, Bonthe, and Kenema offer programs at the Higher National Diploma level. Thus access to TVET at the

Figure 3.14   TVET Institutions by Ownership, 2004

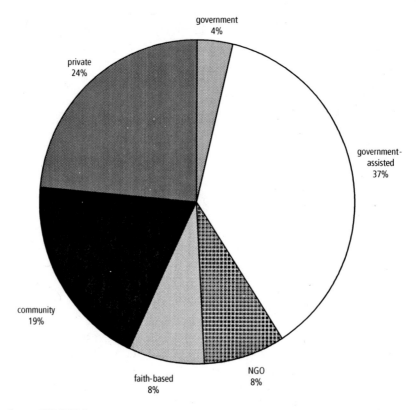

Source: 2004 TVET Survey.

Diploma and Higher Diploma levels (especially with technology options) is still a problem. In fact, some districts do not have technology-related programs beyond the level of the community education center (CEC).

The TVET system is largely supply oriented and has not responded quickly to the job market, tending to react rather than anticipate needs. In addition, the socioeconomic history of Sierra Leone is such that the country has not been able to develop an economic niche and so has not been able to plan for the future skill requirements.

QUALITY OF PHYSICAL RESOURCES

The poor physical condition of TVET structures is highlighted in table 3.7. Although the survey on which the table is based was conducted in the early part of 2001, the infrastructure of most of these institutions still remains inadequate for the growing number of trainees. With the growing demand for skills training and the increasing priority given to technical/vocational education by the government, significant funds need to be invested in the TVET structures to make these institutions worth attending. More than 90 percent of the institutions do not possess the minimum laboratory, workshop, or library facilities needed for their programs. It follows, therefore, that courses that require little equipment (such as

Table 3.7 Conditions of TVET Infrastructure by District, 2001

Region	District	Number of institutions	Rooms needing renovation		Additional rooms needed	
			Number of rooms	Percentage of national total	Number of rooms	Percentage of national total
Eastern Region	Kailahun	15	169	20	271	14
	Kenema	13	33	5	196	9
	Kono	6	36	2	86	3
Northern Region	Bombali	7	34	26	121	19
	Kambia	3	n.a.	n.a.	45	3
	Port Loko	10	25	5	91	14
	Tonkolili	10	31	6	144	6
Southern Region	Bo	24	128	2	196	3
	Bonthe	6	12	4	48	6
	Moyamba	9	14	11	38	4
	Pujehun	4	70	5	51	10
Western Area	Waterloo	3	12	2	13	1
	Western Area	27	80	12	101	7
Total		137	644	100	1,401	100

Source: Report of the 2002 MEST survey on Technical vocational institutes.
Note: n.a. = not applicable.

business studies or gara tie/dye) are common. The equipment for such technology options as automobile, welding, and electronics are not readily available because of the cost. Only the Western Area, Bo, and Kenema have access to the Internet, so access to Internet-related information is very limited.

TEACHING STAFF

Quality of Teaching Personnel. There are more than 2,000 teaching and administrative staff members in the TVET sector, of which more than 70 percent are male. Figure 3.15 profiles the teaching and administrative staff in TVET institutions.[6] Only 28 percent of teachers and administrators in the TVET sector have professional training. Considering that many of those who are classified as professional teachers may not be teaching TVET subjects but support subjects, such as English, the percentage of staff qualified to teach TVET subjects may be even lower. About 50 percent of those with TVET qualifications have Trade Certificates. Because the Trade Certificate is the minimum TVET qualification, this is an indication that a significant number of staff in TVET institutions (especially at the CEC level) have qualifications that are only marginally above the level of some trainees.

Figure 3.15 Staff Profile in TVET Institutions, 2002

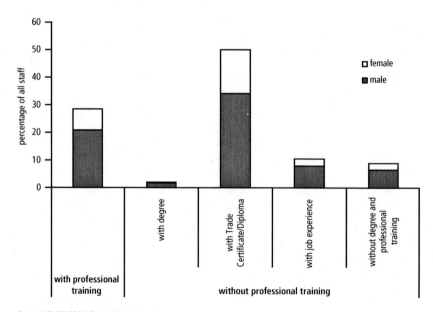

Source: TVET 2004 Survey Report.

Most TVET staff need further training but many do not possess the minimum requirement for entry into teacher training institutions and those who do find more lucrative opportunities on completion of training. The TVET teacher training programs that culminate in HTC-S and Bachelor of Education in technical or commercial studies in the polytechnics are limited in scope and too general for the training of teachers that service nonsecondary institutions. Most staff of these teacher training institutions lack the necessary practical skills. In addition, the institutions have limited practical facilities. Njala University trains teachers for the commercial options, targeting the lower secondary schools, but there are no programs for training technology-related teachers within the university system. Distance education and effective part-time pedagogic training, as well as refresher courses, is one way of developing TVET personnel in the short term. A long-term strategy for adequately and effectively staffing the TVET sector needs to be developed. Such a strategy should raise the number of training institutions across the country and improve the quality of training programs and their relevance to the labor market. Furthermore, an enabling environment should be created to attract and retain more qualified staff (especially women) in this sector.

Quality of Graduates and the Labor Market. With the exception of Community Education Center–B (CEC-B), trainees entering TVET institutions generally meet national entry requirements for having completed basic education. In reality, there is widespread use of a variety of entrance examinations for access or certificate courses in TVET institutions. These entrance examinations create avenues for greater access; however, the quality of intakes is poor, as reflected by the high failure rate at the certificate level. Most entrants into the diploma program (especially in technology options) are those who have gone through access or certificate courses.

At the institutional level, no proper quality assurance system is currently in place. Some limited quality assurance through inspection by the administrative and heads of departments is done occasionally. The Inspectorate Directorate of MEST is overwhelmed, understaffed, and poorly equipped. There are no special inspectors for TVET and no provision for external inspectors. The student learning outcomes are poor, as evidenced by the poor performance of candidates at the NCTVA examinations, particularly at the lower level.

The limited TVET curriculum development process sometimes includes key stakeholders, such as personnel of employment entities. The Professional Engineers Registration Council and Sierra Leone Chamber of Commerce, Industry and Agriculture are represented on the NCTVA Council, and the Institute of Chartered Accounts participates in the curriculum and systems review teams set up by NCTVA. There is urgent need to develop an arm of NCRDC exclusively for TVET or to establish a national training authority to act as the agency for developing and monitoring the TVET curriculum.

TERTIARY EDUCATION

POLICY CONTEXT AND GENERAL CHARACTERISTICS

Tertiary institutions tend to overlap in their offerings, but each has specialties for which it is recognized. For example, Fourah Bay College of the University of Sierra Leone is renowned for its natural sciences, engineering, economics, and arts programs; the College of Medicine and Allied Health Sciences is the only institution offering medical degrees; the Institute of Public Administration and Management is renowned for its business and accounting programs; and Njala University is recognized for its programs in agriculture and education.

The tertiary institutions have heeded the calls for reform in recent years, and changes have been made to programs and methods of assessments. There has even been a change from the traditional English structure to a more modular system.

The Western Area provides significantly greater tertiary education than do the other regions. The Eastern Region in particular is lacking in tertiary institutions. With the establishment of the Eastern Polytechnic, the rebuilding of the Bunumbu Campus in Kailahun District, and the establishment of the Woama Campus in Kono District, teriary education is being enhanced in the Eastern Region. In the Southern Region, Bo Teachers College, the Paramedical School, the School of Hygiene, and Njala University College have now combined to form Njala University (2006). Bonthe Technical College has also been made an affiliate of Njala University.

Given that the combined output of tertiary-level institutions is small and the programs they offer are still not properly aligned with the needs of the nation, the extent to which tertiary education contributes to the overall development of Sierra Leone is in question. The government has considered this issue and has instituted the reforms mentioned earlier in this chapter.

POLYTECHNICS AND TEACHER COLLEGES

Structures and Facilities. All educational structures suffered attacks during the civil conflict, with tertiary institutions being no exception. Njala

University was almost burned to the ground; Makeni Teachers' College and Magburaka Technical Institute were badly vandalized and parts were set ablaze; Freetown Teachers' College and the former Bunumbu Teachers College were looted and vandalized. However, a remarkable transformation has taken place in the past 5 years, with large-scale rehabilitation of most tertiary institution buildings through support from the Arab Bank, European Union, World Bank, and African Development Bank. Some, however, are still awaiting intervention, and most lack the equipment and materials necessary for good quality teaching and learning. Some have used self-help and assistance from alumni associations to generate funds or obtain needed materials, but the equipment in the majority of schools is still deplorable.

Student-Teacher Ratios. Table 3.8 shows the number of staff in tertiary education. About 30 percent of the 3,500 staff members are academic staff and the rest are administrative. Such a high percentage of nonacademic staff consumes a large proportion of scarce financial resources. It would be worthwhile to examine whether savings can be made so that extra resources are available to improve teaching and learning.

Student-teacher ratios vary greatly across departments.[7] For some science courses, the ratio is much lower than 10, whereas for some popular arts courses, the ratio exceeds 30 (table 3.9). The average student-teacher

Table 3.8   Number of Academic and Nonacademic Staff in Tertiary Education, 2004/05

Institutions	Academic staff			Nonacademic staff			Total staff		
	Male	Female	Total	Male	Female	Total	Male	Female	Total
Tertiary education total	1,009	149	1,158	1,926	407	2,333	2,935	556	3,491
Teachers colleges	192	36	228	342	54	396	534	90	624
Polytechnic institutes	159	13	172	197	33	230	356	46	402
University of Sierra Leone	658	100	758	1,387	320	1,707	2,045	420	2,465
Distribution of academic and nonacademic staff (%)	n.a.	n.a.	33	n.a.	n.a.	67	n.a.	n.a.	100

Sources: Payroll data; Higher Education Directorate; MEST.
Note: n.a. = not applicable.

Table 3.9   Student-Teacher Ratios in Tertiary Institutions, 2004/05

Indicator	Teacher training colleges	Polytechnic institutes	University of Sierra Leone
Number of students	2,577	2,104	9,689
Number of teaching staff	228	172	758
Student-teacher ratio	11	12	13

Source: MEST.

ratios are lower than most Sub-Saharan countries, indicating adequate teaching staff in tertiary institutions on average, although there is large variation across subjects. However, most departments are struggling to attract and retain quality personnel, primarily because of the salaries and conditions they can afford to offer. Only the most patriotic, those with strong family ties, and those returning home for other reasons are filling the various positions at the universities. Most of the best and the youngest are tempted by lucrative overseas offers and move away.

Until very recently, most staff members at teacher colleges held undergraduate degrees. Only the requirements of the reforms and the establishment of polytechnics caused many to pursue masters programs and upgrade their qualifications.

Staff development possibilities exist through scholarships from Commonwealth and other countries and through distance education. University lecturers also have sabbaticals, which they use to upgrade their knowledge and/or to conduct research. To minimize the number who go to study in other countries (and subsequently never return), scholarships for study in other African countries are now emphasized.

Curriculum. Unlike schools, curriculum at the tertiary level is not set by MEST. The Tertiary Education Commission has the responsibility of ensuring that tertiary-level institutions offer programs and courses of acceptable standard and quality and to advise government accordingly. Thus, although tertiary institutions have some discretion setting the content of their courses, they must meet the minimum standard set by the Tertiary Education Commission. The government can, however, influence the courses on offer by the scholarships it awards and by targeted funding of programs and courses.

Learning Outcomes and the Labor Market. Most who gain entrance to tertiary institutions successfully complete their courses. At the universities, however, the degrees awarded are mainly lower second-class and third-class degrees. At the Teacher Colleges, many students have final-year papers that they must retake before receiving their certificates. In general, the quality of graduates from tertiary institutions is satisfactory, but there is some concern about the quality of Teacher Certificate graduates.

POLICY IMPLICATIONS

The key issues having implications for further policy development on the learning environment and outcomes are outlined here.

Adequate Classroom Conditions for Effective Learning. Classroom conditions are grossly inadequate, reflected in the high percentages of damaged school infrastructure, overcrowded classrooms, and shortage of teaching materials. The government has made efforts to improve classroom conditions after the war ended, but progress so far has been slower than anticipated. Preparation of the education sector plan is a good opportunity for the government to review the current policies and practices and learn lessons from the past few years to shed light on how to move forward more rapidly.

Qualified and Motivated Teachers. Teaching methodologies need to be revisited, and teachers and principals should be trained for effective classroom management. The high proportion of unqualified teachers should be redressed. Development is needed of a comprehensive and sustainable strategy that comprises preservice training; in-service training; and recruitment, deployment, and retention of motivated, well-paid, and well-resourced professional teachers.

Quality Assurance. Now that great progress has been made on access, the focus should be on ensuring quality. Periodic evaluation of the system and its different levels of education is required, as is the ability to make recommendations and suggest policies for improvement. These requirements necessitate the establishment of a reliable and effective education management information system (EMIS). Integrating quality assurance with EMIS provides a system that ensures that information gathering and analysis go beyond planning to evaluating and reporting on the performance of the system.

National Student Learning Assessment System. Currently there is no true student learning assessment system in the country. The WAEC examinations are designed for selecting individual students to be promoted to the next level of the education, not for evaluating the system. The pass rates do not indicate the level of education achieved by students because the rates are affected by the available space in the next level of the system. A true assessment system should be able to determine whether the system is performing well in terms of learning outcomes, identify the strengths and weaknesses of the system, track the performance of subgroups, determine whether curricula are well designed, and identify factors associated with learning outcomes. Such assessments in developing countries are usually sample based and test students at certain critical grades every few years. A good assessment system helps greatly in the diagnosis of students' performances and in shedding light on the improvement of education quality.

Taking Advantage of Decentralization. Sierra Leone is moving toward decentralization. Local councils will be held accountable for government and government-assisted primary schools and JSS. Their responsibilities will include payment of teachers and student fees, provision of teaching materials, rehabilitation of schools, and inspection of teachers and students. The local councils are moving rapidly to exercise their new powers. It is important for the central government to help strengthen the capacity at the local level and make local councils accountable for delivering education services and diligently supervising schools, so that the learning environment and learning outcomes can in turn be improved.

Setting Higher Standards for TVET. The quality of TVET nationwide is patchy. The condition of buildings is generally appalling, the equipment and other training materials are either obsolete or inadequate, and most teachers—especially for the technology options—are not properly trained. A minimum standard should be set for each level of institutions, their programs, and tutors. This effort could include the establishment of a body responsible for monitoring TVET delivery systems. The country could learn from existing models, such as the National Training Authority or National Commission for TVET in sister African countries.

Promoting More Effective Public and Private Partnerships. TVET is largely in the hands of private providers. Even though some receive subventions and other assistance from the government, their fees make them out of the reach of many potential students. Part of the reason for technical/ vocational centers being able to levy high fees is that demand for places is great. By encouraging and hence increasing the number of centers, competition should lead to an overall reduction in fees and more youth being able to access the programs on offer. Through model centers, the government can set the standards that the private institutions would be required to follow. Given the resources available, the government would do well to focus the funds available for TVET on the lower and upper levels, leaving the middle primarily to private providers while setting the standards, conducting examinations, and assuming responsibility for monitoring. The lower-level skills training could be the responsibility of the local councils while the central government takes responsibility for the upper levels in a manner similar to that for schools. The indications are that the government does not have the resources to take over all levels of TVET, because of the demands of the other sectors of education. It makes sense for the government to focus on those TVET subjects that the private sector is not investing in; those that involve high quality laboratories and equipment with skilled technicians. The government could ensure that there is one such center in each local government area. Most of the business and other vocational courses could be left to the private sector.

Improving Efficiency and Quality. Recent legislation has opened up tertiary education and made it more responsive to national needs, but quality (both learning environment and learning outcomes) is still a problem because of available resources. However, the low student-teacher ratios and high proportion of nonteaching staff in the system indicates low efficiency, which can be a potential area for saving resources. Upgrading teaching facilities and equipment and recruiting high quality teaching staff are areas requiring urgent attention and more resources. It is also necessary to develop a clear strategy for distance education, especially for teacher training. More innovative methods should be explored for the enhancement of the quality and quantity of staff in tertiary institutions, especially in areas such as science and technology.

Modernizing Curriculum and Increasing Relevance. Tertiary institutions should be more proactive in developing programs that respond to the urgent needs of national development. Innovative procedures, such as providing special grants for attracting staff to underserved areas, should be instituted. More encouragement should be given to girls and women who wish to pursue careers in science and technology. MEST should encourage the establishment of an arm of the Tertiary Education Commission that will focus on quality assurance and provide incentives, such as research and development grants, for departments that meet minimum national and international standards. Best practice could be borrowed from such countries as India and South Africa.

CHAPTER 4

Expenditure and Financing

Expansion and quality improvement of the education system, highlighted in the preceding two chapters, indicate an increasing demand
for educational resources in Sierra Leone. Adequate mobilization of
resources and careful management of them is crucial to achieving Sierra
Leone's educational goals. Spending on education by the government has
increased rapidly since 2000. In relation to total government expenditure
(current and development) and to GDP, it remained relatively steady over
that time. In terms of current government spending, the share devoted to
education was about 19 percent between 2001 and 2004, the largest share
for any sector, and very close to the Education for All (EFA) Fast Track Initiative (FTI) benchmark of 20 percent. About half of current government
expenditure on education goes to preprimary and primary education;
about 20–25 percent is earmarked for secondary education. The share for
secondary education has fallen slightly in recent years despite the expansion that will be required because of the recent increases in primary
enrollments. The portion for technical and vocational education also fell
in recent years from the already low 9 percent in 2000 to 4 percent in
2004. Tertiary education consumes about 20 percent of the education
resources, a share that has risen somewhat in recent years.[1] Household
contributions to education are very high. Support from external donors is
an important part of the funding of education in Sierra Leone, although
there are relatively few donors. Because households are already contributing a large amount (and many of those not yet in school come from
the poorest families) and public resources are stretched, increased donor
funding will be needed to increase the coverage of education.

This chapter begins by examining recent trends in expenditure on education from government, household, and donor sources, including the allocation across different levels of education. It then examines the structure of

the 2004 expenditure in more detail, including salary and nonsalary costs, a breakdown of the unit cost, and the factors that influence unit cost.

TOTAL EXPENDITURE ON EDUCATION

This section examines the total amount of government expenditure on education, as well as its distribution across the different levels of schooling. It also relates these figures to the GDP and total government expenditure, and describes trends over the past 5 years. Finally, it examines the contributions made by the international community and by households.

TOTAL PUBLIC SPENDING ON EDUCATION

In line with the significant increase in government revenues and expenditure (see chapter 1), there has been a rapid increase in spending on education since 2000, with an average real increase of 11 percent per year (figure 4.1). However, given the increase in total government expenditure, the share devoted to education remained steady over this period at about 16–17 percent. Estimates from the Ministry of Finance for 2005–08,

Figure 4.1 Government Expenditure on Education, 2000–08

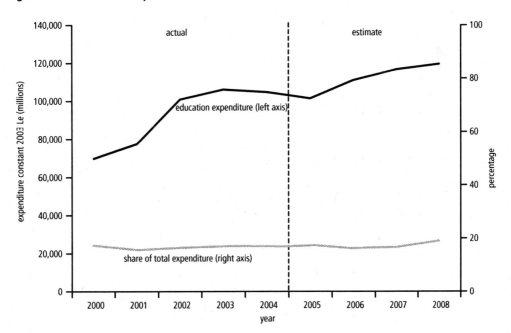

Source: Table 4.1.

although tentative, suggest that government expenditure on education will continue to increase but at a much slower pace (3 percent per year), with the share of total expenditure unchanged.

Government expenditure on education remained stable at about 4.2–4.9 percent of GDP between 2000 and 2004 (see table 4.1). This percentage compares favorably with other postwar countries, such as Burundi (3.9 percent in 2002/03), Rwanda (2.8 percent in 2000/01), and Mozambique (2.4 percent in 1999/2000). The range for other countries in Sub-Saharan Africa is from 0.6 percent of GDP (Equatorial Guinea in 2002/03)

Table 4.1 Government Expenditure on Education, 2000–08

Indicator	Actual					Estimate[a]			
	2000	2001	2002	2003	2004	2005	2006	2007	2008
Current Le (millions)									
Total education expenditure	65,842	74,347	93,268	106,092	121,580	133,395	165,184	188,714	208,725
Current	65,428	73,685	86,901	101,464	113,110	132,594	163,484	187,014	207,875
Development	414	662	6,367	4,628	8,470	805	1,700	1,700	850
Constant 2003 Le (millions)									
Total education expenditure	69,867	77,525	100,935	106,092	104,799	101,454	111,040	116,749	119,592
Current	69,428	76,834	94,045	101,464	97,498	100,844	109,898	115,698	119,105
Development	439	690	6,890	4,628	7,301	612	1,143	1,052	487
Education expenditure as a percentage of GDP	4.9	4.6	4.7	4.6	4.2	3.8	3.9	—	—
Education current expenditure as a percentage of GDP	4.9	4.6	4.4	4.4	3.9	3.8	3.8	—	—
Education as a percentage of total government expenditure	17.2	15.7	16.6	17.0	16.9	17.4	16.4	16.6	19.0
Education as a percentage of total government current expenditure[b]	21.7	18.6	18.3	19.9	19.4	20.8	22.8	24.0	24.7
Percentage of domestically generated current resources for education[c]	25.3	24.3	21.7	21.7	18.4	19.0	17.8	—	—
Education current expenditure per school-aged population (6–21 years; constant 2003 Le)	40,848	44,249	53,015	55,988	52,661	—	—	—	—

Source: Ministry of Finance
Note: — = not available.
a. Figures from 2006 to 2008 include transfers to local councils for areas of education expenditure that have been decentralized.
b. The FTI benchmark for the share of current spending in domestic revenues is 20 percent.
c. Estimates based on the proportion of total public resources that are domestic and donor.

to 10.4 percent (Lesotho in 2001/02), with a median for the region of 3.5 percent (UNESCO Institute for Statistics 2005).

Both current and development spending on education have risen since 2000, though at different rates. In line with the reconstruction and expansion required after the war years, table 4.1 shows that development expenditure increased in real terms, from the low of about Le 400 million in 2000 to Le 7,300 million in 2004 (the bulk of the increase taking place in 2002). This is an increase of more than 16 times the 2000 level. Current expenditure makes up the bulk of the education expenditures, increasing at an average rate of 9 percent per year between 2000 and 2004 in real terms.

To account for changes in the size of the target population over time, table 4.1 shows current expenditure on education per school-aged person. For this purpose, the target population is approximated as individuals between the ages of 6 and 21 years. The expenditure shows an average real increase between 2000 and 2004 of 7 percent per year, from Le 41,000 per school-aged person to Le 53,000. Such numbers indicate a gradual but substantial improvement (about 30 percent over 4 years) in the capacity of the government to provide educational services to its population.

The share of total government current expenditure allocated to the education budget has fluctuated around 19 percent between 2001 and 2004. Figure 4.2 presents comparable figures for other countries in the Sub-Saharan region, showing a wide range from as much as 29 percent in Malawi, Zambia, and Niger down to just 12 percent in Burundi and the Seychelles. The EFA FTI set a benchmark of 20 percent. Sierra Leone is very close to this benchmark.

DISTRIBUTION BY LEVEL OF EDUCATION

About half of all government resources for education goes to primary education (including the preprimary level; figure 4.3).[2] The priority given to this subsector increased between 2000 and 2001 from 44 to 51 percent, falling slightly to 48 percent in 2004. Estimates for 2005 to 2007 (shown in appendix table D.10) suggest that the share for primary will remain stable at about 50 percent.

The share for secondary education fell from 25 percent in 2000 to 20 percent in 2002 and then rose slightly to 22 percent in 2004. The share for tertiary and teacher's education increased from 17 percent in 2002 to 22 percent in 2004. Estimates for 2005 to 2007 indicate that the share of spending for the tertiary sector will remain at about 20 percent of current education expenditure. Finally, the allocation to technical and vocational

Figure 4.2   Education Share of Current Budget in Sub-Saharan Africa

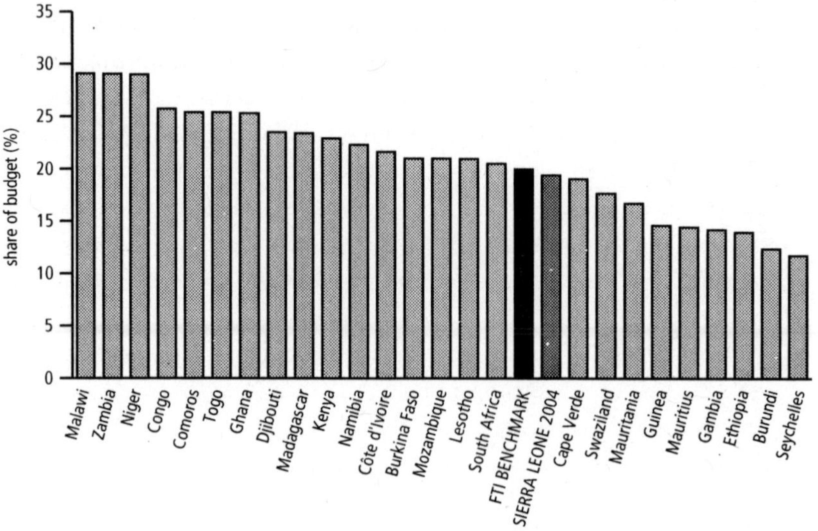

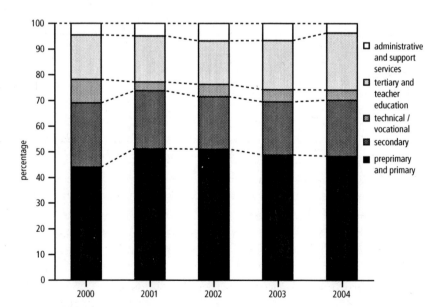

Sources: UNESCO Institute for Statistics 2005; EFA FTI Country Profiles http://www.fasttrackinitiative.org/
education/efafti/keydocuments.asp; The Budget Bureau, Ministry of Finance.
Note: 2004/05: Djibouti, Madagascar, and Kenya; 2003/04: Mauritania and Guinea; 2001/02: Congo,
Mozambique, Burkina Faso, South Africa, and Ethiopia; 2000/01: Togo, Lesotho, and Côte d'Ivoire;
1999/2000: Namibia; 1998/99: Malawi, Zambia, and Seychelles.

Figure 4.3   Share of Current Expenditure by Level of Education, 2000–04

Source: Appendix table D.10.

education decreased substantially, from 9 percent in 2000 to 4 percent in 2004. Even with the overall increase in education expenditure, this reduction equates to a drop in real terms of nearly 25 percent over 4 years.

The final category for allocation of expenditure is administrative and support services, which includes the Office of the Permanent Secretary, Planning and Development Services, Physical and Health Education, the Inspectorate Division, Non-formal Education, and the Tertiary Education Commission. Expenditures in this category more than doubled between 2000 and 2003 in real terms, making up about 7 percent of the total current expenditure on education. It dropped back down in 2004 to 4 percent of education expenditure (although there may be some uncertainty about the accuracy of this figure, because estimates for 2005–07 indicate that spending in this category will increase to about 8 percent of total current education expenditure).

The way in which countries distribute their public expenditure across the different levels of education varies greatly (figure 4.4). For example,

Figure 4.4   Share of Current Expenditure by Level of Education in Sub-Saharan Africa, circa 2003

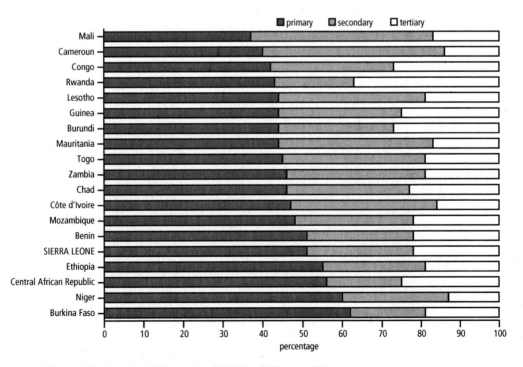

Sources: Table 4.6, EFA Dakar +5, UNESCO-Breda and World Bank Education CSRs.
Note: Sierra Leone primary share includes preprimary (expected to be small). For Sierra Leone, the amounts for administrative and support services have been distributed across the levels of education. Therefore, the percentages differ from those shown in figure 4.3.

Burkina Faso and Niger allocate about 60 percent of their spending on education to the primary level, whereas Mali and Cameroon allocate only about 40 percent to that level. Similarly, for tertiary education, some countries spend more than 25 percent of their current education budget whereas others spend less than 15 percent.

HOUSEHOLD CONTRIBUTIONS TO FINANCING EDUCATION

Households in Sierra Leone spend considerable amounts on the education of their children. Parents who send their children to private school cover the full cost of education. Those with children in government and government-assisted schools also report spending on fees, even though fees were officially abolished in all primary schools and for junior secondary school (JSS) girls in the Eastern and Northern Regions in 2001. In this section, data from the Sierra Leone Integrated Household Survey (SLIHS 2003/04) are used to explore the magnitude of household spending on education.

The total amount households spend on primary education is substantial (table 4.2). In secondary education, the contribution of households is even larger, reaching about 60 percent of total spending. Chapter 2 showed that coverage of education in Sierra Leone has recovered quite rapidly after the war; but this outcome is significantly influenced by the strong motivation of households to put their children in school and contribute to the costs when public financing was lacking.

Households pay tuition and other education-related costs, such as supplying uniforms, books, and transportation for their primary-school children (table 4.3). At primary level, tuition is paid primarily by children

Table 4.2 Household Spending on Primary and Secondary Education, 2003/04

Level	Number of students	Mean household spending Per student (Le)	Mean household spending Aggregate (Le millions)	Government spending (Le millions)	Total spending (Le millions)	Share of financing by households (%)
Primary[a]	989,337	50,872	50,330	49,542	99,871	50.4
Secondary	162,141	196,478	31,857	21,009	52,866	60.3
JSS	125,956	178,306	22,459	—	—	—
SSS	36,185	259,732	9,398	—	—	—
Primary and secondary	1,151,478	71,375	82,187	70,551	152,737	53.8

Sources: SLIHS 2003/04; table D.10.
Note: — = not available.
a. Includes preprimary.

Table 4.3 Distribution of Household Spending per Primary Education Pupil by Category, 2003/04

Indicator	Tuition	Uniforms	Books	Transport	Food	Extra-curricular activities	Other	Total
Mean household spending (Le)	5,787	11,535	6,806	2,612	7,046	6,698	10,387	50,871
Percentage of total	11	23	13	5	14	13	20	100

Source: SLIHS 2003/04.

in private schools and some community schools. Many schools, regardless of ownership, ask parents to contribute to extracurricular activities, such as sports. The category "other" includes contributions to the Community Teachers Association. Payments for uniforms (23 percent of total household spending on primary education), books, food, and extracurricular activities still constitute a large financial burden on parents.

The number of households in the SLIHS (2003/04) with students in the tertiary sector was too small to infer anything about their contributions to tertiary education. However, institutional data on tuition and other fees provide a conservative estimate of these costs. Direct payments to the institutions range from about Le 750,000 at the Milton Margai Teacher's College to Le 3.2 million at the College of Medicine and Applied Health Services.

EXTERNAL DONORS

As shown in chapter 1, Sierra Leone receives a substantial level of donor funding, which peaked at the end of the war in 2001 and 2002. This section examines the amount of external funding that supports education.

External sources of funding include loans, grants, and in-kind contributions from multilateral organizations, bilateral agencies, international NGOs, international religious institutions, and individuals. Some of this funding is channeled through the government, and some goes directly to educational institutions and individuals (for example, scholarships). Because of the wide variety of sources and types of funding, it is not easy to quantify funding for education from international sources. Approximately 40 percent of the overall government budget comes from external support (Budget Bureau staff, Ministry of Finance; chapter 1). This percentage includes heavily indebted poor countries (HIPC) funds targeted toward poverty-related expenditures, including education. The support that is channeled to local and international NGOs working in Sierra Leone is much more difficult to quantify, and some of it may not be

Figure 4.5   Donor Funding for Education, 2000–04

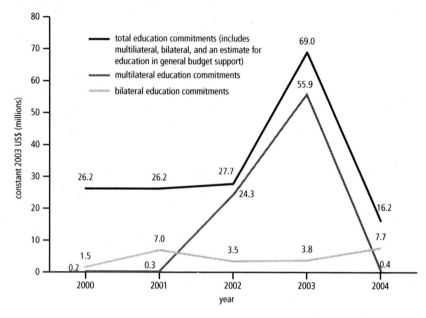

Source: Creditor Reporting System (CRS) Online Database on Aid Activities (www.oecd.org/dac/stats/idsonline), table 2. Last updated January 30, 2006.
Note: From DAC countries and multilateral agencies. Includes an estimated 17% of general budget support commitments (this being the share to education of the total 2004 government expenditure in Sierra Leone).

captured in the Organisation for Economic Co-operation and Development (OECD) Official Development Assistance[3] (ODA) figures from Development Assistance Committee (DAC) member countries[4] and multilateral organizations. Nevertheless, these databases have a consistent series of data for commitments to education that allow an examination of trends in recent years.[5] Figure 4.5 shows the amount of bilateral and multilateral commitments for education, an estimate for the portion of general budget support that goes to education, and the total (which combines the education commitments and a portion of the general budget support). The data show that education commitments peaked in 2003 due to International Development Assistance (IDA) commitments of US$55 million. Over 2000–04, the largest multilateral donors to education in Sierra Leone were the World Bank (through IDA), the African Development Fund, and the European Community; the largest bilateral donors were the United Kingdom (through general budget support), Germany, and Norway.

The majority of donor funding for education is aimed at basic education: more than 90 percent of the 2002 and 2003 commitments and 75 percent of the 2004 commitments were for basic education (CRS 2006).

Currently, the largest basic education project in Sierra Leone is the Rehabilitation of Basic Education Project (commonly known as Sababu) for which US$40 million was committed by the World Bank and the African Development Bank.

In comparison to other countries, the EFA FTI Secretariat found that Sierra Leone had relatively few donors for education. The analysis found that bilateral agencies tend to congregate in the same countries. In fact, Sierra Leone was one of only 11 countries that had no bilateral partners contributing more than an annual average of US$1 million in 2002 and 2003.[6]

RECONSTRUCTING RESOURCES MOBILIZED FOR EDUCATION

This section combines information presented in the previous sections to summarize the mobilization of resources for education and examine prospects for the coming years. Table 4.4 presents a reconstruction of the resources and expenditure for 2003. Total expenditure on education was about Le 188 billion, of which Le 65 billion was from domestic sources, Le 41 billion was from donor sources, and Le 82 billion from private sources (households).[7] Thus domestic public funding represents only 35 percent of total spending on education; contributions from donors are about 22 percent; and the main contributors (with 44 percent of the total) are households.[8] In primary education, households finance about half of total current spending, this proportion rises to over 60 percent in secondary education.

The level of domestic public resources available for education in the coming years will depend on (1) the change in GDP over time; (2) the change in public domestic resources as a percentage of GDP (fiscal pressure); (3) the change in donor assistance to the country and to education; and (4) the change in the priority given to education within public funding (as assessed by the proportion of public resources, both from domestic and external origins, allocated to the sector).

Assuming that (1) GDP grows at an average real rate of 5 percent per year during the coming years;[9] (2) domestic public resources increase from about 12 to 14 percent of GDP; (3) the proportion of external funding remains at about the 2003 level (38 percent of total public resources); and (4) the priority for education remains at the 2003 level (22.7 percent; see table 4.4), the amount of public resources for the sector could rise from Le 106 billion in 2003 (US$40 million) to about Le 160 billion (US$60 million) in 2009, an increase of more than 50 percent over 6 years (or about 7 percent per year) in real terms. However, such an

Table 4.4   Resource Mobilization for Education, 2003

| Indication | Resources and expenditure (Le millions) | | | | |
| | Public | | | Household contributions | Total |
	Domestic public	External donors	Total public		
GDP	2,323,667				
Domestic revenues	287,657				
As % of GDP	12.4				
Donor support		179,344			
As % of domestic revenues		62.3			
Total public resources			467,001		
Public spending on education					
Domestic sources[a]	65,349				
Donor sources[a]		40,743			
Total			106,092		
As % of GDP			4.6		
As % of total resources			22.7		
Capital spending on education			4,628		
Current spending on education			101,464		
Primary education (including preprimary)			53,068		
Secondary education (general and TVET)			27,637		
Tertiary education			20,760		
Private resources for education[b]				82,187	
As % of public spending on education[b]			77.5		
As % of domestic public financing of education			125.8		
Total resources for education	65,349	40,743		82,187	188,279
Percentage distribution	35	22		44	100

Sources: Tables 1.9, 1.11, 4.1, and 4.2.
a. Estimates based on the proportion of total public resources that are domestic and donor (62 percent and 38 percent, respectively).
b. Does not include household contributions to tertiary education.

increase is not likely to be sufficient to adequately expand and upgrade the education system (see chapter 7).

In terms of household resources for education, the levels of contributions are already fairly high, both in terms of total amounts (as described above) and in per-pupil units, because household contributions correspond to about 10 percent of the per capita GDP for primary education, rising to 40 percent for secondary education. Given equity concerns (which are outlined in chapter 5), it is unreasonable to expect that universal primary completion can be financed by an increase in household contributions, particularly since the poor are underrepresented in school and will have the most difficulty covering the costs. Because it appears unlikely that additional public domestic resources, beyond what has been suggested above, can be mobilized, an increase in external funding will be necessary. This is particularly true in the context of the Millennium Development Goal to achieve universal primary completion by 2015.

ANALYSIS OF EDUCATION EXPENDITURE IN 2004

This section provides a more detailed analysis of current spending on education for 2004 and provides an estimate of unit costs at different levels of education. It then examines unit costs in detail to identify the key components.

SALARY AND NONSALARY EXPENDITURE

The salaries of school and central services staff make up 74 percent of the total current spending on education (table 4.5).[10] It is highest at the tertiary level (78 percent), followed by secondary education (75 percent), primary education (72 percent), and technical and vocational education (68 percent). It is not currently possible to separate the teaching and nonteaching staff from the salary expenditure at the school level.

The figures for salary expenditures represent only those teaching and administrative personnel on the government payroll in both government and government-assisted schools. However, a survey of government and government-assisted schools showed that up to 10 percent of teachers are community teachers that are not paid by the Ministry of Education, Science and Technology and therefore are not on the government payroll (Glennerster, Imran, and Whiteside 2006). These teachers either volunteer or are paid by the community. The government is currently trying to place teachers from recognized schools (including community schools) on the payroll, but the process is slow.

With regard to nonsalary current expenditure, table 4.5 shows that capitation grants make up almost half of the nonstaff current spending in primary education (48 percent) and about 40 percent in secondary education. These grants include payments to provide free primary schooling for all and free junior secondary schooling for girls in the Eastern and Northern Regions. Other transfers, such as payment of student examination fees to the West African Examinations Council, are also provided by

Table 4.5 Distribution of Personnel and Current Expenditure by Education Level and Type of Expenditure, 2004

	Number of personnel		Salary expenditure (Le millions)			Nonsalary expenditure (Le millions)						Total cost
	School level	Services	School level	Services	Total	Transfers	Materials & textbooks	Capitation grants	Scholarships	Other	Total	(Le millions)
Primary	17,668	192	39,605	1,518	41,123	510	6,548	7,754	..	1,444	16,257	57,380
Secondary[a]	5,791	178	18,248	1,109	19,357	1,852	576	2,720	..	1,434	6,582	25,939
JSS	4,389	135	13,830	841	14,671	1,438	447	2,113	..	1,112	5,111	19,781
SSS	1,402	43	4,418	269	4,686	413	129	607	..	322	1,471	6,157
Technical or vocational	769	81	2,697	440	3,137	1,031	..	..	88	328	1,446	4,583
Nonformal	..	..	..	..	..	122	..	..	..	..	122	122
Tertiary	..	3,481	..	19,606	19,606	..	..	..	3,774	1,705	5,479	25,086
Total	28,160		..	..	83,224	3,514	7,124	10,474	3,862	4,911	29,885	113,109
Percentage distribution of costs												
Primary			69	3	72	1	11	14	..	3	28	100
Secondary			70	4	75	7	2	10	..	6	25	100
JSS			70	4	74	7	2	11	..	6	26	100
SSS			72	4	76	7	2	10	..	5	24	100
Technical or vocational			59	10	68	22	..	..	2	7	32	100
Nonformal			..	..	..	100	..	..	..	..	100	100
Tertiary			..	78	78	..	..	..	15	7	22	100
Total			..	74	74	3	6	9	3	4	26	100

Sources: Authors' estimates based on MOF Recurrent and Development estimates, financial years 2005–07 and the Budget Bureau, Ministry of Finance.

Note: Amounts for general administration, planning, and development, and the inspectorate are distributed across the levels of education. Therefore, the totals by level are different from those shown in appendix table D.11. Numbers of personnel are for the 2003/04 academic year. .. = nil or negligible.

a. The Ministry of Finance does not report spending at the JSS and SSS levels of secondary education, so the breakdown has been calculated using the estimated number of teachers in the JSS and SSS levels for salaries and benefits and the number of students in JSS and SSS for nonstaff current spending.

the government. Only 6 percent of the current expenditure goes to teaching and learning materials and other school inputs.

ESTIMATES OF THE UNIT COST

From the data presented in table 4.5 and information on enrollment, the cost per student (unit cost) is calculated and shown by level in table 4.6. For primary education, the cost was about Le 53,000 per student in 2004, an equivalent of 9.2 percent of GDP per capita. The unit cost increases with higher levels of schooling: in secondary education, the cost was around Le 156,000 per JSS student and Le 169,000 per SSS student, representing 26.8 and 29.1 percent of per capita GDP, respectively, and around three times the cost for primary school students. For technical and vocational education, the unit cost was roughly double the cost of secondary education, or Le 355,000 per student (or 61.0 percent of the per capita GDP). For tertiary education, the unit cost was substantially higher at Le 1.6 million (2.8 times the per capita GDP), which was about 30 times higher than the cost per student in primary schools and 10 times higher than the cost per student in secondary schools.

For selected countries in Sub-Saharan Africa, table 4.7 shows that there is a very wide range in unit cost in relation to economic development. In particular, Sierra Leone spends relatively less per student on senior secondary school and technical and vocational education in relation to its wealth. Primary education is also relatively low, with Kenya, Niger, and Burkina Faso spending more than twice that (in relation to their wealth) of Sierra Leone on primary students.

Table 4.6   Unit Cost Estimates for Education by Level, 2004

	Primary	JSS	SSS	Technical and vocational	Tertiary
Education current expenditure (Le millions)	57,380	19,781	6,157	4,583	25,086
No. of students in government-assisted institutions[a]	1,078,074	126,731	36,408	12,919	15,497
Unit cost (Le)	53,224	156,090	169,125	354,746	1,618,736
Unit cost as a % of per capita GDP	9.2	26.8	29.1	61.0	278.3
Ratio of unit cost to primary	1.0	2.9	3.2	6.7	30.4

Sources: Ministry of Finance; MEST.
a. Enrollment figures are for school year 2003/04. Enrollments in government and government-assisted institutions have been estimated at 95 percent of total primary and secondary enrollments and about half of technical/vocational enrollments. All tertiary enrollments are in government institutions.

Table 4.7 Unit Cost as a Percentage of GDP Per Capita in Sub-Saharan Countries by Level, circa 2000–04

Primary[a]		JSS		SSS		Tech / vocational		Tertiary	
Kenya	25.2	Niger	49.0	Niger	157.0	Mali	202.6	Rwanda	786.0
Niger	20.0	Rwanda	47.4	Burundi	135.5	Chad	192.1	Burundi	718.7
Burkina Faso	19.2	Burundi	41.6	Mali	117.1	Burundi	188.4	Niger	515.0
Ghana	16.5	Mauritania	39.6	Ghana	85.2	Mauritania	188.0	Chad	412.1
Burundi	15.1	Burkina Faso	39.0	Burkina Faso	84.0	Guinea	121.0	Kenya	409.2
Côte d'Ivoire	13.0	Côte d'Ivoire	35.0	Côte d'Ivoire	72.0	Côte d'Ivoire	111.0	SIERRA LEONE	278.3
Mauritania	12.0	Uganda	34.9	Senegal	70.3	Togo	104.0	Senegal	257.0
Uganda	11.6	Cameroon	31.6	Madagascar	64.4	Senegal	95.0	Gambia, The	229.7
Mali	11.1	Ghana	29.9	Rwanda	64.3	Madagascar	83.0	Guinea	220.0
Madagascar	11.0	SIERRA LEONE	26.8	Benin	56.2	Benin	78.0	Togo	215.0
Togo	11.0	Chad	26.8	Cameroon	37.1	SIERRA LEONE	61.0	Uganda	194.1
Benin	10.8	Madagascar	26.7	Congo	36.8	Cameroon	61.0	Madagascar	190.0
Senegal	10.7	Mali	26.5	Chad	35.8			Mali	173.9
SIERRA LEONE	9.2	Kenya	25.1	Togo	34.1			Zambia	168.2
Guinea	8.7	Togo	22.0	Mauritania	33.8			Benin	149.0
Rwanda	8.1	Zambia	19.9	SIERRA LEONE	29.1			Côte d'Ivoire	126.0
Zambia	7.3	Benin	15.8	Guinea	15.7			Mauritania	120.0
Cameroon	7.1	Senegal	14.7					Cameroon	83.0
Gambia, The	7.1	Guinea	13.4						
Chad	7.0	Congo	12.7						
Congo	4.0	Gambia	8.7						

Sources: Various World Bank CSRs and SEIA study, 2000–04.
a. Includes preprimary for Sierra Leone.

DETAILED ANALYSIS OF THE UNIT COST

This section examines the unit cost in further detail to identify the factors affecting variation in unit cost across different levels of education and between countries. A close analysis of these factors may indicate areas in which Sierra Leone can improve the coverage and effectiveness of the education system within the budgetary constraints.

In the previous section, unit cost was calculated as the total current public spending on education, divided by the total number of students in government-assisted schools. Key variables affecting unit cost are the average salary of personnel in each level and the pupil-personnel ratio (see appendix C for the formula to decompose the unit cost). Both of these variables are examined below.

The average salary of personnel is calculated as the total salary costs for each level of education divided by the total number of personnel at each

Table 4.8   Teacher Salary and Pupil-Personnel Ratio by Level, 2004

	Primary	JSS	SSS
Expenditure on personnel salaries at school level (Le millions)	39,605	13,830	4,418
Number of personnel in schools	17,668	4,389	1,402
Average salary of personnel at school level (Le millions)	2.2	3.2	3.2
Ratio of average salary of personnel at school level to GDP per capita	3.9	5.4	5.4
Number of pupils in government-assisted schools	1,078,074	126,731	36,408
Pupil-personnel ratio	61	29	26

Source: Table 4.5.
Note: The pupil-personnel ratio is of the academic year 2003/04 and therefore differs from those presented in chapter 3.

level. Table 4.8 shows that the average annual salary of personnel is Le 2.2 million in primary schools and Le 3.2 million in JSS and SSS, or 3.9 and 5.4 times the GDP per capita, respectively. The average salary masks the wide variety in pay scales within each level of education. For example, the starting salary of a principal in SSS is 8.3 times the GDP per capita, compared with 1.7 times the GDP per capita for an untrained teacher (see appendix table D.12). In 2004, 15 percent of school personnel in primary schools and 4 percent in secondary schools were principals or vice principals. About 4 percent in both primary and secondary schools were on paid study leave.

The information and analysis required to determine whether teacher salaries and benefits are appropriate, given the demand and supply factors of the labor market, are not currently available (for example, a comparison between the level of remuneration of teachers and the market equilibrium salary of other individuals holding similar credentials). However, by comparing with other countries, particularly those within the same region, it is possible to determine whether the remuneration of teachers in Sierra Leone is within the norm. Table 4.9 compares average teacher salaries in relation to GDP per capita in Sierra Leone with other countries in Sub-Saharan Africa (for which suitable data are available). Sierra Leone is similar to other countries in that the teacher salaries increase with the higher levels of education. Teacher salaries in Sierra Leone are on the low side relative to GDP per capita compared to the other countries.

Another reference, which is perhaps more useful in the context of the Millennium Development Goal of universal primary completion, is the benchmark from the EFA FTI framework. This framework suggests that

Table 4.9   Ratio of Average Teacher Salary to GDP Per Capita in Sub-Saharan Africa, circa 2000–04

Primary[a]		JSS		SSS	
Burundi	6.8	Burkina Faso	13.0	Burkina Faso	19.8
Burkina Faso	6.1	Burundi	9.4	Niger	10.2
Niger	5.5	Niger	8.5	Burundi	9.4
Kenya	5.3	Togo	7.6	Mauritania	8.7
Senegal	4.6	Uganda	7.4	Senegal	8.7
Gambia, The	4.5	Mauritania	7.0	Benin	8.6
Madagascar	4.4	Mali	6.8	Mali	8.3
Mali	4.4	Cameroon	6.5	Togo	7.9
Togo	4.4	Gambia, The	6.5	Madagascar	7.7
Zambia	4.4	Côte d'Ivoire	6.4	Uganda	7.4
Benin	4.3	Senegal	5.8	Côte d'Ivoire	7.1
Côte d'Ivoire	4.3	SIERRA LEONE	5.4	Cameroon	6.8
Mauritania	4.1	Madagascar	5.1	Chad	6.8
Cameroon	3.9	Rwanda	4.5	Gambia, The	6.5
Ghana	3.9	Chad	4.4	Ghana	5.9
SIERRA LEONE	3.9	Zambia	4.4	SIERRA LEONE	5.4
Rwanda	3.8	Benin	4.3	Rwanda	5.2
FTI benchmark	3.5	Ghana	3.9	Zambia	4.5
Uganda	3.2	Congo	3.6	Congo	3.8
Congo	2.4	Guinea	2.9	Guinea	3.2
Chad	2.3				
Guinea	2.1				

Sources: Various World Bank CSRs, 2000–04.
Note: Includes nonteaching school staff in Sierra Leone.
a. Includes preprimary in Sierra Leone.

teacher salaries should not be too high (to allow the recruitment of the number of teachers needed to fulfill the objective within a reasonable level of public resources) nor too low (to ensure that candidates of high quality are recruited). The FTI benchmark for teacher salaries in primary schools, which is based on the structural parameters observed in countries that have demonstrated the best performance in achieving universal completion of primary school, is 3.5 times the GDP per capita. Sierra Leone is very close to this benchmark, with primary teacher salaries at 3.9 times the GDP per capita.

The second important factor for unit cost (and ultimately for coverage and quality of services, given the budgetary constraints) is the pupil-personnel ratio at the school level. In Sierra Leone, the pupil-personnel

Table 4.10 Pupil-Teacher Ratio in Sub-Saharan Africa, 2000–04

Primary[a]		JSS		SSS	
Congo	74	Togo	53	Chad	48
Chad	72	Burkina Faso	50	Guinea	36
Rwanda	65	Mali	46	Burkina Faso	32
Mali	63	Burundi	43	Togo	30
SIERRA LEONE	61	Congo	40	Zambia	30
Cameroon	61	Guinea	40	Cameroon	29
Benin	54	Niger	40	SIERRA LEONE	26
Uganda	54	Chad	39	Côte d'Ivoire	24
Burundi	52	Benin	38	Mali	23
Senegal	51	Côte d'Ivoire	38	Mauritania	23
Zambia	51	Mauritania	36	Rwanda	22
Madagascar	50	Senegal	36	Burundi	20
Guinea	47	Cameroon	31	Ghana	19
Côte d'Ivoire	46	Gambia, The	30	Benin	17
Burkina Faso	45	Rwanda	29	Gambia, The	17
Niger	43	SIERRA LEONE	29	Senegal	16
Mauritania	42	Zambia	24	Congo	15
FTI benchmark	40	Madagascar	22	Niger	13
Gambia, The	38	Ghana	19	Madagascar	12
Togo	37				
Ghana	33				
Kenya	32				

Source: Various World Bank CSRs, 2000–04.
Note: Includes nonteaching school staff in Sierra Leone.
a. Includes preprimary in Sierra Leone.

ratio is estimated at 61 in primary school and 29 in JSS (see table 4.8). The optimal pupil-personnel ratio is very difficult to determine; it should not be so high as to degrade the quality of education nor so low as to absorb all resources for education. As before, a comparison with other countries and the FTI benchmark indicates where Sierra Leone stands.[11] Compared to other countries in Sub-Saharan Africa, the pupil-personnel ratio in primary school is on the high side (table 4.10). At 61 pupils per school-level personnel, it is also high in relation to the FTI benchmark of 40. It is clear that a reduction in the pupil-personnel ratio (an increase in the number of teachers) should be considered in the coming years.

For secondary education, the pupil-personnel ratio in Sierra Leone is somewhat lower than the comparison countries for JSS and near the median for SSS. However, the figures for Sierra Leone include all school staff, regardless of whether they have teaching duties. Studies conducted in some of the comparison countries indicate that support staff may exist in significant numbers (between 20 and 25 percent of the personnel at the school level). If this estimate is applied to the Sierra Leone figures, the comparable pupil-teacher ratio would be about 37 in JSS and 34 in SSS, placing it near the median of the comparison countries for JSS and toward the high end for SSS.

For tertiary and technical and vocational education, comparative data are scarce. The student-personnel ratio is about 4–5, and support staff represents roughly two-thirds of all tertiary staff, so the student-teacher ratio is approximately 13. This value is low in comparison to other countries: student-teacher ratios are closer to 20 in Anglophone countries and 30 in Francophone countries in Sub-Saharan Africa. Therefore, the comparison suggests that savings could be made by increasing the student-teacher ratios and the student-personnel ratios at the tertiary and technical and vocational education levels.

Table 4.11 presents the unit cost decomposed into salary (school level and services), goods and services, and scholarships. The school-level salary unit cost has been calculated using the above information on the average salaries of personnel at the school level and the student-personnel ratio (see appendix C for the formula for decomposition). This calculation shows that about 70 percent of the unit cost in primary and secondary schools is for the salaries of personnel at the school level. For technical and vocational education, the salaries of personnel at the school level are lower at 59 percent (it is not possible to obtain this figure for tertiary education).

Table 4.11 Decomposition of Unit Costs by Level, 2004

	Primary	JSS	SSS	Technical/ vocational	Tertiary
Total unit cost	53,224	156,090	169,125	354,746	1,618,736
Salary (school-level) unit cost[a] (Le)	36,737	109,129	121,342	208,717	1,265,168
Average salary of personnel at school level (Le million)	2.2	3.2	3.2	3.5	5.6
Student-personnel ratio (Le)	61	29	26	17	4
Salary (services) unit cost (Le)	1,408	6,635	7,377	34,072	x
Goods and services unit cost[b] (Le)	15,079	40,326	40,405	105,184	110,015
Scholarships unit cost	..	..	..	6,773	243,554
Salary (school-level) unit cost as a percent of total unit cost (Le)	69	70	72	59	—

Sources: Tables 4.5, 4.6, and 4.8.
Note: X = data included in another category or column, . . = nil or negligible, — = not available.
a. Calculated as average salary of personnel at school level, divided by student-personnel ratio (see appendix C).
b. Includes transfers, materials and textbooks, capitation grants, and other costs.

As expected, table 4.11 shows that the larger the student-personnel ratio, the smaller the unit cost.

POLICY IMPLICATIONS

The key issues that have implications for further policy development on education expenditure and finance are outlined here.

Increasing the Resource Envelope through Further Donor Support. Expansion of the education system will require additional funding. The government is already allocating a proportion of its expenditure to education in line with the FTI benchmark and, given the postwar needs of all sectors, there may be little scope for the government to increase the share of budget that goes to education. Households are already contributing a substantial amount to primary and secondary education. Therefore, further funding will need to be mobilized from the donor community, especially in relation to the Millennium Development Goal of universal primary completion.

Aligning Public Spending with Stated Policy. If the government is to prioritize technical and vocational education, as stated in the Poverty Reduction Strategy Paper (Government of Sierra Leone 2005), then the share of education spending that goes to this subsector will need to be increased. The technical and vocational education sector has experienced a recent decrease in expenditure in absolute terms (a drop of 40 percent between 2000 and 2004), and in the percentage share (from 9 percent of education spending in 2000 to 4 percent in 2004). Prioritizing this area will require a change in this general trend.

Accounting for Projected Needs in Subsectors. The rapid expansion in enrollments at the primary level means that there will be many students in the coming years requiring places in junior secondary education. Currently, the junior secondary education system does not have the places to support this large influx, or to sustain the numbers that should be coming through when the primary system stabilizes and achieves universal primary completion. The secondary level has experienced an increase in real spending that is disproportionate to that of other subsectors. The percentage share of current expenditure on secondary has actually decreased from 25 percent in 2000 to 22 percent in 2004. To adequately supply the resources needed for this subsector, this allocation will likely need to increase.

Reducing Costs to Households for Basic Education. The Constitution and Education Act of Sierra Leone makes reference to free and compulsory basic (primary and junior secondary) education. Yet the contribution of households to education in Sierra Leone is very high (50 and 60 percent of total education expenditure in primary and secondary schools, respectively). To ensure that all children are able to access basic education, the cost to individual households, particularly poor households, will need to be reduced.

Promoting Public-Private Partnerships at the Tertiary Level. Given the competing demands for public funds at the different levels of education, there is scope for seeking alternative ways of financing education, such as promoting private schools and universities and recovering the costs of tertiary education. There are many different models of public-private partnership and cost recovery operating in other countries that could be examined and considered for Sierra Leone.

Increasing Student-Teacher Ratios. As a key component of unit costs, the student-teacher ratio is low in tertiary education, and savings could result by increasing it. It may also be possible to reduce the number of nonacademic staff, given that a high proportion (two-thirds of all tertiary staff) are nonacademic. Although there are trade-offs for every policy choice, the currently modest values of the pupil-teacher ratio in JSS and SSS and the requirement for a large expansion in capacity at these levels suggest that an increase in the pupil-teacher ratio at these levels could be considered.

CHAPTER 5

Disparity

Although significant progress has been made in primary school enrollment, there are still many children who never attend school. These children are likely to be from rural areas, from outside the Western Area, and from poorer households. Gender disparities in initial access to the primary level are not large, perhaps a result of the government's effort to enroll girls in primary education; but as with other disparities, they become greater as the level of education increases. In general, however, socioeconomic and geographic disparities are greater than those related to gender. There are particularly large differences at the district level for JSS and SSS.

Examining student flow data, this chapter finds that gender differences emerge some time after entrance to primary grade 1 but before completion of primary school and that urban and rural disparities exist at all stages of schooling. The same disparities exist across different levels of household wealth. Inequalities by region are particularly high with respect to entrance to primary grade 1 and completion of JSS.

Household expenditure on education varies by relative wealth, as expected, but poorer households spent a greater proportion of their household expenditure on education. They also spent a greater proportion of their education expenditure on uniforms, books, and contributions to the Community Teachers Association.

There are significant inequalities in the distribution of public spending on education: poor householders benefit much less from public education expenditure than do rich households. This inequality could be addressed by increased access to schooling and a more equitable distribution across educational levels.

This chapter examines disparities that exist between groups within the population, including girls and boys, rural and urban localities, different geographic regions, and levels of wealth. The chapter is divided into three main sections that examine inequalities in the coverage of the education system; in household expenditure on education; and in public spending on education across the different groups.

DISPARITY IN SCHOOLING

Disparities exist in schooling. Girls, rural children, those outside the Western Area, and children in less wealthy households all have lower likelihoods of participating in formal education. The process by which these differences materialize is not always the same across groups. In some cases, disparities occur in initial access to schooling and in other cases they arise during the course of schooling.

EDUCATION COVERAGE

Age-Specific Enrollment Rates. There is a clear differential by gender and urban/rural locality in enrollment rates by single year of age (figures 5.1 and 5.2). According to the SLIHS (2003/04), a gender divide does not emerge until age 12, with girls being less likely than boys to be in school.[1] There are two possible ways to interpret this divide. It is possible that girls initially have equal access to education and then start to drop out faster when they reach age 12. A second possibility is that there were gender disparities when the current cohort of students aged 12 and older first entered school (several years ago) and subsequent cohorts do not have a gender disparity in initial access. If the latter is the case, then the current pattern of gender disparity will disappear over time. Evidence from the SLIHS (2003/04) and the Population Census (2004) suggest that the main cause of the current gender enrollment differential for 15- to 17-year-olds was a lack of initial access to education (years ago), but early drop out by girls may also be a contributing factor.[2]

Gross Enrollment Ratios. A measure of education coverage, the GERs show that the more favored subgroups are boys, urban children, those residing in the Western Area, and children from the richest quintile. For each of these groups, table 5.1 presents the parity index, which is the ratio of the GER of the lagging subgroup to that of the more favored subgroup. A parity index of 1 indicates perfect parity (that is, the two groups have the same GERs). For instance, the gender GER parity index of 0.74 for JSS as a whole implies that JSS coverage for girls is only 74 percent as high as it is for boys.

From table 5.1, it can be seen that the gap in each set of comparisons is smallest at the primary education level. The gap between the lagging group and the favored group widens rapidly as the level of education rises. For example, the lowest GER parity index among all the sets of comparisons at

Figure 5.1 Enrollment Rates by Age and Gender, 2003/04

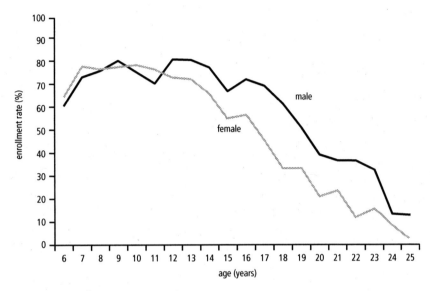

Source: SLIHS 2003/04.
Note: The rates have been smoothed using 3-point rolling averages for age (equally weighted).

Figure 5.2 Enrollment Rates by Age and Urban/Rural Locality, 2003/04

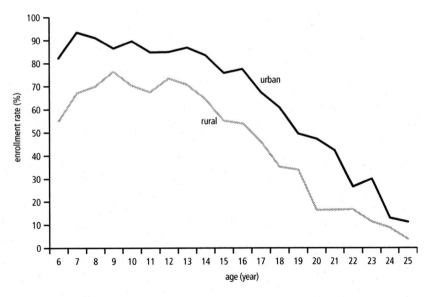

Source: SLIHS 2003/04.
Note: The rates have been smoothed using 3-point rolling averages for age (equally weighted).

Table 5.1 GERs by Gender, Locality, Region, and Household Expenditure Quintile, 2003/04

Percent indicator	Primary	JSS	SSS
Sierra Leone	123	50	32
By gender			
Boys	125	57	36
Girls	121	42	29
Parity index (girls/boys)	0.97	0.74	0.81
By locality and gender			
Rural	113	29	12
Boys	111	40	14
Girls	115	17	10
Urban	142	81	58
Boys	145	86	66
Girls	138	77	51
Parity index (rural/urban)	0.80	0.36	0.21
Parity index (rural girls/urban boys)	0.79	0.20	0.15
By region			
Southern Region	126	51	32
Eastern Region	125	33	9
Northern Region	115	39	12
Western Area	138	89	83
Parity index (Northern/Western)	0.83	0.44	0.14
By household expenditure quintile			
Q1 (poorest)	113	26	9
Q2	117	42	13
Q3	124	43	17
Q4	130	54	30
Q5 (richest)	135	86	84
Parity index (poorest/richest)	0.84	0.30	0.11

Source: SLIHS 2003/04.

the primary education level is 0.79 (the ratio of rural girls to the urban boys). At the JSS level, the parity index for the equivalent comparison is much lower at 0.20 and lowest yet at SSS level (0.15). Although there are still challenges for completely closing the gaps in primary education coverage among different subgroups, the disparities at the JSS and SSS levels are much larger. Tertiary education is almost exclusively accessible to those who are from urban rich families, most of whom are from the Western Area.

The overall gender gap is not as large as the disparities caused by socioeconomic and geographic differences. However, gender gaps exacerbate the

differences in the other characteristics. For example, at the JSS level, the
GER for rural girls is only 20 percent that of urban boys, considerably
lower than the 36 percent differential between urban and rural children as
a whole. The Western Area has very good educational coverage compared
to the other regions, with the Eastern Region having the lowest coverage in
JSS and SSS. There is a very apparent gradient in educational coverage by
household expenditure quintile, with children from poorer households
being much less likely to be enrolled at school, particularly at the JSS and
SSS levels. The parity indexes show that educational coverage for JSS and
SSS for those from the poorest quintile is just 30 percent and 11 percent
that of those from the richest quintile, respectively.

At the district level, primary GERs are all high (mostly more than 100
percent), and consequently the disparities are small. JSS and SSS GERs
have much larger disparities, with parity indexes of 0.12 (JSS) and 0.08
(SSS) between the districts with the highest and lowest GERs (figure 5.3).

Figure 5.3 Gross Enrollment Ratios by District, 2003/04

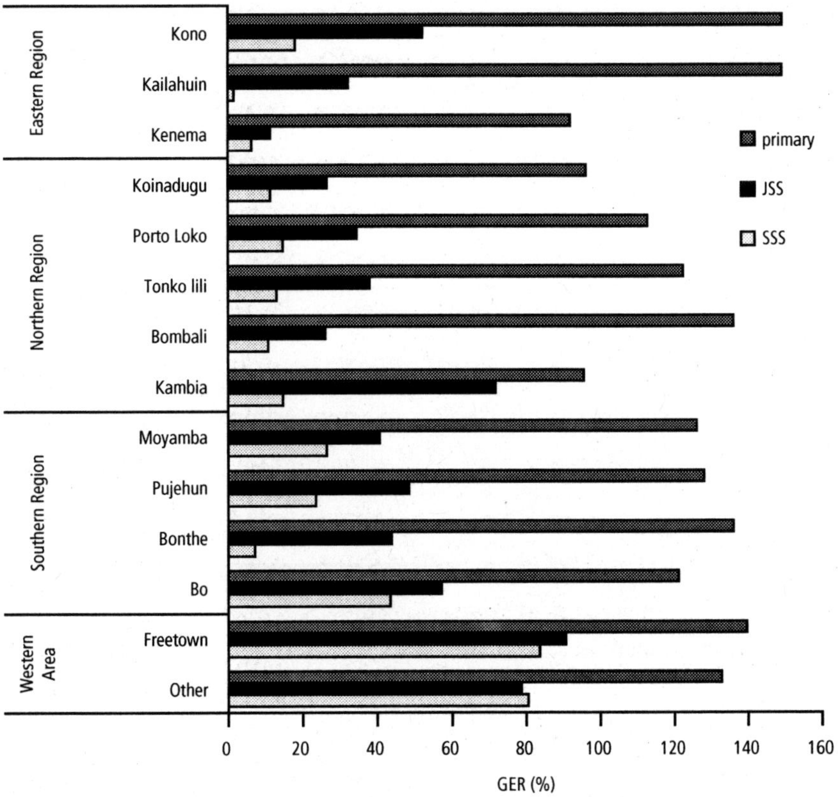

Source: SLIHS 2003/04.

The war-affected, street, and disabled children may account for many of the out-of-school children from the disadvantaged groups discussed above. Unfortunately, there is currently no data available to quantify their schooling status.

Out-of-School Children. The Population Census (2004) indicates that 31 percent of 6- to 11-year-olds were out of school. Of these, almost all (30 percent) had never been to school. The proportions for boys and girls were approximately the same (see appendix table D.14). However, for the older groups, girls were more likely than boys to have never attended school. For 12- to 14-year-olds, 26 percent of girls compared to 19 percent of boys had never attended school, rising to 44 percent of girls compared to 28 percent of boys in the 15- to 17-year age group.

The SLIHS (2003/04) found fairly similar rates for out-of-school children, with most of these children never having attended school and increasing gender disparity with age. It also found large discrepancies between children from rural and urban areas, from different regions, and from different household expenditure quintiles (see appendix table D.15). For example, 12- to 14-year-old girls from rural areas were almost four times as likely as urban boys of the same age to be out of school.

STUDENT FLOW

This section examines disparities in student flow between subgroups of the population, including cohort access rates, gross intake ratios to primary grade 1, completion rates in primary school and JSS, and transition rates from primary school to JSS.

Cohort Access Rates. CAR measures the proportion of an age group (9–13 years in this case) that have ever attended school. No significant disparity exists in CARs between boys and girls, with the possible exception of the poorest households (figure 5.4).[3]

There is a significant divide in cohort access rates by urban/rural locality (figure 5.5). This divide is large regardless of the household expenditure quintile the child comes from. Taken together, figures 5.4 and 5.5 demonstrate that children from households in the lower quintile expenditure brackets are much more likely to never attend school than those in the upper quintile brackets.[4] This difference holds true regardless of gender and urban/rural locality.

Gross Intake Ratios. Table 5.2 shows that GIRs to primary grade 1 were approximately the same for boys and girls.[5] Children in rural areas are less likely to start primary grade 1 than their counterparts in urban areas, and children in the Western Area are more likely than those from other regions to start primary grade 1, with parity indexes of about 0.8.

Figure 5.4   Cohort Access Rates for 9- to 13-Year-Olds by Household Expenditure Quintile and Gender, 2003/04

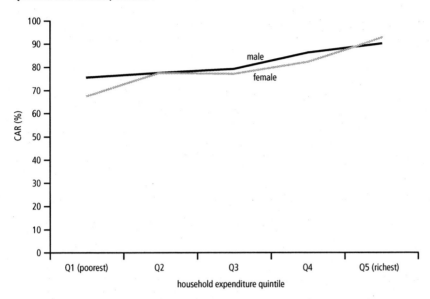

Source: SLIHS 2003/04.
Note: Cohort access rate (CAR) is the proportion of 9- to 13-year-olds that have ever been to school.

Figure 5.5   Cohort Access Rates for 9- to 13-Year-Olds by Household Expenditure Quintile and Urban/Rural Locality, 2003/04

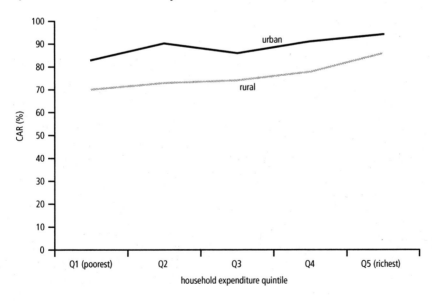

Source: SLIHS 2003/04.

Table 5.2 Student Flow Rates by Gender, Locality, Region, and Household Expenditure Quintile, 2003/04

Percent	CAR[a]	GIR to primary	Completion rate[b]		Primary-to-JSS transition rate
			Primary	JSS	
Sierra Leone	81	151	60	32	77
By gender					
Boys	81	150	64	35	78
Girls	80	153	54	28	76
Parity index (girls/boys)	0.98	1.02	0.84	0.80	0.97
By locality and gender					
Rural	75	140	49	15	58
Boys	75	140	53	22	67
Girls	73	140	45	7	45
Urban	90	175	77	58	97
Boys	92	171	85	59	90
Girls	89	179	68	57	105
Parity index (rural/urban)	0.83	0.80	0.64	0.26	0.60
Parity index (rural girls/urban boys)	0.80	0.82	0.53	0.12	0.50
By region					
Southern Region	81	136	71	15	89
Eastern Region	78	146	52	20	48
Northern Region	76	154	43	15	91
Western Area	93	187	92	99	71
Parity index (northern/western)	0.82	0.82	0.47	0.15	1.28
By household expenditure quintile					
Q1 (poorest)	72	101	42	9	69
Q2	78	114	57	18	73
Q3	78	117	57	14	92
Q4	84	118	68	34	67
Q5 (richest)	91	132	77	90	83
Parity index (poorest/richest)	0.79	0.77	0.55	0.10	0.83

Source: SLIHS 2003/04.
a. CAR is the proportion of 9- to 13-year-olds that have ever been to school.
b. Completion rates are the numbers enrolled in the final grade of the level (primary or JSS), less repeaters, as a percentage of the official age (11- or 14-year-olds). The number of repeaters was determined by applying the percentage of repeaters from MEST administrative data.

Primary Completion Rates. From the SLIHS (2003/04), proxy Primary Completion Rates (PCRs) are calculated as the number enrolled in primary grade 6 (less repeaters) as a percentage of 11-year-olds (the official age for primary grade 6). Nationally, the PCR was 60 percent; however, it was lower for girls (54 percent), children in rural areas (49 percent), and children from the poorest three quintiles of household expenditure. The Western Area had a PCR that was roughly double that of the Eastern and Northern Regions (at 92 percent). Even though the Southern Region had the lowest GIR for primary grade 1 (136 percent), it had one of the highest PCRs (71 percent), suggesting that the few who start attending tend to stay at school.

Transition Rate from Primary School to JSS. According to the SLIHS (2003/04), the transition rate from primary school to JSS was 77 percent, with about the same proportion of boys and girls who were enrolled in primary grade 6 moving on to JSS grade 1 (although, as noted above, there was a lower proportion of girls completing primary grade 6). The equivalent figure from MEST data was fairly close at 73 percent in 2004/05. Table 5.2 shows that the parity index for the transition rate in rural and urban areas was low (0.60). The worst situation is endured by rural girls, being only 50 percent as likely as urban boys to go on to JSS from primary school. The pattern of transition rates by region appears to be very different, with the Northern and Southern Regions having higher rates than those of the Western Area. However, the rates of entering and completing primary school are much lower in these regions, so there are fewer pupils in primary grade 6 who would be eligible to go on to JSS grade 1.

JSS Completion Rates. The rate of JSS completion in the SLIHS (the number of students enrolled in JSS grade 3, less repeaters, as a percentage of 14-year-olds) was 32 percent; close to the MEST figures of 27 percent in 2003/04 and 31 percent in 2004/05. The parity indexes for JSS completion are extremely low. Pupils from rural areas are only 26 percent as likely as those from urban areas to complete JSS. The JSS completion rate is only 15–20 percent in all regions except the Western Area, where it is 99 percent; and all household expenditure quintiles have rates less than 35 percent except the richest quintile, which has a rate of 90 percent.

These rates of student flow suggest that gender disparities begin after entrance to primary grade 1 but before completion of primary school. As mentioned above, these results may be driven primarily by historical inequities in initial access to schooling. The disparities between urban and rural areas and across different levels of family wealth exist at all the stages of schooling: entrance to primary grade 1, completion of primary school, transition to JSS, and particularly completion of JSS. Disparities between the regions are especially marked at entrance to primary grade 1 and on completion of primary school and JSS.

DISPARITY IN HOUSEHOLD EXPENDITURE ON EDUCATION

This section examines the distribution of household spending on education across rich and poor households. As expected, the richer quintiles

Table 5.3   Average Household Spending on Primary Education by Household Expenditure Quintile and Expense Type, 2003/04

Quintile	Tuition	Community Teachers Association	Uniforms	Books	Transport	Food	Extra-curricular activities	Other	Total
Le									
Q1 (poorest)	1,169	2,109	8,183	3,414	44	1,370	1,801	1,527	19,617
Q2	1,500	2,347	9,283	4,057	115	2,256	2,252	3,007	24,817
Q3	3,080	2,330	11,020	5,660	728	4,418	3,718	3,989	34,942
Q4	4,007	2,999	13,549	7,296	1,086	6,755	7,749	6,581	50,022
Q5 (richest)	22,998	3,317	20,116	19,399	11,925	22,522	22,954	11,993	135,224
Percentage distribution									
Q1 (poorest)	6	11	42	17	0	7	9	8	100
Q2	6	9	37	16	0	9	9	12	100
Q3	9	7	32	16	2	13	11	11	100
Q4	8	6	27	15	2	14	15	13	100
Q5 (richest)	17	2	15	14	9	17	17	9	100

Source: SLIHS 2003/04.

spend almost seven times more on primary education than do the poorer households (table 5.3). The distribution of spending across education categories varies by household expenditure. Households in the richest quintile spend a greater share of their primary education expenditure on tuition, extracurricular activities, uniforms, and books. The large share for tuition may reflect parents' willingness and ability to pay high tuitions to enroll their children in better private schools. In contrast, households in the lower quintiles spend a greater share of their education expenditure (up to 70 percent for the poorest quintile) on school uniforms, books, and the Community Teachers Association.

Even though poorer households spend less in absolute terms on primary education, they spend more relative to their overall household expenditure. Figure 5.6 shows that the difference between the poorest and richest households in average expenditure on education as a share of total household expenditure per adult equivalent is stark for those with children in secondary schools. For example, households in the lowest expenditure quintile report spending 43 percent of household expenditure per adult equivalent on a secondary student compared to 20 percent for those in the highest expenditure quintile. Sending children to JSS and SSS for poor households requires a much greater effort and commitment compared to richer households. Furthermore, one potentially high cost is missing from this analysis: the opportunity cost of the extra services a

Figure 5.6   Average per Student Spending on Education as a Percentage of Total Household Expenditures per Adult Equivalent, by Level and Household Expenditure Quintile, 2003/04

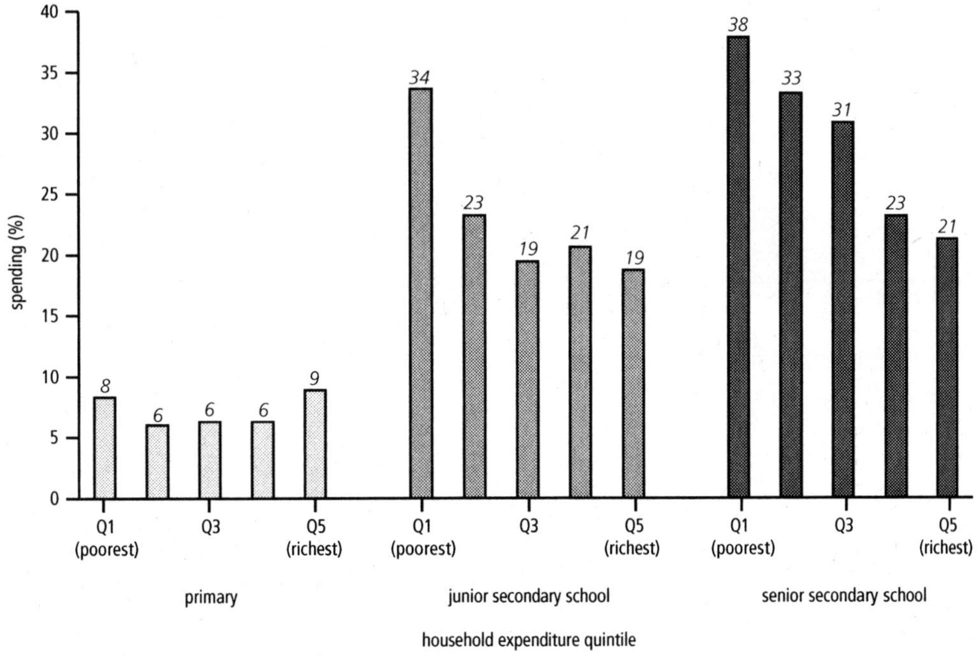

Source: SLIHS 2003/04.

child may provide to the household (or wages they may receive) if they do not attend school are not included.

DISPARITY IN DISTRIBUTION OF PUBLIC EXPENDITURES

This section examines the distribution of public expenditure on education for individuals reaching different levels of schooling as well as for individuals with different characteristics (including gender, urban/rural locality, and household expenditure quintile).

Using information on unit cost at different levels of education (see chapter 4), number of years of education (including repetition), and levels of schooling attained (from MEST),[6] the distribution of public resources for the education of a theoretical cohort of 100 children is shown in table 5.4. Individuals who never attend school do not directly benefit from the public education resources. The longer individuals are enrolled in education, the more they absorb resources. From the initial cohort of 100 children, about 20 end up with no schooling and therefore

Table 5.4 Distribution of Public Education Expenditures in a Cohort of 100 Children, 2003/04

Level	Grade	Unit cost per year (% of GDP per capita) (a)	Average number of years (b)	Level of schooling attained (% of cohort)	Final level attained (% of cohort) (c)	Accumulated resources absorbed by 1 student (% of GDP per capita) (d) = (a) × (b)	Resources absorbed by the cohort (% of GDP per capita) (c) × (d)	Share of resources absorbed (%)
No schooling		..	..	19.5	19.5	..	..	..
Primary	1	9.2	1.16	80.5	7.1	10.7	75.7	0.7
	2	9.2	1.16	73.4	5.7	21.3	122.2	1.1
	3	9.2	1.14	67.7	8.7	31.8	275.7	2.4
	4	9.2	1.12	59.0	6.2	42.1	259.3	2.3
	5	9.2	1.10	52.9	12.1	52.3	633.6	5.6
	6	9.2	1.06	40.7	10.9	62.0	678.4	6.0
JSS	1	26.8	1.15	29.8	3.5	92.8	326.8	2.9
	2	26.8	1.18	26.3	0.5	124.5	58.3	0.5
	3	26.8	1.15	25.8	12.1	155.3	1,882.5	16.7
SSS	1	29.1	1.14	13.7	0.8	188.4	151.5	1.3
	2	29.1	1.12	12.9	0.8	221.0	177.9	1.6
	3	29.1	1.08	12.1	7.8	252.5	1,962.3	17.4
Tertiary		278.4	3.00	4.3	4.3	1,087.7	4,679.6	41.5
Total		n.a.	16.56	n.a.	100.0	n.a.	11,283.8	100.0

Source: Authors calculations based on SLIHS 2003/04 data and MEST administrative data from 2003/04 and 2004/05.
Note: .. = nil or negligible, n.a. = not applicable.

absorb no resources for education. About 7 of them enter primary grade 1 but do not continue their education. These people consume a very small share of the resources (less than 1 percent). At the other end of the education hierarchy, about 12 of the 100 reach the end of SSS (8 attain SSS grade 3 and 4 reach the tertiary level). These students absorb more than half of all public spending on education (almost 60 percent).

Because many children in Sierra Leone never attend school and most never reach SSS, public resources for education are targeted at a small portion of the population. The unit cost for different levels of education also affects the distribution of resources. Unit costs in JSS and SSS are not excessive in Sierra Leone (see table 4.7). Thus concentrating on improving access to primary school and JSS and increasing primary completion rates would be appropriate ways to ensure more equitable outcomes at the primary and secondary levels. In contrast, the unit cost for just 1 year of tertiary education is greater than the cost of educating a student from primary school through SSS. In other terms, the cost of 4 years of tertiary education for one student could pay for about 120 children to attend 1 year of primary schooling. More than 40 percent of all resources for education for the cohort of 100 in table 5.4 go to a mere four children who reach tertiary education; or about 10 percent each. To the extent that those gaining tertiary education are important for the development of Sierra Leone, this initial inequity in resource distribution may be justified. However, a more equitable distribution of education resources can be obtained by ensuring that tertiary education is targeted toward the skills required by the country, and efficiently uses public expenditure. Furthermore, some saving of public expenditure on tertiary education can be made by promoting public-private partnership and a cost recovery system.

LORENZ CURVE AND GINI COEFFICIENT

The degree of inequity in the distribution of public expenditure on education can be displayed graphically using the Lorenz curve (figure 5.7; for primary and secondary education). The Lorenz curve shows the percentage of resources used against the percentage of the cohort. If the resources were distributed evenly across the entire cohort, the Lorenz curve would be a straight line with a slope of 45 degrees (cutting the graphic quadrant in equal halves). Figure 5.7 shows that the Lorenz curve is actually far from perfect equality. At the bottom end, 50 percent of the cohort receives only about 10 percent of the resources. At the top, only 10 percent of the population receives 54 percent of the public resources for education.

Figure 5.7. Lorenz Curve for the Distribution of Public Education Expenditures on Primary and Secondary Education, 2003/04

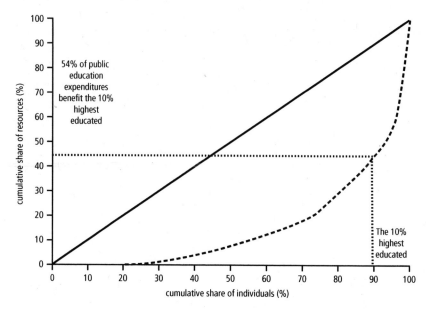

Source: Table 5.4.

Table 5.5 International Comparisons of the Inequality of Distribution of Public Education Expenditures, circa 2002/03

Region	Percentage of resources absorbed by the 10% highest educated	Gini coefficient
Sierra Leone (2003/04)	**57**	**0.68**
Sub-Saharan Africa (low income countries)	39	0.46
Francophone Africa	44	0.56
Anglophone Africa	33	0.36

Sources: UNESCO Pole de Dakar 2005; Authors' calculations based on SLIHS 2003/04.

The Gini coefficient is a measure derived from the Lorenz curve that allows a comparison of inequality with other countries. It represents the area between perfect equality (the 45-degree line) and the Lorenz curve, so that perfect inequality equals 1 and perfect equality equals 0. At 0.68, the Gini coefficient for Sierra Leone is higher than the average for Sub-Saharan countries of 0.46 (table 5.5).[7] Therefore, the distribution of public education expenditure in primary and secondary schools is more inequitable than it is on average in other countries in the region. On average in Sub-Saharan Africa countries, the 10 percent of the population with the highest education attainment absorbs 39 percent of the education resources, while Sierra Leone spends markedly higher at 54 percent of the public resources.

DISTRIBUTION OF PUBLIC SPENDING ON EDUCATION

By combining information on the proportion of population groups accessing different levels of education from the SLIHS (2003/04) and data on unit costs, it is possible to determine how equitably the resources are distributed among these groups. Table 5.6 shows the percentage of education resources that are consumed by different subgroups of the population, including gender, urban/rural locality, and household expenditure quintile. For example, about 40 percent of expenditure goes to students in rural areas, with the rest (60 percent) spent on students in urban areas. Table 5.6 also shows the relative size of each of the population groups for 5- to 24-year-olds. For example, 60 percent of this age group lives in rural areas and 40 percent in urban areas. The final column of table 5.6 shows the relative consumption of resources for a student belonging to a particular group compared to a student belonging to another group. For example, a male student consumes almost 30 percent more resources than does a female student. A student from an urban area consumes 2.3 times the resources of a student from a rural area. One from the richest quintile consumes 2.9 times the resources that a student from the poorest quintile consumes.

Table 5.6 Disparity in the Consumption of Public Education Resources, 2003/04

Cohort	Percentage of education expenditures consumed by group (a)	Percentage of population aged 5–24 years (b)	Ratio (a) / (b)	Index of resources consumed
By gender				
Female	43	49	88	100
Male	57	51	112	128
By locality				
Rural	40	60	66	100
Urban	60	40	150	226
By household expenditure quintile				
Q1 (poorest)	14	21	63	100
Q2	14	19	72	113
Q3	16	20	82	130
Q4	19	20	98	154
Q5 (richest)	38	20	184	291

Sources: Authors' calculations based on SLIHS 2003/04 for no schooling to SSS; MEST data for tertiary; unit cost estimates from chapter 4.
Note: Includes all levels of education (for breakdowns by locality and expenditure quintile, tertiary figures have been estimated).

The disparity by gender should naturally improve over time as the new cohort of girls 12 years of age and younger advances to higher levels of education.[8] Ensuring successful transitions to secondary schooling for this cohort of girls is vital to closing this gender gap (although the high costs of university make increasing the female presence in tertiary education the most efficient way to narrow this gap).

POLICY IMPLICATIONS

The key issues that have implications for further policy development on disparities are outlined here.

Reducing Gender Differences. The government must build on the efforts to reduce gender disparity in access to primary schooling by extending these efforts to secondary-level education. Gender disparities are still very large at the JSS and SSS levels. As increasing numbers of students in primary school graduate to JSS, it is important to ensure that transition and completion rates for girls maintain parity with those for boys. MEST has already abolished fees for girls to attend JSS in the Eastern and Northern Regions, but this effort should be extended if cost considerations allow it.

Lowering Urban-Rural Disparity in Access to Education. This urban-rural divide persists at the primary level and dramatically worsens at the JSS and SSS levels. Likewise, despite improvement in all regions, there are still stark disparities in educational outcomes across regions. To achieve universal primary completion, narrowing the gap between urban and rural areas in entry and survival rates needs to be a priority.

Investigating District Inequalities. In contrast to differences between urban and rural areas, the district-level disparities did not appear to be systematic, with some districts having mixed performance for the different levels. These variations should be explored for possible lessons to be learned and applied to other districts.

Investigating Household Expenditure Differences. Further analysis of household survey data is needed to investigate how the lower quintile households can be encouraged to send their children to school.

Making the Distribution of Resources More Equitable. A large share of the resources for education in Sierra Leone goes to a small portion of the school-aged population who are from wealthier households in urban areas. Improvement in the distribution of public resources requires the allocation of public expenditure to the levels with the highest proportion of poor children. The prime target should include primary and JSS education in general but also technical and vocational training. Cost recovery at the tertiary level and scholarship schemes for students from poor families would contribute to a more equitable distribution.

Improving Information Gathering from Household Surveys. To fully understand issues of educational inequalities, data are needed that track students over time (at least for two consecutive school years. Ideally, children's literacy and numeracy skills would be assessed as a part of the survey to allow more effective analysis of the quality of education students are receiving.

CHAPTER 6

Governance and Management

Good governance and management of the education sector is critical for the efficient delivery of education services. Education governance typically refers to the way in which authority is exercised to steer the education system: the mechanisms, processes, and institutions that allow for the setting of goals and the monitoring of the process of achieving those goals. Governance is also very closely related to issues of management and accountability. Education management refers to the effective implementation of education goals, whereas accountability refers to the mechanisms that stakeholders use to assess the system's performance and advocate for better representation of their interests (World Bank 2000).

The political and social attitudes toward governance and management are changing profoundly in Sierra Leone. The local governance reform enacted in 2004 has had significant implications for the education sector because management and control of basic education have devolved to local government. MEST has been mandated to focus on monitoring and policy making for all sectors and retains management responsibility for senior secondary and tertiary education. The governance reform is part of a larger state decentralization process that was undertaken to improve overall financial and administrative efficiency, political participation, and economic and social development.

Successful decentralization will lead to efficient and effective delivery of educational services. Careful planning now, at the early stages of decentralization, will facilitate the process. The devolution schedule for the education sector is ambitious and full of challenges, but there are signs that MEST favors a much more cautious approach to decentralization. Lines of authority and accountability need to be more clearly defined. Most importantly, capacity building must be aggressively pursued at both the central and local levels. But capacity building is not enough; effective incentives and institutional structures are needed to enable the education sector to retain trained individuals and promote good performance. The issue of accountability must not be overlooked: accountability systems that ensure effective service delivery are essential.

This chapter, describing governance and management issues in the delivery of education in Sierra Leone, is organized as follows. First, it provides a brief review of the legal and governance environment within which the education system operates, highlighting a major governance reform effort that is characterized by a move toward decentralization of education services. Second, it discusses management capacity of the education sector in the changing environment.

THE CHANGING LEGAL AND GOVERNANCE ENVIRONMENT

Following the Education Act of 1964, there were no policies embedded in the legal framework until the substantial post-war reforms starting in 2001. After the war, the legal environment underwent substantial reforms, and between 2001 and 2004 six acts were passed that directly affect the education sector (table 6.1).

FROM CENTRALIZED TO DECENTRALIZED GOVERNANCE

Of the acts listed in table 6.1, the Education Act and the Local Government Act (LGA) are the two most important for understanding the system of governance and management (Government of Sierra Leone 2004a,b). The LGA provided the legal basis for the reform project that reestablished local governance after more than 30 years of centralized governance and transferred part of the management and administrative responsibilities of the central government to local councils. The decentralization of education is part of this larger state decentralization reform. The LGA calls for the transfer of the authority for administering basic education to the local governments as outlined below.

Educational decentralization is on an aggressive 3-year schedule, starting with the devolution of the management of District Education Council (DEC) and city/town council schools in the 2005 academic year. These schools were previously governed by local councils during the first period of decentralization in the 1960s and early 1970s. Control and supervision of all preprimary, primary, and junior secondary institutions should be under the purview of the local councils by 2008. Statutory Instrument No. 13 of the LGA outlines the schedule of activities to be devolved in education (table 6.2). According to this schedule, management and control of basic

Table 6.1 Summary of Key Education Acts, 2001–04

Act (year passed)	Key issues
National Council for Technical, Vocational, and other Academic Awards (NCTVA) Act (2001)	Established the NCTVA, an independent body, whose main functions are to validate and certify awards in technical and vocational education and teacher training; accredit technical and vocational institutions; and advise MEST on curriculum areas.
The Polytechnics Act (2001)	Established the polytechnic institutions and the polytechnic councils. Functions of polytechnic councils are to: control and supervise polytechnic institutions; grant diplomas and certificates through the NCTVA; determine the content of instruction; manage student admission; and hire administrative staff.
Tertiary Education Commission Act (2001)	Established the Tertiary Education Commission (TEC) for the development of tertiary education. Functions include: advising the government on tertiary education; fund-raising for tertiary education; vetting the budgets of tertiary institutions; ensuring relevance of offerings; ensuring equity in admissions, conditions of service, and staff promotions.
University Act (2004)	The colleges of the University of Sierra Leone (Njala and Fourah Bay College) were constituted into two new universities—Njala University and the University of Sierra Leone. Allows for university autonomy in matters of administration and academics. Allows for the creation of private universities.
Education Act (2004)	Replaced the Education Act of 1964 and outlines the structure of the education system, management and control, and the role of various actors in the system including local authorities. Major points covered are the legalization of the 6-3-3-4 education system; and free and compulsory basic education. Ultimate authority for management and control of schools lies with the minister of education, but school management committees and board of governors will manage primary and secondary schools respectively. Local authorities recognized, but existence of education committees within local councils dependent on approval of the minister.
Local Government Act (2004)	Established local councils and local governments and marks the return to decentralization in education after over 30 years of centralized governance. Transfers the management and supervision of basic education from the central to local governments.

Source: Authors.

education schools, including recruitment and payment of teachers, provision of textbooks and teaching materials, payment of school fee subsidies, and school supervision should move from the central to the local level. The role of the central ministry in basic education is to focus on policy making and monitoring the performance of the local governments.

The literature on decentralization of educational services worldwide shows that decentralization can lead to improved efficiency and effectiveness, improved delivery of services, and increased school performance linked to higher levels of parental and community participation. However, these outcomes do not automatically follow from decentralization. The international experience with decentralization of education suggests that efficiency and effectiveness improve only when service providers are held accountable for results. Accountability in turn requires well-defined lines of authority and good information on results (Winkler 2005). Furthermore, for countries to realize the gains of the process, the new actors must have

Table 6.2 Schedule for the Devolution of Functions of MEST to Local Councils

Main functions	Activities to devolve	Year
Management and control of council schools (district, town, and city) from the preprimary to JSS levels	Recruitment of teachers Payment of salaries of teachers and staff Provision of teaching and learning materials Payment of school fee subsidies Provision of furniture Rehabilitation and reconstruction of schools Staff development (study leave matters)	2005
Management and control of other government and government-assisted schools (primary to JSS)	Payment of examination fees Payment of salaries of staff Provision of furniture Provision of subsidized textbooks	2005 2006
School supervision	Inspection of teachers and school curriculum Inspection of pupils	2007
Management and control of government libraries	Establishment of boards Supervisory monitoring Training of staff	2007

Sources: The Local Government Act 2004; Statutory Instrument no. 13; local government (assumption of functions) regulations.

the necessary skills and training to perform their new duties, especially in leadership and management. The central ministry must also be willing to make changes in its structure and processes, and the issue of resource flows to local councils must be carefully considered for its effect on equity.

The transformation process is long, complex, and fraught with challenges. For example, presentations and discussions at a seminar on national experiences with decentralization concluded that "despite the great efforts of Latin American countries, problems of social, geographic and economic inequality and of the quality of education services have remained" (UNESCO 2005, 10). Sierra Leone can learn from the experiences of these other countries.

CHALLENGES OF DECENTRALIZATION

Sierra Leone's decentralization process has good potential for success, but some issues need to be addressed to achieve a smooth implementation. First, the laws governing the process must be unambiguous. At present there are some contradictions between the Education Act and the LGA. For example, the Education Act (Government of Sierra Leone 2004a, 8, section 6(3)) states that "primary education, and hence all primary schools, shall be controlled and caused to be inspected by the Minister." The same document also says that the local authorities can only set up education committees with the approval of the minister of education. However, the LGA states that all functions pertaining to primary education are to be devolved to the local councils. MEST is to be responsible only for policy making, providing technical guidance to the local councils, and monitoring their performance (Government of Sierra Leone 2004b, 19, section 20(3)). The ambiguities in the laws pose a challenge for successful devolution of tasks and responsibilities, because some of the legal provisions are being interpreted in a discretionary manner (Barrie 2005).

In general, the Education Act envisions a gradual decentralization in which responsibilities are transferred to local authorities that have demonstrated the capacity to assume them. Officials at MEST and the Ministry of Local Government are working together on reconciling the LGA and the Education Act, because they realize that collaboration is essential for successful devolution.

The slow response of MEST is not unique to this ministry, and it highlights one of the challenges of the reform agenda: commitment to decentralization reform by the various stakeholders. A review of the process in Sierra Leone, presented at the Poverty Reduction and Economic Management Network 2005 conference (hosted by the World Bank), finds that ministries, departments, and agencies are generally weak champions of decentralization. The strong champions are the Ministry of Finance (MOF), the president, the people of Sierra Leone, and external donors (Barrie 2005).

A second cause for concern, related to the first, is that clear lines of responsibility between MEST, the district education offices, school managers, and the local governments do not yet exist. For example, even though the devolution schedule described above stipulates that the provision of textbooks and learning materials should devolve to the local governments, a document from the Ministry of Education recommends that the selection and procurement of textbooks and teaching materials remain at the central ministry (MEST 2005). At present it is unclear where this responsibility will lie. The procurement of the materials is still being done centrally, but the Ministry of Finance has already started the transfer of the financial resources for these materials to the local councils.

Building capacity at the local councils to manage their new responsibilities is a critical concern. Sierra Leone has weak human capacity at all levels of the public service—a situation brought on by many years of corrupt governance compounded by 10 years of civil war (World Bank 2003a). The devolution of key tasks to local government has simply exacerbated the need for capacity building at all levels of government. Thorough assessments of the capacity-building needs of local educational authorities are necessary, and the local institutions to support the devolved functions should be developed as soon as possible. The issue of capacity is one of the most critical challenges facing Sierra Leone today. Addressing this challenge will take not only an aggressive capacity-building agenda but also a transformation in public sector pay and incentive structures.

A third challenge posed by decentralization is to ensure that disparities among localities are reduced, in the transition to local governance. A baseline survey of public services in local councils carried out by the Institutional Reform and Capacity Building Project (IRCBP) in 2005 showed differences among councils in terms of access to and satisfaction with public services. Table 6.3 shows the results from the survey regarding access to primary schooling, opinions on school quality, and the level of government that should be responsible for running the education system. The table also shows reported level of trust of local governments, central government, and teachers. The indicator for access to schooling is the percentage of households that have primary schools within 30 minutes of their homes. Kono District Council in the Eastern Region and Bonthe and Pujehun District Councils in the Southern Region are particularly disadvantaged in terms of access: less than 50 percent of surveyed households reported having a primary school within 30 minutes. The national average is 66 percent of households, and in the larger towns, such as Makeni, Bonthe, and Freetown, more than 75 percent of households have easy access to primary schools.

In addition to inequalities in access to primary schooling, there are also differences in satisfaction with the current level of educational quality and on which level of government should run the school system. Satisfaction with the quality of primary schooling is generally high. The lowest level of satisfaction is among households in Kailahun District in the Eastern Region and Freetown City Council. The survey also showed some support for local governments managing schools. In thirteen of nineteen local councils, the majority of households surveyed expressed support for local government taking over control of schools. The only exceptions are households in Pujehun District, Bonthe Town, Freetown, Makeni Town, Western Rural, and Tonkolili District.

Given the different starting positions of the local councils, one of the central government's challenges is to develop a distribution of resources that would ensure equity in access and opportunity for all children. So far, the allocation formula in place is simply based on the number of students in the system. A more equitable distribution of resources would take into account the starting position and differing needs of the various councils.

Finally, although the focus has been on the devolution of tasks to local councils, issues related to school-based management and autonomy are

Table 6.3   Baseline Snapshot of Local Councils: School Availability, Quality, and Management, 2005
(percent)

Region	Local council	Primary school within 30 minutes	Satisfied with education quality	Feel local government should run schools	Trust local government	Trust central government	Trust teachers
SIERRA LEONE		66	86	58	72	63	82
Eastern	Kono District	42	86	66	79	64	91
	Kenema District	64	92	60	71	75	85
	Kenema Town	77	92	60	71	75	85
	Kailahun District	72	73	71	73	72	82
	Koidu Town	74	85	66	75	66	89
Northern	Koinadugu District	63	86	73	80	63	98
	Tonkolili District	72	88	39	72	59	89
	Port Loko District	58	93	57	74	63	88
	Bombali District	70	92	49	70	49	83
	Kambia District	65	93	70	73	70	89
	Makeni Town	90	100	64	72	35	84
Southern	Bonthe District	47	90	47	64	73	83
	Pujehun District	47	97	38	67	80	93
	Bo District	66	91	69	80	67	90
	Bo Town	70	82	69	69	57	78
	Moyamba District	59	94	66	76	63	91
	Bonthe Town	78	100	42	79	72	86
Western	Western Area Rural	78	86	49	70	56	89
	Freetown	78	80	46	58	44	82

Source: IRCBP Baseline Survery of public services in Local Councils 2005.

even more important. MEST had devised several initiatives to give schools and communities more autonomy in decision making and management of funds. Devolution of responsibilities to local authorities should not erode some of these initiatives. For example, MEST started a process to transfer capitation grants directly to schools, giving head teachers and School Management Committees (SMCs) the authority to manage school funds. The decentralization of basic education functions to local governments could actually erode this initiative if capitation grants are transferred to local governments instead of to schools. The overall goal of the reform process should be that schools receive the funds needed to operate on time and in full, and that there are accounting systems in place to ensure that the funds are spent wisely.

MANAGEMENT OF EDUCATION SERVICE DELIVERY

The governing bodies of the education sector have established several goals for the sector, one of which is that every Sierra Leonean child will receive at least 9 years of education (basic education). The implementation of this goal will depend on the management capacity of the bodies responsible for education from the central to local levels. As mentioned in the section above, technical and management capacity was a casualty of the long civil war and the preceding years of corrupt government. The education sector, like other sectors, suffers from a dearth of highly skilled professionals and managers. A review of the education sector for the Poverty Reduction Strategy Paper (Bennell, Harding, and Rogers-Wright 2004, 101) found planning and management capacity was "weak at all levels of the education sector—schools, district, and ministry headquarters." This section analyzes the capacity for managing different components of the education sector, from information to resources. The focus is on basic education, although the discussion is pertinent to other sectors.

INFORMATION MANAGEMENT AND COMMUNICATION

Good information on the education sector is critical for planning, monitoring, and evaluating the system. It is also crucial for accountability. Currently, data on enrollment and schools are collected by school officials and collated by the Inspectorate Division. Because of a lack of institutional capacity and poor transportation and communication infrastructures, the data collected are sparse and inferior. What does exist is not readily accessible, and without good data, planning and implementation of sector goals is difficult. Furthermore, it is difficult to hold institutions accountable when information on the system is not available to stakeholders.

The Planning and Budgeting Department of MEST is planning the development of an EMIS. For the system to be successful, the Central Ministry must work in concert with local governments to coordinate data collection and analysis. Capacity building on the development and use of such a system will have to be undertaken. A baseline census of schools should be performed as soon as possible to plan for and monitor progress toward universal basic education.

TEACHER MANAGEMENT

Teachers are crucial to the delivery of a quality education system because they are directly responsible for equipping students with the necessary skills and knowledge. Furthermore, teacher salaries account for the largest share of current educational expenses, so it is crucial that they are managed effectively. Teacher management functions—recruitment, deployment, transfer, replacement, promotion, and supervision—are carried out in an ad hoc manner.

Fully cognizant of this problem, the New Education Policy recommended the establishment of a Teacher's Service Commission, which would take overall responsibility for teacher management functions, but this commission does not yet exist. According to the LGA, responsibility for the recruitment, payment, and supervision of teachers lies with the local councils.

Recruitment. At present the responsibility for recruiting and hiring teachers lies with individual schools and SMCs. When a teacher is hired, the school applies to MEST for the teacher to be added to the government payroll. Once the hire is approved by MEST and the teacher has gone through a photo verification process, the new employee is added to the payroll. This process can take a long time, resulting in a backlog of teachers to be added to the government payroll.

Deployment. Figure 6.1 shows the relationship between teacher numbers and enrollments in JSS and depicts patterns of teacher allocation among schools. The number of teachers in school increases with the number of students, as expected. Regression analysis quantifies this relationship: on average a new teacher is added for every 32 students in the junior secondary level. The R^2 statistic (0.71) means that 71 percent of the variation in the number of teachers in schools can be explained by differences in the sizes of schools. Thus about 29 percent of the variation comes from randomness in allocation. A degree of randomness of 30 percent for

Figure 6.1   Teacher Deployment in JSS, 2003/04

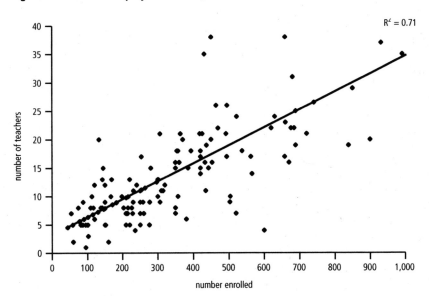

Source: Authors' computation based on data from MEST.
Note: Includes schools with JSS only (i.e., not combined schools).

JSS is in line with teacher deployment in Ethiopia, Madagascar, Burkina Faso, and Côte d'Ivoire, but is much larger than in Guinea, Mozambique, and Namibia. Unfortunately, data do not exist to carry out this analysis for SSS or primary schools.

Better deployment and placement procedures are also needed to alleviate the acute shortages of qualified teachers in the rural district areas. Because teachers can apply directly to their schools of choice and the incentives to work in rural areas are few, the more qualified teachers tend to work in the larger towns. A disproportionate number of community teachers work in rural schools.

Monitoring and Supervision. Monitoring and supervision of teachers is primarily carried out by the head teachers themselves and boards of governors in the case of JSS. However, most head teachers and members of SMCs have had little or no training in this area. Absenteeism and persistently late teachers are a problem in schools in many areas even though teachers are required to sign attendance registers. The IRCBP (2005) baseline survey involved two unannounced visits to primary schools, and the results showed that absenteeism is a serious issue in many schools (figure 6.2). Twenty-two percent of teachers in the sample schools were absent on the day of the survey. The rate of teacher absenteeism varies from 10 percent in Bo Town Council to almost 40 percent in Moyamba District Council.

Figure 6.2   Teacher Absenteeism by Local Council, 2005

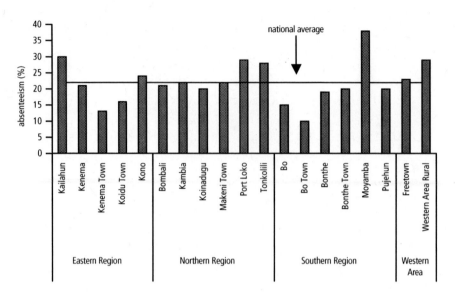

Source: IRCBP Baseline Survey of Primary Schools 2005.

In addition to tallying teachers who were absent, the IRCBP (2005) *Baseline Survey of Primary Schools* documented the activities of teachers during surprise visits to classrooms. The results show that much could be done to improve the performance of those teachers who do show up. In the sample, fewer than half the classrooms had teachers who were actively engaged in teaching. There were wide variations among the local councils; in Freetown about 80 percent of classrooms had teachers engaged in teaching, whereas in Kenema and Moyamba districts only about 20 percent of teachers in classrooms were engaged in teaching. Many teachers were engaged in nonteaching activities, such as doing paperwork, and disciplining students (figure 6.3). Again, many class-rooms simply had no teachers in them (close to 30 percent in Kenema, Bonthe District, Koinadugu District, and Pujehun District councils).

These findings point to the need for monitoring and supervising teacher activities at the school level. The most common disciplinary mea-sures taken against teachers who were repeatedly late or absent were to issue verbal and, to a lesser extent, written warnings. Head teachers are sympathetic to the plight of other teachers because they know that work-ing conditions are poor. Late payment of salaries, poor housing condi-tions, and low salaries compared to the private sector have all contributed to a lack of motivation among teachers (Harding and Mansaray 2005).

Figure 6.3   Teacher Activities during Surprise Visit to Classrooms, by Local Council, 2005

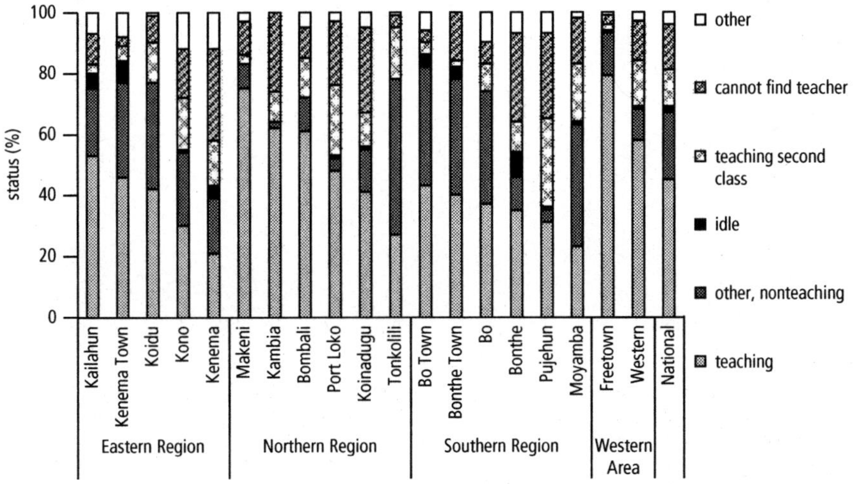

Source: IRCBP Baseline Survey of Primary Schools 2005.

SCHOOL MANAGEMENT

SMCs are responsible for the day-to-day activities of government and government-assisted schools. According to the Education Act of 2004, the members of an SMC are the head teacher, the inspector of schools or his or her representative, the proprietor's representative, the chairman of the Community Teachers Association, the traditional ruler of the village or area concerned, a female member or representative of the Chiefdom Education Committee, and a prominent educator. The SMCs are charged with managing the school in accordance with the laws laid down by the Education Act. With the establishment of decentralization, it is not clear what the role of the SMCs is with respect to the local education authorities. It is expected that there should be a member of the Local Government Education Committee on the SMC.

In government and government-assisted JSS, the board of governors manages the school. According to the Education Act, six members of the board of governors, including the chairman, are appointed directly by the minister to represent the interests of MEST. Four members are nominated by the proprietor of the school and one member by the local authority in which the school is located. These members have to be approved by the MEST minister. The remaining members are the school principal and an ex-student. It will be important to clarify the role of the board of governors under decentralization. However, none of the documents on decentralization mention the role of the board of governors under the new governance structure. The most likely outcome is that the boards will continue to exist, and the minister's role in appointing members to them will be diminished. For the SMC and the board of governors to perform effectively, their new roles and responsibilities under decentralization must be clarified.

RESOURCE MANAGEMENT

This section considers the management and flow of financial resources, teaching and learning materials, and furniture necessary for a well-functioning education system. The ongoing process of decentralization means that many of the existing processes and institutions are changing even as this document is being written. As much as possible, this section distinguishes between written policies and actual practices. Prior to decentralization, resources flowed from MEST to the schools, but the devolution of basic education means that resources will flow directly to local governments for disbursement to schools.

Financial Resources. The share of funds going to education is determined as part of the government's Medium Term Expenditure Framework (MTEF). MTEF is a tool that enables the government to allocate available resources to the different sectors and subsectors in line with its priorities. It also affords the government an opportunity to plan over a 3-year period.

As part of MTEF, the International Monetary Fund and the government of Sierra Leone agree on budget ceilings for the year and quarterly allocations. Through budget hearings and discussions, the annual expenditure is allocated across all government ministries and departments. There are several major expenditure items for basic education: teacher salaries, fee subsidies for students, examination fees, and teaching materials (including textbooks and furniture). As a result of decentralization, the Local Government Grants Distribution Formula and Allocations for 2006 (Ministry of Finance 2006) specifies that school fee subsidies are given to local councils to be paid directly to schools; examination fees are paid to WAEC upon validation of the number of pupils taking exams; and textbooks and teaching materials are procured and distributed to local councils. In addition, local councils have to provide a detailed plan of activities with costing to MoF; submit an acceptable monthly financial report; and provide data on key education indicators, including enrollment at each level, number of teachers, and number of schools.

Fee subsidies. For the first term of the 2005/06 academic year, MEST distributed checks prepared by the Accountant General's Department (AGD) at MoF for primary school fee subsidies to the private audit firm KPMG, which had been hired to pay the school fee subsidies directly to schools over the past few years. KPMG deducts 10 percent for the administration costs of this exercise. This processing is currently being reviewed. Under decentralization, school fee subsidies are expected to be paid directly into school bank accounts once those are established.

Public Expenditure Tracking Surveys conducted in 2002 suggest that when KPMG took over disbursement of subsidies, leakages from the flow of funds were reduced greatly, from 54 percent during the last two terms of 2001/02, to 21 percent in the first term of 2002/03. The added complexity involved in deliberations among local councils, MEST, and KPMG will therefore have to be managed carefully to avoid a rise in leakages.

The situation is further complicated because enrollment statistics and hence calculations of fees to be paid to each school are still currently done by MEST. Currently vouchers for the payment of subsidies are prepared by MEST and forwarded to AGD, which prepares checks for disbursement to schools. In principle, vouchers should be prepared by the local councils. In practice, capacity constraints in many regions prevent this.

One solution is the ongoing project by AGD to ensure that all schools open a bank account. Well over half of all schools now have accounts, making direct transfers to schools from the central government a possibility. However, this solution has not been universally adopted, and local councils will have to be involved in these deliberations.

Teacher Salaries. Teacher salaries flow through a consolidated fund directly through MEST. Vouchers are sent by MEST directly to AGD. For schools with bank accounts, salaries are paid directly to the school's account. For those without bank accounts, head teachers must collect teacher pay from the provincial headquarters. In many cases, payments do not reach teachers on time, and late payment of salaries is one of the many challenges facing teachers in Sierra Leone. The decentralization schedule calls for the devolution of the payment of salaries, but it has not yet happened. One role of local governments would be to ensure that all schools in their locality open bank accounts so that monies can be transferred directly. Until that time, monies can be transferred to local governments, which would be responsible for transfers to schools.

Examination Fees. Examination fees will be paid directly to the WAEC for the local council by MoF. It is expected that the local councils will furnish data on the number of candidates for the national exams to MoF. This arrangement has not changed with decentralization, except that the responsibility for furnishing the number of candidates taking the exam lies with the local councils.

Figure 6.4 summarizes the proposed financial flows to the schools. Revenues available for the sector come from taxes (some of which are

Figure 6.4 Flow of Resources in the Education Sector

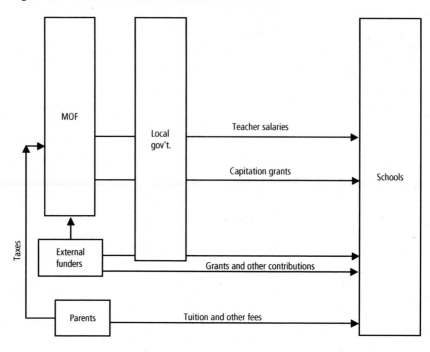

Source: Economic Policy and Research Unit.

paid by parents) and other domestic revenue sources and from external funding agencies that provide budget support. For schools with bank accounts, the capitation grants and teacher salaries would be transferred directly to the school accounts. Otherwise, they would go through local governments, who would be responsible for getting them to schools. Parents and communities also make direct contributions to schools through fees and other voluntary contributions.

Textbooks, Teaching Materials, and Furniture. The procurement and distribution of textbooks, teaching materials, and furniture are currently the responsibility of the central government and its district and zonal offices. In 2004/05 MEST awarded three contracts through a competitive process for the supply of primary school textbooks. The contractors delivered the textbooks to the MEST central warehouse in Freetown for storage, and these books were subsequently sent to school inspectors in the districts and zonal heads in the Western Area for distribution to head teachers of primary schools (figure 6.5).

The 2004 Public Expenditure Tracking Survey (PETS), which tracked the distribution of textbooks from MEST to schools, found that all books were successfully transferred from the MEST central warehouse to the

Figure 6.5   Current Mode of Procurement and Distribution of Primary School Text-books, Procurement Reform Unit

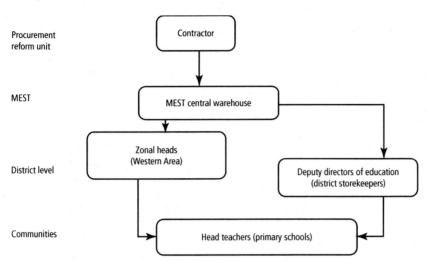

Source: Ministry of Education Science and Technology.

zonal heads and district education offices in 2004/05. However, there were problems with the transfer of books from the district and zonal offices to the schools; about 10 percent of the books did not make it to the schools, and those that were delivered came in late. Furthermore, record keeping at the local and school levels was found to be much weaker than at the central level.

Earlier PETS surveys that tracked the transfer of teaching materials (PETS 2002) and school furniture (PETS 2003) found significant leakages in the transfer of these resources from the central to the local levels. Many resources do not reach the intended schools. As mentioned earlier, one of the many reasons for the decentralization reform is to reduce these wastages in the transfer of resources from the central government to the intended recipients. The devolution schedule for MEST states that the provision of textbooks, furniture, and teaching materials in primary schools and JSS will be the responsibility of the local councils starting in 2006. If local governments provide an enabling environment (trained personnel; logistical support; improved record keeping, monitoring, and oversight) then the effectiveness of public resources in education can be improved.

MONITORING AND EVALUATION

Before decentralization, monitoring schools was the responsibility of school inspectors and supervisors from the district education offices of

MEST. Inspection was organized at the district level, and supervisors monitored specific primary schools within a district. Monitoring tended to be limited to enrollment, attendance, teacher numbers, teaching practices, and the school curriculum. Monitoring of furniture and structures is primarily the responsibility of the Facilities Unit of the Planning Department. However, school monitoring has been largely ad hoc, because district education officers lack transportation and other resources needed for systematic monitoring. Annual monitoring and inspection reports are not published by the inspectorate, but this matter is now the subject of discussion at MEST.

Under decentralization, supervision and monitoring of basic education schools are to be devolved. The document also stipulates that school supervisors should be under the employ of local councils; supervisors are expected to bring much needed technical expertise. However, the transition is not slated to take place until 2007; at present the relationship between the local government education authorities and MEST district education officers is unclear.

The IRCBP (2005) baseline survey shows that 86 percent of the schools surveyed were visited by a MEST official (an inspector or teacher supervisor from the District Education Office); 50 percent of the schools had been visited by a local council representative; 56 percent by a religious figure; and 65 percent by NGO representatives (table 6.4). These visits typically include a conversation with the head teacher and inspection of students, classrooms, and supplies. Eighty percent of the schools surveyed had SMCs that met at least once during the school year, but some local councils (for example, Bonthe) have very inactive SMCs.

The performance of government and government-assisted schools at the WAEC examinations is also monitored, but it is not clear how the information garnered is used to improve schools. The monitoring is carried out by the Secretariat of the National Commission for Basic Education, which creates a league table of schools based on the performance of candidates. The top performers are usually exclusive private schools, with small class sizes and children from high socioeconomic backgrounds, and a few elite government and government-assisted schools with a more diverse student body. The good practices employed by the successful government and government-assisted schools are being studied so that they can be implemented at other schools.

Student learning is supposed to be monitored by continuous classroom assessments. Other than determining whether students transition from one class to the next, these assessments do not seem to be used. Although schools are now required to carry out very elementary

Table 6.4 **Share of Primary Schools Visited, by Stakeholder and Local Council, 2004/05**
(percent)

Region	Local council	MEST official	MP	Local councillor	Religious figure	NGO Rep.	SMC meeting[a]	No. of schools
SIERRA LEONE		86	13	50	56	65	80	279
Eastern Region	Kailahun	94	13	75	44	56	80	16
	Kenema	87	7	44	56	69	93	15
	Kenema Town	93	8	79	57	71	85	14
	Koidu Town	83	13	82	67	92	67	11
	Kono	67	14	60	47	80	80	15
Northern Region	Bombali	100	13	46	71	100	100	16
	Kambia	94	13	63	31	38	93	16
	Koinadugu	86	7	60	53	60	87	15
	Makeni Town	93	6	33	53	93	64	13
	Port Loko	100	7	6	94	100	87	15
	Tonkolili	69	..	29	50	50	94	16
Southern Region	Bo	81	6	75	88	63	100	16
	Bo Town	88	..	31	44	13	69	16
	Bonthe	81	44	63	31	31	67	16
	Bonthe Town	78	13	38	11	33	22	8
	Moyamba	67	13	53	53	67	100	16
	Pujehun	64	13	40	60	73	71	14
Western Area	Freetown	100	13	25	81	69	60	15
	Western Rural	100	11	50	63	75	88	16

Source: Glennerster, Imian, and Whiteside 2006.
Note: .. = nil or negligible.
a. Percentage of schools surveyed with an SMC that met during 2004–05.

rating of specific psychomotor and affective skills, and MEST has created a new position of Continuous Assessment Teacher for each school, many schools do not comply with these broader assessment requirements. In addition, MEST does not have the capacity to monitor noncompliance.

Monitoring the school curriculum is primarily the responsibility of the National Curriculum Research and Development Center. This agency reviews the curriculum at least once every 3 years and makes recommendations. It also makes those changes to the curriculum deemed necessary by MEST. Little systematic evaluation of the curriculum is carried out by the National Curriculum Research and Development Center or any other entity. Only after WAEC results have been received are references sometimes made to the contents of specific syllabuses.

PLANNING AND DEVELOPMENT CAPACITY

The Planning Department of MEST, responsible for planning and decision making, suffers from inadequate capacity, as do other MEST departments. Furthermore, because of poor information and communication infrastructure, the ability of this department to perform its task is limited. For MEST to focus on its new roles of policy making, monitoring, and supervision, this Planning Department must be strengthened considerably. MEST would have to train a cadre of professionals and managers tasked with overall management of the education system to ensure that the goals of the sector are met. MEST must also provide the information and communication infrastructure that would enable better performance. In addition, the right incentives must be instituted to lower the attrition rate of these professionals, whose skills would be in demand in other sectors.

POLICY IMPLICATIONS

The key areas for further policy development on education governance and management are as summarized here.

Defining Responsibility and Authority. One of the lessons learned from international experience with decentralization is that clear delineation of the lines of responsibility and authority is required for effective service delivery. The laws governing the sector must be clarified and the assignment of responsibilities made transparent. It is important that all parties cooperate to work out the details of the transfer of responsibilities, including the transfer of human and financial resources.

Building Capacity. Once the responsibilities have been assigned, it is imperative that responsible parties acquire the skills and knowledge required to carry out their tasks. The issue of capacity building, as mentioned throughout this chapter, is one that is critical for the success of the decentralization process. For capacity building to be successful, it must go hand in hand with public service pay reform, because salaries in the public sector are low compared with the private sector. Public service reforms are currently under way, which will have an impact in the sector. The salaries of senior managers and professionals at MEST must be increased to make them competitive with those in the NGO and private sectors. Donor resources could be used to support temporarily these salaries. The decentralization and reform should be seen as an opportunity for a needs assessment on the current and desired levels of both management and technical capacity. An effective continuous professional development program would be a worthwhile investment. The capacity building agenda should also include training for managers of schools (head teachers and members of SMCs and boards of governors) and parent-teacher associations.

Improving Data. Throughout this report, the lack of good data on the education sector has been highlighted. Data are important for various reasons; planning, monitoring and evaluation, management, and policy making all call for timely, accurate, and reliable data on the education sector. In a decentralized system, it is particularly important that all subnational regions provide timely and quality data for MEST to perform its primary role of monitoring and supervision. In addition to EMIS, financial and human resource management systems would improve fiscal management and accountability systems. Furthermore, teachers could be allocated to local councils in a manner that ensures equity in terms of the distribution of trained teachers.

Managing Teachers. The management of teachers is important for the effective delivery of education services. Decentralization poses certain challenges for the allocation and deployment of teachers, issues that are linked to those of teacher qualifications and professional development in the different localities. Under LGA, the legal responsibility for teacher recruitment, supervision, and payment lies with the local government.

In many countries, the management of teachers has typically been one of the major functions of the central government. In Sierra Leone, there has been de facto decentralization of teacher management, because recruitment and deployment of personnel was left to the schools themselves due to weak capacity at the central level. A Teaching Service Commission is being established at MEST to assume teacher management tasks. With decentralization, responsibilities for recruitment and deployment now lie with the local government. However, nothing has been stipulated concerning the establishment of standards for recruiting and training of teachers. The responsibility for ongoing professional development of teachers is another function that needs to be allocated to a particular level of government.

Reducing Inequities. Although not explicitly acknowledged in any of the decentralization documents, reducing inequalities among localities will be one of the challenges of MEST. There are several policy options available to MEST to ensure that every child obtains a good education regardless of region of residence. Fiscal transfers to local governments may be determined by transparent formulas designed to promote equity. The equity component could ensure that all children receive a minimum level of education. MEST could also allocate additional monies to local councils on the basis of need.

CHAPTER 7

Improving Education: Policy Choices

Given limited resources, difficult choices have to be made to balance the needs of subsectors, population groups, and the various components of the education system. This chapter uses a simulation model as a tool to facilitate discussion about long-term, sustainable development of the education system to meet the needs and aspirations of the people of Sierra Leone. It presents the financial consequences of several policy scenarios to illustrate how such a tool can aid sectorwide planning.

CONTEXT

Since the country emerged from the devastating civil war, demand for education and the consequent expansion in the system have been astonishing. The expansion has been accompanied by a rapid increase in primary school population, overcrowded classrooms, high pupil-teacher ratios, large numbers of untrained and unqualified teachers, and a paucity of teaching materials and furniture. The expansion at the primary level has not been matched by provision at the postprimary level, which has resulted in an educational bottleneck compounded by a relatively sluggish economy in which youth unemployment or underemployment is high.

The PRSP indicates that 70 percent of Sierra Leoneans are unable to meet their basic needs in terms of safe water and sanitation, shelter, health care, and education (Government of Sierra Leone 2005). Thus in the medium term, the provision of free primary education for those in government and government-assisted schools must continue if the MDG of universal primary completion is to be met. Expanding this provision to the JSS level and thus covering basic education as required by the Constitution and the Education Act is a concern for the future.

Even though school enrollment has increased tremendously in the past few years, a large number of school-aged children are still not in school. Achievement of the MDGs for education could require a further expansion to absorb those presently out of school, even if the number of over-aged students in the system naturally decreases. If more students transit from primary school to JSS and beyond, the whole system will expand. However, given the restriction on available funds, such expansion is likely to be untenable without external funding, particularly if quality is not to be sacrificed. Even should increased external funding materialize, the government must consider how the education system can be sustained once the external funding ends.

FINANCING SCENARIOS

A simulation model helps describe alternative scenarios for the allocation of limited resources. The scenarios are based on policy options that are guided by many factors:

1. The legal framework (the constitution and legislation, such as the Education Act, the Universities Act, and LGA)
2. Commitments to the MDGs, EFA, and girls' education
3. Affordability and sustainability of choices given the status of the country
4. Developmental objectives and targets (such as government strategic plans)
5. The needs of the economy and society
6. The capacity to absorb, implement, and sustain inputs

The scenarios presented in this chapter should be seen as examples of how a simulation model can be used to support evidence-based decision making. As such, they are merely illustrative of the use of such a tool. The model uses all relevant available data, and the results are dependent on the quality of that data. As education data in Sierra Leone improve the parameters used in the model can also be improved. As for all simulations, because the model is based on assumptions, estimates, and perhaps questionable data, the results may not be a fully accurate prediction of future needs and costs. Furthermore, the model does not fully capture qualitative factors. However, by taking account of pupil-teacher ratios, class sizes, intake, repetition and completion rates, and spending on inputs other than the salaries of teachers, the model does address some issues that affect quality.

The key parameters examined in the model are listed here.

Duration of Compulsory Education. The constitution of Sierra Leone and the Education Act both call for compulsory basic education (6 years of primary school and 3 years of JSS). The EFA goals and MDGs for education call for universal *primary* education. Achievement of universal basic education may have to be phased because the government may not have the funds to implement universal basic education simultaneously with universal primary education. By varying the transition rate from primary to JSS in the model, the cost implications of having more students completing basic education can be discerned.

Expansion of Preprimary Schooling. To date, preprimary education has been provided mainly by the private sector. With a significant percentage of the population now living in urban areas, the gradual move away from extended families, and the perceived benefits of early structured learning, the government has been encouraging government and government-assisted primary schools to offer preprimary classes for children 3–5 years old. The cost of increased government involvement is examined in the model.

Targets for Repetition, Completion, and Transition Rates. High repetition rates have meant that the system has been inefficient. The cost implications of different rates of repetition, completion, and transition are examined in the model.

Enrollment Targets. By setting the target of 100 percent primary completion by a certain date, the corresponding enrollment targets can be determined. The cost effects of varying the date for achievement of 100 percent completion are examined using the model.

Imbalances in Level Allocations. Expansion at the lower levels of education necessitates increased output at the higher levels to provide the personnel required for maintaining and improving quality at the lower levels. There is some doubt as to whether the required balance has been achieved, judging by the high percentage of unqualified and untrained teachers at the primary level, the increasing number of underqualified teachers at the secondary level in the rural areas, and the high failure rate at the end of SSS. Getting the balance of funding right could have a marked effect on the quality of the outputs of the system.

Service Delivery at the School Level. Whereas a reasonably low pupil-teacher ratio may be a desirable educational goal, it is heavily dependent on available financial resources. The higher the teacher count, the larger the payroll; the more highly qualified and experienced the teacher, the greater the salary. With salaries and emoluments being major areas of expenditure at all levels of education, arriving at a sustainable balance is difficult but necessary. Scenarios with different teaching loads and different numbers of teachers are examined.

Rehabilitating and Reconstructing Education. The extensive destruction of educational institutions, massive population movements, and surging school enrollments have forced the reconstruction of many schools and colleges over the past few years. The model considers the cost of further construction work to accommodate expanding enrollments within the various scenarios.

Allocating Internally Generated Funds. As an economic consequence of the civil conflict of the 1990s, every sector, including education, is in dire need of funds. The present government has allocated a greater percentage of its current expenditures to education than to any other single sector for many years. But the share of current expenditures devoted to education is slightly below that for countries that have met EFA FTI goals. Adjustments to ensure that the country meets the benchmark for EFA FTI are considered in the model. The effect of a variation in the share of domestically generated resources allocated to education is examined in some of the scenarios.

All the scenarios require achievement of a 100 percent primary school completion rate by 2015, in line with the MDGs and the PRSP targets. In addition, for all the scenarios, the assumptions are made that the population will grow steadily at 1.8 percent per year (which was the annual average growth between 1985 and 2004) and GDP will grow at an average of 5 percent per year.[1] Should population growth decelerate (highly unlikely) or the growth in GDP accelerate (quite possible), then the financing gaps predicted by the scenarios would ease. A further assumption in all the scenarios is that the percentage of domestically generated resources allocated to education increases to 20 percent by 2015 (from a base of 18 percent in 2004). The key parameters and targets for the four illustrative policy-based scenarios are presented in table 7.1.

All scenarios are built on the assumption that at least 6 years of primary education are required to reach literacy and numeracy for life and to equip children with the skills they need to contribute to the development and growth of the society. The scenarios differ with regard to the resources and targets for pre- and postprimary education. All scenarios take into account the existing policies and the goals of education in Sierra Leone. But each scenario concentrates on different targets—thus the share of resources devoted to each level of education distinguishes the scenarios (table 7.2). A summary of the costs and the financing gaps that develop under each of the four scenarios is shown in table 7.3. Details of each of the scenarios are presented in the following section.

Table 7.1 The Scenarios: Key Parameters

Parameter	Base year (2003/04)	2015 targets			
		Scenario 1	Scenario 2	Scenario 3	Scenario 4
Preprimary					
GER (%)	4	100	50	50	50
Percentage government or government-assisted	8	80	10	20	10
Subsidy to private (US$ millions)	..	..	3.8	3.4	3.8
Primary					
GER (%)	145	105	105	105	105
GIR (%)	191	100	100	100	100
GCR (%)	63	100	100	100	100
Number of teachers (including head teachers)	17,668	24,080	20,278	22,812	20,278
Pupil-teacher ratio	61	40	45	40	45
Percentage of pupils private	5	5	10	10	10
Spending on inputs other than teachers (% of total current)	31	33	33	33	33
JSS					
GER (%)	40	105	55	66	61
Transition rate primary–JSS (%)	65	95	50	60	60
Survival rate (%)	87	90	90	90	90
Repetition rate (%)	14	14	14	14	7
Number of teachers (including head teachers)	4,389	13,770	5,187	7,278	6,131
Pupil-teacher ratio	29	31	39	35	38
Percentage of pupils private	5	5	15	10	10
Spending on inputs other than teachers (% of total current)	30	50	50	50	50
SSS					
GER (%)	12	48	19	22	24
Transition rate JSS–SSS (%)	53	53	40	40	45
Survival rate (%)	100	90	90	90	90
Repetition rate (%)	11	11	11	6	5
Number of teachers (including head teachers)	1,402	7,881	2,542	2,927	3,214
Pupil-teacher ratio	27	23	27	27	27
Percentage of pupils private	1	3	10	10	10
Spending on inputs other than teachers (% of total current)	28	50	50	50	50
Technical and vocational centers					
No. enrolled in technical & vocational courses for primary school leavers	n.a.	4,635	53,418	45,571	41,722
No. enrolled in technical & vocational courses for JSS leavers	n.a.	41,164	29,029	35,675	30,814
No. enrolled in technical & vocational professional courses	n.a.	25,000	25,000	25,000	25,000

Table 7.1 *(continued)*

Parameter	Base year (2003/04)	2015 targets			
		Scenario 1	Scenario 2	Scenario 3	Scenario 4
Tertiary					
Number enrolled	15,497	33,416	33,416	33,416	42,529
Percentage of pupils private	. .	3	3	6	5
Subsidy to private (US$ millions)	. .	0.5	0.5	1.0	1.0

Source: Authors.
Note: . . = nil or negligible, n.a. = not applicable.

Table 7.2   Distribution of Current Costs by Subsector, 2015
(percent)

	Scenario 1	Scenario 2	Scenario 3	Scenario 4
Preprimary	9.9	5.0	4.9	4.5
Primary	22.7	37.7	39.2	35.2
JSS	30.5	15.4	17.9	16.6
SSS	20.1	10.0	10.4	10.5
Technical and vocational centers	5.3	9.3	8.5	8.2
Literacy and nonformal education	0.0	0.1	0.1	0.1
Higher education and research	11.5	22.5	19.1	25.0

Source: Authors.

Table 7.3   Cumulative Cost Implications of the Scenarios, 2007–15
(US$ millions)

Indicator	Scenario 1	Scenario 2	Scenario 3	Scenario 4
Domestic current resources for education[a]	401.3	401.3	401.3	401.3
Primary education[b]	179.7	179.7	179.7	179.7
Other levels of education	221.7	221.7	221.7	221.7
Current costs	1,275.1	705.0	843.2	757.9
Primary education	328.9	261.9	320.3	269.4
Other levels of education	946.2	443.1	522.9	488.6
Current gap (resources – costs)	−873.7	−303.7	−441.8	−356.6
Primary education	−149.2	−82.2	−140.6	−89.7
Other levels of education	−724.5	−221.5	−301.2	−266.9
As a percentage of total current resources for education	217.7	75.7	110.1	88.9
Primary education	83.1	45.8	78.3	49.9
Other levels of education	326.9	99.9	135.9	120.4
Development costs (classroom construction)	237.2	59.8	100.1	79.0
Primary education	72.6	40.8	61.8	40.8
Other levels of education (JSS + SSS)	164.7	19.0	38.3	38.1

Source: Authors.
a. Based on reaching a target of 20 percent of domestically generated resources devoted to education by 2010.
b. Based on the FTI indicative framework of 20 percent of domestically generated resources to education and 50 percent of this to primary by 2015.

FOUR SCENARIOS

SCENARIO 1: EFA ACTION PLAN

In scenario 1, many of the targets given in the national EFA Action Plan (MEST 2003a) are implemented (see table 7.1). This scenario assumes that the government continues to be the predominant provider of education at all levels; the percentage of private providers is minimal. The desired increase in enrollment at the school level is very large, as are the transition rates. Little account is taken of in-country absorptive capacity, the size of the financing gap, and subsequent sustainability when external support decreases. Class sizes and pupil-teacher ratios are relatively low, but are obtained at a high cost. The cost implications for selected years and each level are shown in table 7.4.

Among other things, Scenario 1 calls for a 100 percent GER in preprimary education and for 80 percent of those enrolled to be in government and government-assisted schools by 2015. This target is particularly ambitious, given that the GER in 2003/04 was 4.3 percent and only 7.9 percent of pupils were enrolled in government and government-assisted schools. The scenario also optimistically assumes a 95 percent primary-to-JSS transition rate by 2015, even though the transition rate in 2003/04 was only 65 percent and the government is contemplating raising the pass mark for the NPSE. The targets within this scenario are desirable, but they are unlikely to be achievable given the time frame without significant donor support.

Table 7.4   Annual Cost Implications of Scenario 1: EFA Action Plan, 2004–15 (US$ millions)

	2004	2006	2007	2010	2012	2015
Total current cost	41.8	64.7	74.7	114.6	156.5	229.1
Preprimary	0.0	0.6	1.2	5.0	9.9	22.6
Primary	21.2	24.1	25.7	30.9	38.8	52.1
JSS	7.3	15.1	18.7	33.7	48.3	69.8
SSS	2.3	8.9	11.1	20.8	30.3	46.0
Technical/vocational	1.7	3.8	4.4	6.6	8.5	12.1
Tertiary	9.3	12.3	13.5	17.6	20.8	26.4
Current gap (resources − costs)	−17.6	−35.7	−43.0	−73.4	−109.1	−170.5
Preprimary	0.0	−0.4	−0.8	−3.6	−7.7	−18.4
Primary	−8.9	−10.0	−10.7	−12.5	−17.8	−26.4
JSS	−3.1	−9.6	−12.4	−24.5	−37.4	−56.8
SSS	−1.0	−5.6	−7.4	−15.1	−23.5	−37.5
Technical/vocational	−0.7	−2.4	−2.9	−4.8	−6.6	−9.9
Tertiary	−3.9	−7.8	−8.9	−12.8	−16.1	−21.5

Source: Authors.

The financing gap would be US$43 million in 2007 and US$170 million in 2015 (table 7.4).[2] For primary education alone, the financing gap would be US$11 million in 2007 and US$26 million in 2015. These estimates do not include the cost of training teachers (although it is partly accounted for under the costs of higher education and research) and the capital cost of constructing classrooms. The cost of classroom construction under this scenario could be as much as an additional US$26 million in 2015.

The annual financing gap for achieving universal primary education by 2015 under this scenario is large, and fiscal sustainability would clearly be an issue of concern. In fact, it is extremely unlikely that the government would be able to sustain the program from domestic resources alone, and to depend so heavily on external funding for education is a significant risk. Furthermore, in-country capacity to accomplish all that needs to be done to meet the targets indicated in this scenario by 2015 is questionable. Although the desire to meet the targets may exist, the reality is that many targets are unlikely to be met.

SCENARIO 2: ACHIEVABLE

In Scenario 2, the focus is on realistic targets based on the current situation in Sierra Leone. Assumptions regarding enrollment rates, transition rates, and the degree of private involvement are all adjusted with in-country absorptive capacity and sustainability in mind. The pupil-teacher ratios and class sizes are slightly larger than desired but are still quite reasonable for Sierra Leone's stage of development. In this scenario, the preprimary GER, percentage of pupils in government and government-assisted institutions, primary-to-JSS and JSS-to-SSS transition rates, and pupil-teacher ratios given in scenario 1 are modified to arrive at more readily achievable goals.

Under scenario 2, the financing gap for education would be US$27 million in 2007 and US$46 million in 2015 (table 7.5), significantly lower than in scenario 1. For primary alone, the gap would be US$8 million in 2007 and US$14 million in 2015. Approximately US$7 million annually from 2005 to 2015 would be added to this gap to finance the construction of classrooms.

Under this scenario, the total enrollment by 2015 at the primary level is the same as for scenario 1 but the financing gap at this level is smaller. Enrollments at other levels are smaller than for scenario 1 but they are more realistic. Additionally, the overall financing gap is significantly smaller than in scenario 1.

Table 7.5 Annual Cost Implications of Scenario 2: Achievable, 2004–15 (US$ millions)

Indicator	2004	2006	2007	2010	2012	2015
Total current cost	41.8	55.3	58.8	70.1	82.1	104.1
Preprimary	0.0	0.6	0.9	2.0	3.0	5.2
Primary	21.2	22.4	23.2	25.2	30.0	39.3
JSS	7.3	10.5	11.1	12.9	14.1	16.0
SSS	2.3	6.1	6.6	8.0	8.9	10.4
Technical/vocational	1.7	3.8	4.2	5.9	7.3	9.7
Tertiary	9.3	11.9	12.9	16.2	18.8	23.4
Current gap (resources – costs)	−17.6	−26.3	−27.1	−29.0	−34.6	−45.5
Preprimary	0.0	−0.3	−0.5	−1.0	−1.5	−2.6
Primary	−8.9	−8.4	−8.1	−6.7	−8.9	−13.6
JSS	−3.1	−5.7	−5.9	−6.4	−7.0	−7.9
SSS	−1.0	−3.3	−3.5	−3.9	−4.4	−5.1
Technical/vocational	−0.7	−2.0	−2.3	−2.9	−3.6	−4.8
Tertiary	−3.9	−6.5	−6.9	−8.0	−9.3	−11.5

Source: Authors.

SCENARIO 3: OPTIMISTIC

Scenario 3 is somewhat more optimistic than scenario 2. In this scenario, government and government-assisted preprimary schools would exist in every district, and class sizes and pupil-teacher ratios at the primary level would be as low as possible. Furthermore, the primary-to-JSS transition rate is higher than in scenario 2, given the goal of achieving universal basic education. Further changes from scenario 2 are based on optimism about the availability of funds and the ability of the government to sustain the provisions required by the scenario. The resulting financial gaps fall between those obtained in scenarios 1 and 2.

The overall effect of the changes under scenario 3 is that the remuneration for all teachers at the school level would increase slightly and pupil-teacher ratios at the primary and JSS levels would decrease. Enrollment in tertiary education programs would also increase relative to scenario 2, at the expense of distance education. The resulting gap would be US$32 million in 2007 and US$69 million in 2015 (table 7.6). For primary alone, it would be US$10 million in 2007 and US$24 million in 2015. In addition, classroom construction would require about US$11 million each year from 2005 to 2015.

Table 7.6 Annual Cost Implications of Scenario 3: Optimistic, 2004–15 (US$ millions)

Indicator	2004	2006	2007	2010	2012	2015
Total current cost	41.8	58.7	64.1	82.9	101.6	127.8
Preprimary	0.0	0.6	0.9	2.2	3.5	6.2
Primary	21.2	23.9	25.5	30.3	37.8	50.1
JSS	7.3	11.6	12.9	17.4	21.0	22.9
SSS	2.3	6.7	7.5	10.0	11.9	13.3
Technical/vocational	1.7	3.8	4.3	6.3	8.0	10.8
Tertiary	9.3	12.1	13.1	16.6	19.4	24.4
Current gap (resources − costs)	−17.6	−29.7	−32.4	−41.7	−54.1	−69.2
Preprimary	0.0	−0.4	−0.5	−1.2	−2.0	−3.6
Primary	−8.9	−9.9	−10.4	−11.9	−16.7	−24.4
JSS	−3.1	−6.6	−7.3	−9.9	−12.3	−13.2
SSS	−1.0	−3.8	−4.3	−5.7	−6.9	−7.7
Technical/vocational	−0.7	−2.2	−2.5	−3.6	−4.7	−6.2
Tertiary	−3.9	−6.9	−7.5	−9.4	−11.4	−14.1

Source: Authors.

For this scenario, the total enrollment by 2015 at the primary level is the same as for scenarios 1 and 2 but the financing gap is smaller. Enrollments at all school levels are higher than for scenario 2, but achieving them would be a challenge, given the relatively short period of time before 2015. Under this scenario, there may still be a concern regarding in-country capacity and sustainability, with financing requirements being more than twice the domestic resources for education by 2015.

SCENARIO 4: EFFICIENT

This scenario is a development of scenario 3 and can be seen as a compromise among earlier scenarios. It requires the system to be more efficient, to reduce the repetition rates, and to have a better balance of teachers in the schools. Whereas scenario 3 has lower pupil-teacher ratios, this scenario has much lower repetition rates and allocates more financial resources to each of the postprimary levels. The underlying principle of scenario 4 is greater efficiency and cost effectiveness and greater emphasis on postprimary education compared to the preceding scenario.

The overall effect of the changes in scenario 4 is that the remuneration for all teachers at the school level would decrease slightly relative to scenario 3, and pupil-teacher ratios at the primary and JSS levels would increase. Total enrollment in tertiary education would increase relative to scenario 3, largely because of anticipated increases in enrollment in

Table 7.7 Annual Cost Implications of Scenario 4: Efficient, 2004–15 (US$ millions)

Indicator	2004	2006	2007	2010	2012	2015
Total current cost	41.8	56.3	60.4	74.4	88.7	115.6
Preprimary	0.0	0.6	0.9	2.0	3.0	5.2
Primary	21.2	22.6	23.5	25.8	30.9	40.7
JSS	7.3	10.6	11.3	13.8	15.7	19.2
SSS	2.3	6.2	6.7	8.4	9.8	12.1
Technical/vocational	1.7	3.7	4.2	5.8	7.1	9.5
Tertiary	9.3	12.6	13.9	18.6	22.3	28.9
Current gap (resources – costs)	−17.6	−27.3	−28.8	−33.2	−41.3	−57.0
Preprimary	0.0	−0.3	−0.5	−1.1	−1.7	−2.9
Primary	−8.9	−8.6	−8.4	−7.4	−9.9	−15.0
JSS	−3.1	−5.9	−6.2	−7.3	−8.5	−10.8
SSS	−1.0	−3.5	−3.7	−4.5	−5.3	−6.8
Technical/vocational	−0.7	−2.1	−2.3	−3.1	−3.8	−5.3
Tertiary	−3.9	−7.0	−7.7	−9.9	−12.1	−16.2

Source: Authors.

distance education. The latter has been made possible by the assumption that a greater percentage of the population will access tertiary education: 700 per 100,000 of population compared to the 550 per 100,000 of population in scenario 3.

Under scenario 4, the financing gap for education would be US$29 million in 2007 and US$57 million in 2015 (table 7.7). For primary alone, the gap would be US$8 million in 2007 and US$15 million in 2015. Classroom construction, in addition, would cost about US$9 million each year from 2005 to 2015.

For this scenario, the total enrollment by 2015 at the primary level is the same as for all other scenarios, but the financing gap is smaller. Only enrollment at the JSS level is less than in scenario 3, and achieving this would be less of a challenge, given the relatively short period of time before 2015.

SUMMARY

This chapter has presented illustrative scenarios that estimate the cost implications of policy choices available to Sierra Leone in its endeavor to meet national and international targets for education. All the scenarios considered aim to achieve 100 percent primary school enrollment and completion for all primary-school-aged children by 2015. The main focus of the model is on the current financing gap of the different levels of education. School classroom construction is included in the model, but there are no other capital costs considered (such as construction for tertiary institutions). Furthermore, by focusing on expansion of the system, the inputs that target improvement in quality (such as libraries or learning resource centers) are only marginally included. Therefore in reality the total financing gap for education in Sierra Leone is higher than the model suggests, and the missing costs should be built into the next phase of the model to be used in the preparation of the Education Sector Plan.

Difficult choices must be made. Although cost is the main factor included in the model used, it is not the only one determining the possible options. Of almost equal importance are issues of sustainability and capacity to carry out the activities that would allow the achievement of targets. Much still has to be done. The government cannot achieve international targets based solely on its domestic resources. Therefore, at least in the near future, Sierra Leone will remain largely dependent on the inputs of its external partners to meet education goals. The simulation tool presented in this chapter can be used as a planning aid, allowing a dialogue among stakeholders on trade-offs and sustainability that can lead to a consensus on a plan for the future of the education sector.

Appendixes

APPENDIX A. SMOOTHING THE DATA FROM THE SIERRA LEONE POPULATION AND HOUSING CENSUS 2004

The final results of the 2004 Population and Housing Census (Statistics Sierra Leone 2004) in Sierra Leone were published on February 23, 2006. For this report, the census results have been examined and smoothed. The following is a description of the methodology used.

Misreporting age in population censuses is very common. Before the data can be used for analysis, the age distribution must be examined to determine whether a smoothing technique should be applied. The procedure used here is based on the Population Analysis Spreadsheets, which were created by the U.S. Bureau of the Census International Programs Center to aid analysis of demographic data and prepare population projections (Arriaga 1994). The programs SINGAGE and AGESMTH (Arriaga 1994) were used on the census data reported for households.[1] The first program examines population figures for each year of age data for digit preference. The second examines irregularities in the data by means of age and sex ratios and applies several smoothing techniques to the 5-year age group data.

The single-age data were found to have significant irregularities stemming from a preference for the digits 0 and 5. The digit preference was detected in charts of the data and in several different indexes used in the SINGAGE program (Arriaga 1994, 18). Age misreporting is also detected by the age ratios for 5-year age groups. This measure is defined as the ratio of the population in a given age group divided by the average population of the two adjacent age groups, multiplied by 100. If fertility and migration have not changed significantly, then the ratios should be close to 100. Some irregularity would be expected in this measure for Sierra Leone because of the civil war; however, the fluctuating pattern of the age ratio across all age groups indicates that age misreporting is a significant problem in the census data. Sex ratios are also used to check for errors in the data. This ratio is calculated as the number of males per 100 females in each 5-year age group. In the case of Sierra Leone, the sex ratio shows a significant dip around the 20- to 40-year age range, which may reflect greater mortality for males than females during the war years. However, even when this disparity is taken into account, it can still be concluded that the census data need to be smoothed because of the significant misreporting of age.

The AGESMTH program was used to obtain smoothed data for 5-year age groups using several methods. Because the age irregularities in the census data are so large, the "strong" method was selected. As its name suggests, this method makes a greater change to the original data than do the "lighter" methods. The method is as follows: (1) the census population is grouped into 10-year age groups; (2) the groups from 10 to 69 are smoothed by averaging three consecutive 10-year age groups with specific weights: $S(0)=[T(-1)+2T(0)+T(1)]/4$ (where S is the smoothed value and T the actual value; (3) the results are adjusted proportionally to equal the census totals; and (4) the 10-year age groups are divided into 5-year age groups using Arriaga's formula (Arriaga 1995, 40).

To obtain single-year data, the smoothed 5-year age groups were plotted and a second-order polynomial was fitted to the male and female data separately. These equations were used to determine values for single ages from 0 to 79. Because the total of these values was slightly higher than the reported total, they were proportionally adjusted to match the totals of the smoothed 5-year age groups.

There were a few "not stated" responses for age in the census (just over 7 per 100,000). These were proportionally distributed across the smoothed data for all ages. In addition, there was a "special population" (just under 1 per 100) which included, for example, prisoners, police and armed forces on duty, and street children. Age and sex information is not known for this group and, based on the nature of the group, it was assumed that they generally ranged in age from 12 to 44 years, with 70 percent of them being male. Therefore this group was proportionally distributed across the 12–44 age range, separately for males and females, to obtain the final estimates.

APPENDIX B. SIERRA LEONE INTEGRATED HOUSEHOLD SURVEY DATA

Data from the Sierra Leone Integrated Household Survey (SLIHS) (2003/04) were used to compute several important measures in this report, including enrollment rates by age, gross and net enrollment rates, gross and net intake rates, and cohort access rates. Prior to constructing these values, the data were modified in the following manner:

1. Respondent's current grade and highest grade completed were made consistent with expected norms (so that they were within one grade level of each other).
2. A maximum educational level threshold was imposed, based on the respondent's age, to correct for apparent coding or respondent errors. For example, a 7-year-old would be reassigned to the fourth grade if the survey identified her as being in a higher grade.
3. An assumption was made that 7.75 percent of students in primary grade 1 were less than 5 years old. Those under 5 were not asked questions regarding their current educational status, but evidence from the primary grade 2 age distribution suggests that a substantial proportion were already enrolled in primary grade 1. This somewhat arbitrary percentage was used independent of gender, location, or other variables.
4. To avoid confusion over year of enrollment status and/or current grade level, data from months when school was not in session were discarded when constructing most estimates regarding current schooling. Because the survey took place over 12 months, with surveys conducted in multiple regions simultaneously, this omission is not expected to bias results. Sample weights are adjusted accordingly.
5. When constructing GERs and similar gross measures, age data were smoothed by taking an equally weighted average population size based on the age in question and the age above and below. The smoothing

process was done separately for each breakout (for example, region, gender, expenditure) but has the favorable property that the age breakouts for higher levels of aggregation are the same as those obtained by adding all subgroups. This property implies that the GERs and other gross figures are additively decomposable: the GER at the national level is just the weighted sum of subgroup estimates. In this case, the weights are the estimated proportion of the population within each subgroup.

6. An asset index was used to test the robustness of various results that were broken out by household expenditure status. The primary asset index used in this analysis is constructed using factor analysis as outlined in Sahn and Stifel (2000). An alternative asset index approach, suggested by Filmer and Pritchett (1998), was also created and gave nearly identical household rankings to that of Sahn and Stifel. Included in the asset indexes are characteristics of the household (shared housing, mud walls, non-earthen flooring, thatch roof, water from closed system [well or pipes], water source more than 50 yards from house, wood fuel, and use of toilet or latrine), a short list of durable goods (ownership of furniture, a radio, and a bicycle), and a dummy variable indicating whether the head of household had any education. Use of information on the value of the durable goods was avoided due to data concerns. As these items are primarily shared among all members without any loss of value, the use of simple dummy variables comes without major concerns about deflating to an appropriate adult equivalent level. A more comprehensive list of household durables was available, but inclusion of the additional durables led to serious violations of underlying assumptions in the factor analysis model. The sparse approach is considered much more suitable.

APPENDIX C. FORMULA TO DECOMPOSE THE UNIT COST

$$UC = \frac{CSE}{ENR}$$

$$UC = \frac{SALBS + SALBA + GS + SCHO}{ENR}$$

$$UC = \frac{SALBS}{ENR} + \frac{SALBA}{ENR} + \frac{GS}{ENR} + \frac{SCHO}{ENR}$$

$$UC = \frac{SALPS \times NPS}{ENR} + \frac{SALBA}{ENR} + \frac{GS}{ENR} + \frac{SCHO}{ENR}$$

$$UC = \frac{SALPS}{PPRS} + \frac{SALBA}{ENR} + \frac{GS}{ENR} + \frac{SCHO}{ENR}$$

Where:

UC = Unit cost

CSE = Current spending on education

ENR = Number of students enrolled

$SALBS$ = Salary bill of personnel at the school level

$SALBA$ = Salary bill of administrative and support services staff

GS = Expenditure on goods and services

$SCHO$ = Expenditure on scholarships

$SALPS$ = Average salary of personnel at the school level

NPS = Number of personnel at the school level

$PPRS$ = Pupil-personnel ratio at the school level

APPENDIX D. FIGURES AND TABLES

Figure D.1   Population Pyramids, 1963–2015

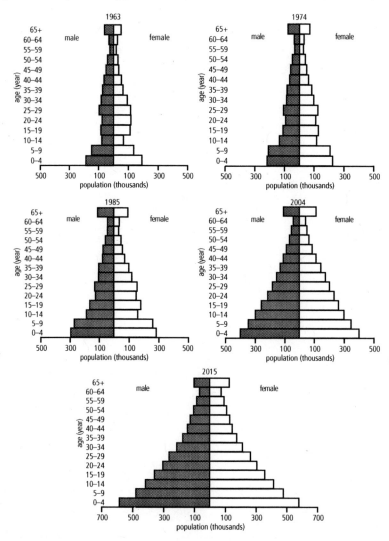

Sources: Statistics Sierra Leone 2004; projected figures from the United Nations Population Division (medium variant).

Table D.1   Significant Events in Sierra Leone's History

Date	Event
1961	Independence from Britan. First prime minister: Sir Milton Margai.
1971	Republican state: first executive president: Siaka P. Stevens.
1972	Dissolution/suspension of local councils.
1977	Declaration of one party rule: all Peoples' Congress Party.
1980	OAU Confab held in Freetown.
1985	Maj. Gen. J. S. Momoh appointed successor to Siaka P. Stevens.
1991 (Mar 23)	Start of Revolutionary United Front (RUF) armed conflict in Bomaru and Sienga in the Kailahun District.
1992 (Apr 29)	Military coup led by Capt. V. E. M. Strasser.
1996 (Jan 26)	Palace coup: Capt. V. E. M. Strasser overthrown by his deputy, Brig. Julius Bio.
1996 (Feb/Mar)	Parliamentary/presidential elections.
1996 (Mar 15)	Ahmad Tejan Kabbah sworn in as president.
1997 (May 25)	Military coup led by Maj. Johnny Paul Koroma.
1998 (Mar 10)	Restoration of democracy: President Kabbah reinstated by the Economic Community of West African States Monitoring Group.
1999 (Jan 6)	Rebel/dissident soldier incursion into Freetown.
2001 (Jan)	Formal declaration of end of conflict.
2002	First postconflict democratic elections: President Kabbah reelected for a second 4-year term.
2004 (May)	First local government elections preceded by promulgation of Local Government Act 2004.

Source: Authors.

Table D.2   Regions, Administrative Districts, Local Councils, and Educational Districts of Sierra Leone

Region	Administrative district	Local council	Educational district
Eastern Region	Kenema	Kenema District	Kenema
	Kailahun	Kailahun District	Kailahun
	Kono	Kono District	Kono
		Koidu / New Sembehun Town	
		Kenema Town	
Southern Region	Bo	Bo District/Bo Town	Bo
	Bonthe	Bonthe District/Bonthe Town	Bonthe 1, Bonthe 2
	Moyamba	Moyamba District	Moyamba
	Pujehun	Pujehun District	Pujehun
Northern Region	Port Loko	Port Loko District	Port Loko 1, Port Loko 2
	Bombali	Bombali District	Bombali
	Tonkolili	Tonkolili District	Tonkolili 1, Tonkolili 2
	Kambia	Kambia District	Kambia
	Koinadugu	Koinadugu District	Koinadugu
		Makeni Town	
Western Area	Western Area	Freetown City	Western Urban East
		Western Area Rural	Western Urban West
			Western Rural

Source: MEST.

Table D.3 Government Revenues and Expenditure, 1996–2006

Indicator	1996	1997	1998	1999	2000	2001	2002	2003	2004	2005(e)	2006(e)
Government revenues											
Current Le millions											
Total government revenues	101,953	50,003	102,286	151,210	258,282	302,692	400,027	467,001	616,342	699,281	920,425
Domestically generated	87,334	45,333	77,199	85,819	152,175	207,669	238,691	287,657	356,966	428,347	538,808
Grants	14,619	4,670	25,087	65,391	106,107	95,023	161,336	179,344	259,376	270,933	381,617
Program	11,887	4,595	22,456	41,628	89,445	57,628	118,199	144,843	206,172	212,251	240,479
Of which HIPC	0	0	0	0	0	0	75,326	106,617	93,650	61,311	50,880
Projects	2,732	75	2,631	23,763	16,662	37,756	43,137	34,501	53,204	58,682	141,139
Constant 2003 Le millions											
Total government revenues	212,978	89,436	144,000	170,261	274,073	315,630	432,913	467,001	531,273	531,838	618,732
Domestically generated	182,439	81,083	108,682	96,631	161,479	216,545	258,314	287,657	307,696	325,779	362,200
Grants	30,539	8,353	35,318	73,629	112,594	99,084	174,600	179,344	223,576	206,058	256,532
Program	24,832	8,219	31,614	46,873	94,914	60,091	127,916	144,843	177,716	161,428	161,656
Of which HIPC	0	0	0	0	0	0	81,519	106,617	80,724	46,630	34,203
Projects	5,707	134	3,704	26,757	17,681	39,370	46,683	34,501	45,861	44,631	94,877
Total revenues as percentage of GDP	—	—	—	—	19.4	18.9	20.4	20.1	21.3	—	—
Domestic resources as a percentage of GDP	—	—	—	—	11.4	13.0	12.1	12.4	12.3	—	—
Grants as a percentage of total revenues	14.3	9.3	24.5	43.2	41.1	31.4	40.3	38.4	42.1	38.7	41.5
Government expenditure											
Current Le millions											
Total government expenditure	146,331	108,223	211,523	265,605	382,343	472,263	562,252	622,392	717,554	767,454	943,276
Current	117,581	96,037	159,384	235,939	301,831	397,186	474,811	509,760	583,519	637,391	718,122
Capital expenditure and net lending	28,750	12,186	52,139	29,666	80,512	75,077	87,441	112,632	134,035	130,063	225,154

Table D.3 *(continued)*

Indicator	1996	1997	1998	1999	2000	2001	2002	2003	2004	2005(e)	2006(e)
Constant 2003 Le millions											
Total government expenditure	305,683	193,568	297,786	299,067	405,719	492,449	608,475	622,392	618,515	583,687	634,093
Current	245,625	171,772	224,384	265,664	320,284	414,162	513,845	509,760	502,980	484,768	482,739
Capital expenditure and net lending	60,058	21,796	73,403	33,403	85,435	78,286	94,630	112,632	115,535	98,919	151,354
Total expenditure as a percentage of GDP	—	—	—	—	28.7	29.5	28.6	26.8	24.8	—	—
Overall balance (revenues — expenditure)											
Current Le millions											
Including grants	−44,378	−58,220	−109,237	−114,395	−124,061	−169,571	−162,225	−155,391	−101,212	−68,173	−22,851
Excluding grants	−58,997	−62,890	−134,324	−179,786	−230,168	−264,594	−323,561	−334,735	−360,588	−339,107	−404,468
Constant 2003 Le millions											
Including grants	−92,705	−104,133	−153,786	−128,807	−131,646	−176,819	−175,562	−155,391	−87,242	−51,849	−15,361
Excluding grants	−123,244	−112,485	−189,104	−202,436	−244,240	−275,903	−350,161	−334,735	−310,819	−257,908	−271,893
Overall balance as a percentage of government revenues											
Including grants	−43.5	−116.4	−106.8	−75.7	−48.0	−56.0	−40.6	−33.3	−16.4	−9.7	−2.5
Excluding grants	−57.9	−125.8	−131.3	−118.9	−89.1	−87.4	−80.9	−71.7	−58.5	−48.5	−43.9

Sources: Ministry of Finance; IMF.
Note: — = not available.

175

Table D.4   Preprimary Enrollment Trends, 2003/04 to 2005/06

Year	Boys	Girls	Total
2003/04	9,906	9,162	19,068
2004/05	10,794	9,838	20,632
2005/06	8,619	9,528	18,147

Source: MEST.

Table D.5   Primary School Enrollment Trends, 1987/88 to 2004/05

Year	Boys	Girls	Total
1987/88	—	—	392,192
1988/89	—	—	367,201
1989/90	—	—	370,564
1990/91	—	—	375,941
1991/92	—	—	315,146
1992/93	—	—	—
1993/94	—	—	—
1994/95	—	—	—
1995/96	—	—	—
1996/97	—	—	367,920
1997/98	—	—	—
1998/99	—	—	—
1999/2000	—	—	548,059
2000/01	369,631	264,489	634,120
2001/02	369,953	289,550	659,503
2002/03	545,109	444,227	989,337
2003/04	618,982	515,833	1,134,815
2004/05	698,387	582,466	1,280,853

Source: MEST.
Note: — = not available.

Table D.6   Secondary School Enrollment Trends, 2000/01 to 2004/05

Year	JSS			SSS		
	Boys	Girls	Total	Boys	Girls	Total
2000/01	36,989	23,256	60,245	12,806	10,123	22,929
2001/02	47,154	29,707	76,861	14,154	8,103	22,257
2002/03	76,444	49,511	125,956	24,825	11,361	36,185
2003/04	80,963	52,438	133,401	26,292	12,032	38,324
2004/05	93,822	61,230	155,052	28,541	16,383	44,924

Source: MEST.

Table D.7   Tertiary Institution Enrollment Trends, 1998/99 to 2004/05

Year	Males	Females	Total
1998/99	4,164	2,265	6,429
1999/00	5,398	2,752	8,150
2000/01	6,381	2,614	8,995
2001/02	9,123	3,772	12,895
2002/03	9,521	4,329	13,850
2003/04	10,128	5,369	15,497
2004/05	10,558	6,067	16,625

Source: MEST.

Table D.8   Tertiary Institution Enrollment Trends by Institution Type, 1998/99 to 2004/05

Year	University of Sierra Leone	Teachers Colleges	Polytechnics	Distance	Total
1998/99	4,141	1,423	865	. .	6,429
1999/00	4,544	2,061	1,545	. .	8,150
2000/01	5,184	2,165	1,646	. .	8,995
2001/02	8,287	2,328	2,080	200	12,895
2002/03	8,462	2,360	2,028	1,000	13,850
2003/04	9,142	2,508	2,047	1,800	15,497
2004/05	9,689	2,577	2,104	2,255	16,625

Source: MEST.
Note: . . = nil or negligible.

Table D.9 Number of Staff in Tertiary Institutions, 2004/05

	Academic staff		Nonacademic staff			
	Full-time	Part-time	Senior staff	Intermediate staff	Junior staff	All Staff
Total						
Teachers colleges	225	3	32	53	311	624
Bo Teachers College	66	3	11	22	78	180
Freetown Teachers College	72	. .	10	16	97	195
Port Loko Teachers College	87	. .	11	15	136	249
Polytechnic institutes	156	16	20	10	200	402
Eastern Polytechnic	91	16	14	. .	105	226
Northern Polytechnic	65	. .	6	10	95	176
University of Sierra Leone	631	127	249	102	1,356	2,465
College of Medicine and Allied Health Science	41	13	10	37	111	212
Fourah Bay College	155	61	50	. .	638	904
Institute of Public Administration and Management	18	9	5	10	28	70
Milton Margai College of Education and Technology	277	. .	32	55	178	542
Njala University College	140	44	22	. .	401	607
University Secretariat	. .	. .	130	. .	. .	130
All institutions	1,012	146	301	165	1,867	3,491
Males						
Teachers colleges	189	3	28	39	275	534
Bo Teachers College	58	3	10	19	72	162
Freetown Teachers College	58	. .	7	10	86	161
Port Loko Teachers College	73	. .	11	10	117	211
Polytechnic institutes	146	13	20	8	169	356
Eastern Polytechnic	85	13	14	. .	83	195
Northern Polytechnic	61	. .	6	8	86	161
University of Sierra Leone	541	117	195	81	1,111	2,045
College of Medicine and Allied Health Science	37	9	10	32	79	167
Fourah Bay College	136	58	36	. .	518	748
Institute of Public Administration and Management	18	8	5	7	25	63
Milton Margai College of Education and Technology	224	. .	26	42	153	445
Njala University College	126	42	19	. .	336	523
University Secretariat	. .	. .	99	. .	. .	99
All institutions	876	133	243	128	1,555	2,935

Table D.9 (*continued*)

	Academic staff		Nonacademic staff			All Staff
	Full-time	Part-time	Senior staff	Intermediate staff	Junior staff	
Females						
Teachers colleges	36	..	4	14	36	90
Bo Teachers College	8	..	1	3	6	18
Freetown Teachers College	14	..	3	6	11	34
Port Loko Teachers College	14	..	..	5	19	38
Polytechnic institutes	10	3	..	2	31	46
Eastern Polytechnic	6	3	..	..	22	31
Northern Polytechnic	4	..	..	2	9	15
University of Sierra Leone	90	10	54	21	245	420
College of Medicine and Allied Health Science	4	4	..	5	32	45
Fourah Bay College	19	3	14	..	120	156
Institute of Public Administration and Management	..	1	..	3	3	7
Milton Margai College of Education and Technology	53	..	6	13	25	97
Njala University College	14	2	3	..	65	84
University Secretariat	..	..	31	..	..	31
All institutions	136	13	58	37	312	556

Source: MEST.
Note: .. = nil or negligible.

Table D.10   Current Expenditure by Level of Education, 2000–07

	Preprimary and primary education	Secondary education	Tertiary / teacher education	Technical or vocational education	Administration and support services, other	Total
Current Le (millions)						
2000	28,833	16,336	11,322	5,959	2,979	65,428
2001	37,740	16,606	13,217	2,495	3,626	73,685
2002	44,385	17,767	14,686	4,155	5,908	86,901
2003	49,542	21,009	19,381	4,792	6,741	101,465
2004	54,702	24,711	25,086	4,418	4,193	113,109
2005 (e)	61,514	22,502	23,039	4,303	9,545	120,903
2006 (e)	68,144	23,627	27,528	4,518	11,640	135,458
2007 (e)	71,755	24,808	28,905	4,744	11,369	141,582
Constant 2003 Le (millions)						
2000	30,596	17,335	12,014	6,323	3,161	69,428
2001	39,353	17,316	13,782	2,602	3,781	76,834
2002	48,034	19,228	15,893	4,496	6,394	94,045
2003	49,542	21,009	19,381	4,792	6,741	101,465
2004	47,152	21,300	21,623	3,808	3,615	97,497
2005 (e)	46,784	17,114	17,522	3,273	7,259	91,953
2006 (e)	45,808	15,883	18,505	3,037	7,825	91,058
2007 (e)	44,392	15,348	17,882	2,935	7,034	87,590
Share of total current education spending (%)						
2000	44.1	25.0	17.3	9.1	4.6	100.0
2001	51.2	22.5	17.9	3.4	4.9	100.0
2002	51.1	20.4	16.9	4.8	6.8	100.0
2003	48.8	20.7	19.1	4.7	6.6	100.0
2004	48.4	21.8	22.2	3.9	3.7	100.0
2005 (e)	50.9	18.6	19.1	3.6	7.9	100.0
2006 (e)	50.3	17.4	20.3	3.3	8.6	100.0
2007 (e)	50.7	17.5	20.4	3.4	8.0	100.0

Source: MOF.
Note: e = estimated.

Table D.11 Commitments for Education and General Budget Support to Sierra Leone, 2000–04
(constant 2003 US$ millions)

	2000	2001	2002	2003	2004
Education commitments					
All donors—total	**1.7**	**7.3**	**27.7**	**59.7**	**8.1**
DAC countries—total	1.5	7.0	3.5	3.8	7.7
Australia	..	..	..	..	..
Austria	0.0	0.0	..	..	0.0
Belgium	..	..	..	..	..
Canada	..	1.5	..	..	..
Denmark	..	..	..	..	..
Finland	..	..	0.8	0.4	0.2
France	0.1	0.1	0.1	0.1	0.1
Germany	0.8	1.0	1.4	2.4	5.3
Greece	..	..	..	..	..
Ireland	..	0.2	0.3	0.8	0.3
Italy	..	0.0	..	..	..
Japan	..	..	..	0.0	0.1
Netherlands, The	..	..	..	..	..
Norway	..	3.5	0.9	..	1.4
Portugal	..	..	..	..	..
Spain	..	..	..	..	0.2
Sweden	..	..	..	..	..
Switzerland	0.6	..	..	..	..
United Kingdom	..	0.0	..	..	..
United States	..	0.7	..	..	..
Multilateral—total	0.2	0.3	24.3	55.9	0.4
AfDF	..	..	23.5	..	..
IDA	..	..	..	55.0	..
UNICEF	0.2	0.3	0.8	0.9	0.4
EC	..	..	..	..	..
General budget support					
All donors—total	**144.1**	**111.5**	**0.0**	**54.7**	**47.6**
United Kingdom	53.5	52.3	0.0	0.5	24.0
Multilateral—total	90.7	59.2	..	54.2	23.6
AfDF	..	..	..	24.2	23.5
IDA	45.3	59.2	..	30.0	..
EC	45.3	..	..	..	0.1
Education commitments + allocation of general budget support (17%)[a]					
All donors—total	**26.2**	**26.2**	**27.7**	**69.0**	**16.2**
DAC countries	10.6	15.8	3.5	3.8	11.8
Multilateral	15.6	10.4	24.3	65.1	4.4

Source: CRS online database on aid activities (www.oecd.org/dac/stats/idsonline), Table 2, last updated January 30, 2006.
Note: .. = nil or negligible.
a. Based on 2004 education spending as a percentage of total government expenditure (17%), MOF.

Table D.12   Basic Salary Scale of Teaching Staff, 2004

Grade	Qualifications	Initial Salary (Le)	Ratio of intital salary to GDP per capita
1	Untrained with No O Level	1,004,676	1.7
2	Untrained with 3+ O levels	1,067,712	1.8
3	R.S.A stage 3 (completed)	1,178,520	2.0
4	TC/TC and graduate trained	1,315,320	2.3
5	TEC/TC/OND/OTD	1,534,200	2.6
6	HTC holder, graduate without diploma, senior teacher (primary)	1,834,800	3.2
7	Deputy head teacher, graduate with diploma	2,157,804	3.7
8	Senior teacher (secondary)/head teacher (primary)	2,534,136	4.4
9	Vice principal SSS	3,656,880	6.3
10	Principal SSS	4,844,520	8.3

Source: MEST.
Note: TC = teaching certificate; OND = ordinary national diploma; HTC = higher teaching certificate; OTD = ordinary teaching diploma.

Table D.13   Number of Personnel and Actual Salary Bill by Educational Level and Rank, 2004

Level	Number of personnel[a]	Percentage of teachers at each level (%)	Total annual wage bill (Le millions)	Average annual salary (Le millions)	Ratio of annual average salary to GDP per capita
Primary education	17,668	100.0	39,605	2.24	3.9
Principal	1,755	9.9	8,823	5.03	8.6
Vice principal	971	5.5	4,588	4.73	8.1
Senior teacher	850	4.8	2,283	2.69	4.6
Teacher	11,052	62.6	19,887	1.80	3.1
New teacher	1,813	10.3	2,356	1.30	2.2
Study leave	767	4.3	1,095	1.43	2.5
CREPS	460	2.6	572	1.24	2.1
Secondary education	5,791	100.0	18,248	3.15	5.4
Principal	193	3.3	1,549	8.03	13.8
Vice principal	24	0.4	185	7.55	13.0
Senior teacher	747	12.9	4,167	5.58	9.6
Teacher	3,921	67.7	10,549	2.69	4.6
New teacher	680	11.7	1,189	1.75	3.0
Study leave	227	3.9	609	2.69	4.6
Technical/vocational education	769	100	2,697	3.51	6.0
Principal	31	4.0	264	8.66	14.9
Vice principal	15	2.0	124	8.14	14.0

Table D.13 (*continued*)

Level	Number of Personnel[a]	Percentage of teachers at each level (%)	Total annual wage bill (Le millions)	Average annual salary (Le millions)	Ratio of annual average salary to GDP per capital
Senior teacher	92	11.9	497	5.42	9.3
Teacher	426	55.5	1,289	3.02	5.2
New teacher	196	25.5	396	2.02	3.5
Study leave	. .	. .	. .	. .	. .
Lecturer	9	1.1	127	14.53	25.0
Tertiary education	1,158	—	—	—	—
All levels	25,386	—	—	—	—

Source: Authors' estimates based on MOF recurrent and development estimates, financial years 2005–07, and the Budget Bureau, Ministry of Finance.
Note: . . = nil or negligible, — = not available.
a. Includes only teachers on the payroll.

Table D.14 School Attendance by Age Group and Gender, 2004
(percent)

Demographic	Attending school	Not attending school	Never attended school
Population Census 2004			
6–11 years old	69	1	30
Males	70	1	29
Females	69	1	30
12–14 years old	75	3	22
Males	78	3	19
Females	71	4	26
15–17 years old	56	8	36
Males	65	6	28
Females	46	9	44
SLIHS 2003/04			
6–11 years old	75	2	23
12–14 years old	76	4	20

Sources: Statistics Sierra Leone Population Census 2004; SLIHS 2003/04.

Table D.15 Percent Out-of-School by Gender, Locality, Region, and Family Wealth, 2003/04

Indicator	Age (years)		
	6–11	12–14	15–17
Sierra Leone	25	24	38
By gender			
Boys	26	19	30
Girls	24	28	46
Parity index (girls/boys)	0.92	1.47	1.53
By locality by gender			
Rural	33	30	47
Boys	34	26	37
Girls	31	34	60
Urban	12	15	26
Boys	12	9	21
Girls	12	20	32
Parity index (rural/urban)	2.75	2.00	1.81
Parity index (rural girls/urban boys)	2.58	3.78	2.86
By region			
Southern Region	24	23	39
Eastern Region	29	27	39
Northern Region	30	27	46
Western Area	19	14	25
Parity index (Northern/Western)	1.58	1.93	1.84
By household expenditure quintile			
Q1 (poorest)	22	12	26
Q2	28	21	32
Q3	25	25	40
Q4	30	29	43
Q5 (richest)	46	30	51
Parity index (poorest/richest)	2.09	2.50	1.96

Source: SLIHS 2003/04.

Definitions of Indicators

Age-specific enrollment rate (AER)
Age-specific enrollment rates are the ratio of the number of students within the age group enrolled in any educational level to the size of the population of the age group, multiplied by 100.

Cohort access rate (CAR)
Cohort access rates are the percentage of an age group that has ever been to school. In this report, the age groups for computing access rates are 13 years (chapter 2) and 9–13 years (chapter 5).

Gross completion ratio (GCR)
Gross completion ratios are the ratio of the total number of students, regardless of age, enrolled in the final grade of an educational level minus the number of repeaters, to the population of the official graduation age, multiplied by 100.

Gross enrollment ratio (GER)
Gross enrollment ratios are the ratio of all students enrolled in an educational level, regardless of age, to the size of the official age population corresponding to that educational level, multiplied by 100. The gross enrollment ratio for the tertiary level is the number of tertiary students of any age as a percentage of 18- to 21-year-olds.

Gross intake ratio (GIR)
Gross intake ratios are the ratio of all new entrants to the first grade of an educational level, regardless of age, to the size of the population at the official age of entry, multiplied by 100.

Net enrollment rate (NER)
Net enrollment rates are the ratio of the number of students in the official age group enrolled in an educational level to the size of the

official age population corresponding to that educational level, multiplied by 100.

Net intake rate (NIR)

Net intake rates are the ratio of new entrants to the first grade of an educational level who are at the official age of entry, to the size of the population at the official age of entry, multiplied by 100.

Official age

The official age groups for each educational level are:

Level	Age (years)
Preprimary	3–5
Primary	6–11
JSS	12–14
SSS	15–17

Primary completion rate (PCR)

The primary completion rate is the gross completion rate at the primary level (see GCR).

Pupil-to-teacher ratio (PTR)

The pupil-to-teacher ratio is the ratio of the number of students in an educational level to the number of teaching staff in that level.

Repetition rate

Repetition rates are the number of pupils who are enrolled in the same grade (or level) as the previous year, expressed as a percentage of the total enrollment in the given grade (or level) of education.

Survival rate

Survival rates are the percentage of a cohort of students enrolled in the first grade of an educational level who are expected to reach successive grades within the stage. Survival rates have been calculated using two methods (see CCM and RCM below.)

Composite cohort method (CCM)

CCM survival rates are obtained for each grade by dividing the number of new entrants to the grade by the number of new entrants in the lower grade in the previous year. The survival rate to the end of primary school, for example, is obtained by multiplying the survival rates for each grade. The result is multiplied by 100.

Reconstructed cohort method (RCM)

The RCM survival rate tracks the flow of a cohort of students based on the observed grade-by-grade promotion, repetition, and implied dropout rates. It gives the percentage of a cohort that would be expected to reach each successive grade with repetition. The method is based on the fundamental concept that for pupils enrolled in a given grade in a certain year, there can be only three eventualities: (1) some of them will be promoted to the next higher grade in the next school year; (2) others will drop out of school in the course of the year; and (3) the remaining will repeat the same grade in the next school year. Based on calculated flow rates, a cohort of 1,000 pupils through the educational cycle may be simulated, with three important assumptions:

1. That there will be no additional new entrants in any of the subsequent years during the lifetime of the cohort;
2. That, in any given grade, the same rates of repetition, promotion, and dropout apply, regardless of whether a pupil has reached that grade directly or after one or more repetitions (hypothesis of homogenous behavior); and
3. That the number of times any given pupil will be allowed to repeat is well defined. In this report, it is defined as a maximum of six repeats.

Because data are not directly available on promotees and dropouts, errors in the data available on enrollment and repeaters affect the estimates derived for these two flows. Errors will lead to biases in indicators of internal efficiency. Since the drop-out rate is determined as a residual, it often serves as a test for some types of error: particularly, a negative dropout rate is a sign of errors in the raw data (that is, enrollment and repeaters reported).

Transition rate
Transition rates are the number of new entrants (nonrepeaters) to the first grade of a higher educational level (regardless of age) in the following year expressed as a percentage of the number of students (nonrepeaters) in the final grade of the lower educational level in the given year.

Notes

EXECUTIVE SUMMARY

1. The high primary GER is mainly due to a large number of older children coming back to school after the war.

CHAPTER 1: POSTCONFLICT CONTEXT

1. Basic education in Sierra Leone includes 6 years of primary and 3 years of junior secondary education.

2. The food/extreme poverty line is defined as the level of expenditures needed to attain the minimum nutritional requirement of 2,700 calories per adult—Le 1,033 per day or US$1 equivalent. A person whose expenditure on food falls below this threshold is considered to be food/extreme poor (PRSP 2005, 21). The full poverty line is defined as the minimum expenditure required for such basic needs as safe water, sanitation, shelter, health care, and education, in addition to that required for food (represented by the food/extreme poverty line). This minimum amounts to Le 2,111 per day (Le 770,678 per year) or approximately US$2 equivalent. A person whose expenditure on food and basic needs falls below this level is considered to be poor (PRSP 2005, 21).

3. The short-lived Lome Peace Accord was signed between the Government of Sierra Leone and the Revolutionary United Front. The two sides agreed to a cease fire and shared governance.

CHAPTER 2: STUDENT ENROLLMENT, COMPLETION, AND TRANSITION

1. The war was not officially declared over until 2002, but it ended in some parts of the country before it did in others.

2. The sampling of institutions in the TVET Survey 2004 was not necessarily nationally representative; combined schools were included in some districts and not in others. The following table summarizes the various TVET program requirements:

TVET Program	Equivalent Education Level
Community Education Center-B (CEC-B)	Nonformal education
Community Education Center-A (CEC-A)	Equivalent to JSS
Vocational Trade Center (VTC)	Between JSS and SSS
Technical/Vocational Center (TVC)	Equivalent to SSS
Technical/Vocational Institute (TVI)	Post-SSS below Tertiary
Polytechnics	Tertiary

3. Even with the assistance provided by the government, many of these institutions are still primarily private. They decide the salary scales for their staff; and they hire and fire staff without much reference to government criteria. They also design their curricula. To a large extent, they also set student fees.

4. See Appendix 2.2 for details on the analysis of SLIHS (2003/04) data.

5. Given the geographically concentrated nature of SSS in Sierra Leone, and the cluster-based sampling approach of the SLIHS, all SLIHS results concerning education at the SSS level are subject to higher sampling error and are therefore less reliable than measures with less across-cluster variation.

6. It is not possible to compute AERs from administrative data because student ages were not recorded.

7. For definitions of the CCM and RCM methods, refer to the Definitions of Indicators appendix.

8. The survival rate exceeds 100 percent from SSS grades 1 to 3 possibly because of problems in the data and limitations of the CCM and RCM methods.

CHAPTER 3: LEARNING ENVIRONMENT AND OUTCOMES

1. The data used for analyzing the learning environment and learning outcomes are from various databases and other sources. Currently, it is impossible to merge the databases for exploring direct relationships between these two factors. Therefore learning environment and learning outcomes are analyzed separately. When a comprehensive database becomes available, the associations between the two factors should be explored.

2. There are some community schools and private schools that are not yet recognized by MEST.

3. Damage index values range from 1 to 4. A classroom in usable condition (no repair needed) is ranked as 1, a classroom in need of minor repair is ranked as 2, one needing rehabilitation is ranked as 3, and one requiring reconstruction is ranked as 4.

4. Evidence suggests that the presence of female teachers has a positive impact on girls' schooling (World Bank 2005a).

5. The findings are from the Basic Education Secretariat, whose staff paid a series of visits to schools and held discussions with school principals.

6. The data do not allow disaggregation of teaching and administrative staff. Although the survey was done in 2002, the situation has not changed much since then.

7. Nonacademic staff are not included in the calculation of teacher-student ratios.

CHAPTER 4: EXPENDITURE AND FINANCING

1. Note that other percentage shares are presented in this chapter in which the administration and support services have been distributed across the levels of education.

2. Note that the proportion devoted to preprimary education is relatively small relative to primary education.

3. Official Development Assistance consists of grants or loans to developing countries that are undertaken by the official sector, with the promotion of economic development and welfare as the main objective, at concessional financial terms (if a loan, having a grant element of at least 25 percent). In addition to financial flows, technical cooperation is included in aid. Grants, loans, and credits for military purposes are excluded.

4. DAC is a key forum of major bilateral donors. Members work together to increase the effectiveness of their common efforts to support sustainable development.

5. Data on commitments are shown because data on disbursements are not currently available by recipient country and sector.

6. The United Kingdom was not included in this count because their funding is provided through general budget support.

7. This breakdown assumes that the percentage of total public resources for education from domestic revenues and donor support is the same as the percentage distributions of domestic revenues and donor support in total public resources.

8. This number may be an underestimate because the contribution of households for students in tertiary education is not included.

9. The International Monetary Fund estimates growth in the GDP between 2003 and 2009 to be about 6–7.5 percent per year. The lower figure of 5 percent per year is used here and in chapter 7 as a conservative estimate.

10. System administration amounts have been distributed across the educational levels.

11. Pupil-teacher ratios for Sierra Leone include nonteaching personnel.

CHAPTER 5: DISPARITY

1. However, the Ministry of Education, Science and Technology (MEST) administrative data finds that there are gender disparities even at the early grades. The difference may arise because the two agencies are measuring different things. The MEST data do not allow an analysis by age, so a large number of older boys in the early primary grades may explain why MEST finds a greater gender disparity. Data from the 2004 census show a similar pattern to the SLIHS data, supporting the conclusion that there is little gender disparity for those younger than 12 but a large disparity at older ages.

2. The SLIHS (2003/04) data suggest that 25 percent of the differential in enrollment ratios for boys and girls 15–17 years old results from differences in the percentage of dropouts, whereas 75 percent is caused by differences in the percentage who have ever attended school. The Population Census (2004) data indicate that these percentages are 16 and 84 percent, respectively.

3. In this analysis, poorest and richest quintiles are determined using household expenditure as a proxy.

4. Because educational expenses are included in total household expenditures, one might be concerned that these relationships are driven by the tendency of households to spend more in years when they have children in school. However, these figures are quite robust to specifications using asset index quintiles rather than household expenditure quintiles.

5. MEST data indicate that the GIR to primary grade 1 was lower for girls than for boys (199 percent and 234 percent, respectively).

6. The final level attained for cohort members is approximated using the reconstructed cohort method for calculating survival rates and MEST administrative data from 2003/04 and 2004/05. The starting assumption is that 80.5 percent of the cohort will have access to primary 1 (this number is the national average cohort access rate for 9- to 13-year-olds estimated from SLIHS 2003/04).

7. Estimates of the Gini coefficient and the percentage of public expenditures that go to the top 10 percent of individuals depend sensitively on the estimate that 4.3 percent of this cohort will attend tertiary education. This estimate was calculated by dividing current tertiary enrollment by the number of 18- to 21-year-olds in Sierra Leone. Like the GERs for primary enrollment, this measure may be inflated by either a backlog of would-be tertiary students flooding into tertiary education in the postconflict era or by students taking more than 3 years to complete (either due to repetition or attending on a part-time basis). However, if this rate were 2.0 percent, the Gini coefficient would still be 0.63 and 10 percent of the population would still be receiving 45 percent of the public expenditures on education.

8. A flaw of this approach is that it cannot fully account for the structural changes taking place, for instance, in the enrollment of female students. For example, we would expect the ratio of women to men in JSS to improve over time because the share of females students in primary schools has grown rapidly in recent years. Thus the method may overstate the disparity that a cohort of current primary school entrants will face. These measures may still be useful in providing a benchmark for progress. Some progress in measures of gender disparity should be expected to occur naturally, but the extent of progress made will depend largely on how many girls in this younger cohort transition to JSS in the next few years.

CHAPTER 7: IMPROVING EDUCATION: THE COST OF POLICY CHOICES

1. The IMF estimates for GDP growth between 2003 and 2009 are about 6–7.5 percent per year. The lower figure of 5 percent per year is used here and in chapter 4 as an indicative and conservative estimate.

2. Note that these financing gaps are annual and not cumulative.

APPENDIXES

1. The "special population" and "not stated" groups were excluded from the data analyzed.

References

Arriaga, Eduardo. 1994. *Population Analysis with Microcomputers, Volume 1: Presentation of Techniques.* Washington, DC: U.S. Bureau of the Census, USAID, and UNFPA.

Barrie, Ousman. 2005. "Sequencing Fiscal Decentralization: Comments Based on the Sierra Leone Experience." *Poverty Reduction and Economic Management Week.* http://www1.worldbank.org/publicsector/PREMWK2005/Sequencing Decentralization/comments.pdf.

Bennell, Paul, Jeanne Harding, and Shirley Rogers-Wright. 2004. *PRSP Education Sector Review.* Prepared for the PRSP Education Sub-Sector Working Group, Freetown, Sierra Leone.

CIA (Central Intelligence Agency). 2005. *The World Factbook.* Washington, DC: Government Printing Office.

CRS (Creditor Reporting System). 2006. *Online Database on Aid Activities.* www.oecd.org/dac/stats/idsonline, table 2. Last updated January 30, 2006.

Evans, Judith, Robert Myers, and Ellen Ilfeld. 2002. *Early Childhood Counts: A Programming Guide on Early Childhood Care for Development.* Washington, DC: World Bank.

Filmer, Deon, and Lant Pritchett. 1998. *Estimating Wealth Effects without Expenditure Data—or Tears: With an Application to Educational Enrollments in States of India.* Washington, DC: World Bank.

Glennerster, Rachel, Shehla Imran, and Katherine Whiteside. 2006. *Baseline Report on the Quality of Primary Education in Sierra Leone: Teacher Absence, School Inputs and School Supervision in District Education Committee and Government-Assisted Schools in Sierra Leone.* Freetown, Sierra Leone.

Government of Sierra Leone. 1991. *The Constitution of Sierra Leone.* Freetown, Sierra Leone.

———. 1995. *New Education Policy for Sierra Leone.* Freetown, Sierra Leone: Department of Education.

———. 2004a. "Education Act 2004." *Sierra Leone Gazette* supplement CXXXV(19).

———. 2004b. "Local Government Act 2004." *Sierra Leone Gazette* extraordinary volume CXXXV(14).

———. 2005. *Poverty Reduction Strategy Paper.* Freetown, Sierra Leone.

———. 2006. *Youth Employment Programme.* Ministry of Youth and Sports, Freetown.

GTZ/MEST (German Technical Cooperation/Ministry of Education, Science and Technology). 2004. *National Survey of Technical and Vocational Institutions.* Freetown, Sierra Leone.

———. 2005. *The Status of Technical and Vocational Education in Sierra Leone: Survey on Technical/Vocational Institutions.* Freetown, Sierra Leone.

Harding, Jeanne Beryl, and Augustine Tejan Mansaray. 2005. *Teacher Motivation and Incentives in Sierra Leone.* Freetown, Sierra Leone.

IRCBP (Institutional Reform and Capacity Building Project) Project Coordination Unit. 2005. *IRCBP Baseline Survey of Primary Schools.* Freetown, Sierra Leone: Ministry of Finance.

Medicins Sans Frontiers. 2006. *Financial Access to Healthcare in Post-War Sierra Leone.*

MEST (Ministry of Education, Science and Technology) 2003a. National Action Plan for Education for All. Freetown, Sierra Leone.

———. 2003b. *Rapid Assessment of Early Childhood Care and Education.* Freetown, Sierra Leone.

———. 2004. *Teacher Ceiling Gazette.* Freetown, Sierra Leone: MEST.

———. 2005. *Assumption of Basic Education Functions by the Local Councils—Rollout Plan: Some Challenges and Suggestions.* Freetown, Sierra Leone.

Ministry of Education. 1989. *External Examinations Task Force Report.* Freetown, Sierra Leone.

Ministry of Finance. 2006. *Local Government Grants Distribution Formula and Allocations for 2006.* Freetown, Sierra Leone. http://www.ircbp.sl/drwebsite/uploads/gazette_final_april_20.doc.

Sahn, David, and David Stifel. 2000. "Poverty Comparisons over Time and across Countries in Africa." *World Development.*

Statistics Sierra Leone. 2003/4. *Sierra Leone Integrated Household Survey.* Freetown, Sierra Leone.

———. 2004. *Population and Housing Census.* Freetown, Sierra Leone.

Stuart, L., Palmer, E., Holt, E., Porter, A. T., and University of Sierra Leone. 1996. *Sierra Leone, Education Review All Our Future Final Report.* Freetown, Sierra Leone: Published under the auspices of the University of Sierra Leone.

UNESCO (United Nations Educational, Scientific and Cultural Organization). 1990. *World Declaration on Education for All: Meeting Basic Learning Needs.* http://www.unesco.org/education/efa/ed_for_all/background/jomtien_declaration.shtml.

———. 2005. *Decentralization in Education: National Policies and Practices.* UNESCO Education Policies and Strategies 7. Paris: UNESCO.

UNESCO Institute for Statistics. n.d. http://stats.uis.unesco.org/ReportFolders/ReportFolders.aspx?CS_referer=&CS_ChosenLang=en.

———. 2004. *Educational Statistics Capacity Building, Diagnostic Report.* Freetown, Sierra Leone: MEST.

———. 2005. *Global Education Digest 2005 CD-Rom.* http://stats.uis.unesco.org/ReportFolders/reportfolders.aspx.

UNESCO Pole de Dakar. 2005. *EFA: Paving the Way for Action.* UNESCO, Dakar.

United Nations. 2000. *UN Millennium Development Goals.* http://www.un.org/millenniumgoals/.

Winkler, Don. 2005. *Understanding Decentralization.* EQUIP 2 Series. Washington, DC: USAID.

World Bank. 2000. *Hidden Challenges to the Education System in Transition Economies.* Washington, DC: World Bank.

———. 2003a. *Sierra Leone: Strategic Options for Public Sector Reform.* AFTPR, Africa Region Report 25110-SL. Washington, DC: World Bank.

———. 2003b. *EFA in Indonesia: Hard Lessons about Quality*. Education Notes Series. Washington, DC: World Bank.

———. 2005a. *Education in Ethiopia: Strengthening the Foundation for Sustainable Progress*. Washington, DC: World Bank.

———. 2005b. *World Development Indicators*. Washington, DC: World Bank.

———. 2005c. *Expanding Opportunities and Building Competencies for Young People: A New Agenda for Secondary Education*. Washington, DC: World Bank.

———. 2006. *Meeting the Challenges of Secondary Education in Latin America and East Asia: Improving Efficiency and Resource Mobilization*. Washington, DC: World Bank.

Index

boxes, figures, notes, and tables are indicated by *b, f, n,* and *t,* respectively

Cantonese Phrases Omniglot

English (Cantonese)

Chinese Language   Cantonese Phrasebook
Province of China Guangdong, China
Hong-Kong South East Asia Kuala Lumpur,
Ho chi Minh City Cantonese dominant
Language Los Angeles, San Francisco Seattle New
York

What is the main lang spoken in Australia

Common phrases chinese phrases/

Cantonese phrases/

English Phrases   Cantonese Phrases/Greetings
① How to introduce Yourself
AQA Communication and culture A level
AS Communication and culture 7th June 2008
by Peter Bennett (Author) Jerry Slater
    (£18.19p) Javier Hernández Mexican
    Carlos Vela   footballer
    Giovani dos Santos   Andres Guardado
            Guillermo Ocha